RELIGIOUS JUDGEMENT

A Developmental Perspective

Fritz K. Oser and Paul Gmünder

Religious Education Press
Birmingham, Alabama

Library of Congress Cataloging-in-Publication Data

Oser, Fritz.
  [Mensch.   English]
  Religious judgement: a developmental perspective / Fritz K. Oser and Paul Gmünder; translated by Norbert F. Hahn.
  Translation of : Der Mensch.
  Includes bibliographical references and indexes.
  ISBN 0-89135-081-0
  1. Judgement—Religious aspects.   2. Psychology, Religious.
  3. Religion—Philosophy.   I. Gmünder, Paul.   II. Title.
  BL65.J8307413   1991
  291.4'2—dc20   91-32908
                                                                          CIP

Religious Judgement: A Developmental Perspective is a translation of *Der Mensch—Stufen seiner religiösen Entwicklung* by Fritz K. Oser and Paul Gmünder (Gütersloh: Gütersloher Verlagshaus Gerd Mohn, 1988). Translated by Norbert F. Hahn

Religious Education Press, Inc.
5316 Meadow Brook Road
Birmingham, Alabama 35242
10 9 8 7 6 5 4 3 2

Religious Education Press publishes books exclusively in religious education and in areas closely related to religious education. It is committed to enhancing and professionalizing religious education through the publication of serious, significant, and scholarly works.

PUBLISHER TO THE PROFESSION

Contents

84321

Translator's Preface

The choice of the Continental spelling of "judgement" (with the "e") in the title of the book and throughout the text, rather than the American spelling (without the "e"), is intentional. It signals the European origins of this book and the European setting of its authors. However, the theoretical body of the book is deeply grounded in North American intellectual heritage, and its practical concerns are relevant to the North American context.

The translator thus tries to do justice to both, the European origin and the North American audience of the book. Apart from a few minor deletions and an occasional additional note, no modifications of the original text have been made. However, a chapter on the practical applications and implications of the theory has been added for the American edition. The translation seeks to honor both style and didactic flow of the German original. Thus, at times, the reader may encounter a sentence or passage with more of a Germanic flavor than he or she might ordinarily be accustomed to. Avoiding such instances would have meant major interventions into the flow of the original text. Thus, the reader is asked to accept such occasions in the spirit that they may serve as a reminder of the function of this book: to build a bridge between theory and research on religious development in Continental Europe and North America.

However, the book's concerns and impact go beyond the field of religious development. Oser and Gmünder are involved in several conversations which they ground in a challenging intellectual framework as well as in a solid empirical base. They converse with and seek to engage educators, theologians, psychologists, sociologists, theoreticians, empiricists, and practitioners. There is enough here to excite and challenge nearly everyone. And there is little reason to doubt that those who accept the authors' invitation to engage their argument with some seriousness will be rewarded.

When possible, quotations from other works have been taken from their English-language translations. Occasionally, when no English edition of the

1

source-quote could be found and a translation had to be made specifically for this volume, references to related works in English by the same author(s) have been added. Similarly, the bibliography lists English-language editions whenever possible. A large number of works cited are not available in English. This, however, may be considered a strength of this volume. It offers direct access to an important body of literature in the fields pertinent to the issues discussed in this book.

A personal note is in order. Ultimately, editors have the final say over the title of a book. However, authors and translators are allowed to dream about their preferred choice. In 1988, over a beer and a sandwich at the train station in Fribourg, Switzerland, Fritz Oser and the translator dreamed up possible titles for the American version of the book. They settled on "Liberation of the Religious Mind." Although that is not the title of the present volume, it could be viewed as the title of Fritz Oser's larger project, of which this book is a part. Reading this book with that larger framework in mind may yield some interesting perspectives and insights.

Gratitude is due to many people involved in seeing this project to its conclusion. A few deserve to be thanked in name: James Michael Lee, editor and publisher of the Religious Education Press, was always helpful and patient. He played a central role in making the theory and research presented in this volume available to a North American audience. Karen DeNicola read and edited the manuscript and made many clarifying suggestions. James W. Fowler encouraged the project at its inception and during its unfolding. Fritz Oser's kind support and Helmut Reich's gentle nudging moved the process along at critical times. Their trust and patience in awaiting the publication was greatly appreciated.

Norbert F. Hahn

Preface

When we first conducted a research project on religious judgement, we noticed that persons would quite frequently take the interview as an opportunity to recount their religious interpretations of the world. They spoke of experiences which had fundamentally altered their religious thinking and which had made them more autonomous, less anxious, more liberated. They noticed change, progress; and they were intrigued by it. They not only spoke of how they were viewing things at the time of the interview but also how they had been viewing them in the past. These experiences of transformation led us to inquire into the development of a general religious judgement.

Since it was possible to extract from the interviews certain regularities, we felt encouraged to develop a stage hierarchy of religious judgement according to the paradigm of structural developmental theory. Initially, we had designed a stage sequence analogous to Kohlberg's. But the data (with the corresponding step-by-step or "bootstrapping" analysis) yielded an independent sequence of discontinuity which correlated with Kohlberg's only at the lower stages. We then tested our own stage theory with new cross-sectional data. The theoretical construct, "religious judgement," proved stable.

Somewhere in the process questions arose about the exact definition of religion and about its motivational aspect. We have tried to determine both from the viewpoint of the person: (a) religion is a person's interpretive struggle with reality in light of an Ultimate which transcends the given reality. This is experienced as the establishing of "absolute" meaning; (b) we have interpreted the motivational aspect via the concept of experience, i.e., that condensed experience which results from the interactions of individuals' life-stories and manifests itself in the structures of religious judgement. We are not discussing "religion" as such or religion in its historical forms, but "religiosity" as a special, subjective form of coping with the contingencies of life.

The theory presented here attempts to sketch the developmental lines of

3

religious judgement from a broad data base. As free from contradictions as possible, terminologically precise, and empirically validatable, this theoretical construct attempts to describe and predict the developmental course of religious judgement. At the same time, it intends to explain the ranges of persons' judgements according to their cognitive limits. The theory, then, yields a better understanding of the relation between persons and an Ultimate (God or a divinity).

No theory can explain everything, and this theory is no exception. Although it understands its modus operandi primarily as explaining phenomena psychologically, it wants to avoid any so-called reductionism. That is, it does not view the idea of God as a human need and does not explain it as a projection. Furthermore, it does not want to uncover the origins of religion. This theory does not comment on religious truth claims nor on the apologetics of faith. It deals with the relation of persons to an Ultimate in concrete situations—as much as such a relation can be grasped on the side of the subject.[1] By far the least amount of attention can and will be paid by this theory to the entity at the other side of the relation, the Ultimate, "God." That would be presumptuous. Rather, this theory wants to investigate how persons integrate this Ultimate into concrete life-situations and how they attempt to comprehend it symbolically and conceptually. And, although the data support the theory, we can never be fully certain that it is correct.

The assumption that structures of religious reasoning undergo a process of progressive construal is indebted, on the one hand, to the genetic epistemology of Jean Piaget and, on the other hand, to the interactionism of George Herbert Mead. This assumption works with three presuppositions. First, it is genuinely possible to "fathom" the structures of religious reasoning by means of the religious judgement. Second, something like a specific religious domain does exist which remains stable in its relational quality—even across the varying contents of different religious creeds and denominations—and that relational quality can be grasped as a general structure of religion. Thereby,

> any generalization or functionialization of the concept of religion . . . (remains) plausible as a concept of *religion* only if the generally postulated functions or contents of religion can still be explained and explicated in concrete relation to particular religious traditions.[2]

---

1. Vergote has clarified this point nicely: "Research of religion . . . allows us to see that the scientific study of religion must refrain from attempting to explain religion, i.e., to reduce it to psychological or sociological causalities. However, the social sciences can investigate those factors which pattern behavior in a religious relationship (1980, p. 51).
2. Rendtorff, 1980, p. 198.

Third, the assumption that structures of religious reasoning undergo a process of progressive construal finally presupposes that the functions of religious reasoning are responsible for the self-regulation of religious interactions in such a way that different structural characteristics clearly can be identified (cf. Piaget, 1965). The last two conditions are dependent upon the first one, i.e., upon the fact that so-called religious structures of reasoning can be grasped. To that end, it is necessary to apply formal characteristics.

The genetic epistemology of Piaget has come to be recognized as the paradigm of a "genetic shift" (Holenstein, 1980, p. 42; cf. also Maier, 1978, Kesselring, 1981). It can be viewed as a "fundamental transformation of modern thought" insofar as it pursues the intent "to bring the philosophy of science and the theory of knowledge—which, since Kant, had occupied the status of the last typically philosophical discipline—into closer proximity to a scientific-empirical mode of inquiry. Put more simply, the global philosophical problem *"what* is knowledge?" (*Was ist Erkenntnis*) is being replaced with the question *"how* does knowledge *develop?"* (*Wie wird Erkenntnis*), and even more precisely "how does knowledge *increase?"* (*Wie wird mehr Erkenntnis;* Fetz, 1979, pp. 221f). In the framework of the Piagetian structural developmentalism the knowing subject is no longer regarded as an entity that IS a certain way. In addition, it is being viewed as an entity that has *become* a certain way, whereby the process of becoming makes it possible to explain a state of existence to the degree that, at all stages, the subject is always the product of its preceding developmental history.

As indicated by its name, genetic epistemology has researched especially the becoming of *episteme*, i.e., the growth of scientific knowledge. The structural-developmental approach, however, has claimed from the beginning its applicability not only to the field of scientific development but also to the various domains of human knowing. With his rather extensive investigations in the 1920s, Jean Piaget was able to prove the existence of fundamental differences between adults and children, not only in regard to logico-mathematical thought and the explanation of nature, but also in regard to the interpretation of reality in general and, thus, also in regard to moral and religious judgement.

The research into these different developmental trajectories of human cognition—i.e., the logico-mathematical, ontological, moral, and religious forms of knowing—possesses its unifying center in the shared approach of genetic structuralism. Their methodologies have another common foundation in symbolic interactionism. As Lawrence Kohlberg states: "My own approach does not go from sign to sign, but rather from expressions or 'symbols' to what is postulated as common theme or 'structure'" (Kohlberg, 1981a, p. 15). The developmental stage of an individual is determined based upon an investigation of the organizational form, or "structure," of his or her expressions or "symbols." It is the intention of the analysis of religious judgement to investigate such structures. Like Kohlberg did in the area of morality, this project intends to fathom and interpret the realm of religion from a structural developmental perspective.

The approach presented here has given rise to a much more comprehensive research project. Its result will be introduced in different publications.

The present volume contains seven chapters. Following upon the introduction, chapter one will explicate the theme of religious identity and the concept of religious judgement. It will also review previous research. The second chapter deals with research concerning the existence of a specifically religious domain. It will introduce the term, "mother-structure." The third chapter is the central one. It presents the stages of religious judgement from various perspectives (e.g., transitions, social perspective taking). Chapter four provides concrete examples corresponding to the stage descriptions of the previous chapter. It will also offer methodological reflections on the empirical basis of religious judgement research. Chapter five summarizes and evaluates the impact of the theory and suggests future directions by reflecting on the theological, epistemological, and pedagogical implications as well as on the limitations of this approach. Chapter six outlines some exciting practical applications of the theory and discusses the relevant educational implications. By describing the empirical foundations and procedures of the theory of the development of religious judgement, chapter seven provides a window into the breadth, depth, and strength of the empirical research underlying the theory. It introduces a cross-sectional research project validating the theoretical construct, "hierarchical stage sequence," surveys the empirical basis and flow of the research program during the last eight years, and lifts up directions for future research.

The authors admit that it was difficult to design the flow of the religion-science debate in such a way that both the religio-philosophical foundation as well as the empirical, religio-psychological validation follow the same language code. For a philosopher of religion, the empirical dimension often appears too simple while the psychologist of religion often considers the religio-philosophical rationality too abstract. However, in the first section, we attempt to connect our empirical work to the current discussion in the philosophy of religion. Empirically oriented readers interested in this connection are referred to the summaries which precede each section, to chapters three and four, and especially to chapter seven. Those readers interested in the philosophical or scientific study of religion and the pertinent lines of argument in this study are encouraged to read critically all introductory segments. They reflect the grounding of the research on religious judgement in the "cognitive paradigm."

Furthermore, the authors' concern is to emphasize the distinct differences between the philosophy of religion and the psychology of religion. Only the former can supply a normative and principled framework, while only the latter is able to validate it empirically. While it is the task of the philosophy of religion to determine the nature of the religious judgement, the psychology of religion is responsible for explaining its functioning. Just as psychology is unable to determine in research on morality what justice is and ought to be, it is equally unable in our case to determine what, in the sense of the development of religious judgement, constitutes higher "religiosity." However, psychology alone can perform reality testing with rational theories. Thus, we ask the reader to accept that theological as well as religio-philosophical elements are contained in our stage concept, while its validation must be achieved with the psychology of religion. In this context, then, it appears that "psychology's challenge to faith" (cf. *Concilium*, vol. 6/7, 1982) remains.

Both authors are equally responsible for the present volume. The major sections were constructed in a cooperative venture. Certain individual sections, however, were edited exclusively by one of the authors. Oser is responsible for "The Development of the Religious Judgement: Educational and Didactic Implications," while Gmünder is responsible for "Implications for Theology: Theological Statements in a Developmental Mode." (Both sections are in chapter five.) Undoubtedly, the reader will sense the particular intention of each author. Furthermore, both authors are well aware of the preliminary character of some of their formulations. This preliminary quality is due to the fact that the structural developmental approach needs a multidisciplinary grounding—as exemplified by genetic epistemology. In religious research, the structural developmental approach needs the cooperation of historians, psychologists, sociologists, philosophers, and theologians. Due to the absence of such cooperation at the time of researching and writing, both authors had to venture into domains outside of their own specialization. This, however, occurred with the authors' explicit understanding that structural developmental research in religion cannot be the subject matter of only one discipline and with their intention to initiate an interdisciplinary discussion of the issues at hand.

Our final task in this introduction is to thank everyone who participated in the creation of this book: First and foremost, Fritz Oser would like to acknowledge Lawrence Kohlberg, for they shared many a scientific argument. For a long time, Kohlberg espoused the conviction that moral structures are "hard structures" while religious structures ought to be counted among the "soft structures." That, however, would mean the dissolution of religion into morality. Furthermore, we would like to thank Ulrich Fritzsche and his many associates who invested three years in this project with the organization and implementation of the empirical research. Ulrich Klaghofer was responsible for the design of the empirical sections as well as for the analysis of the data. Without his rigorous and lucid interpretation this publication would contain many gaps. Anton Bucher's collaboration is acknowledged in the preparation of chapter six. The sketches and graphics in this book were supplied by Eugen Hinder. Additional thanks, for his friendly support and for making the infrastructure available to this project, go to Konrad Widmer who was part of the inception of the project in Zurich. Thanks also to Rainer Döbert and Norbert Mette for critical remarks, to James Fowler for many conversations, and to Clark Power for the initial encouragement and outlines for this project. Wolfgang Edelstein, Reto Luzius Fetz, and Hans Ulrich von Brachel have carefully read the manuscript and provided brilliant suggestions for improvements. Therese Binggeli typed uncounted hours until the book's completion. Finally, this project would not have been feasible without the financial support of the Swiss National Fund.

FRITZ OSER/PAUL GMÜNDER

Chapter One

On the Development of the
Religious Personality

In this first chapter, we would like to outline the nature and developmental unfolding of the religious judgement. When persons work through certain life experiences in a religious fashion, they rely on cognition, language, feeling, and action. These activities are coordinated in a subjective relational pattern between a person and an Ultimate. This pattern constitutes what we call the religious judgement. We will introduce the elements for the "definition" of this judgement, differentiate it from religious knowledge, and supply a preliminary review of the stages of religious development. A section on previous research will indicate how our theory is distinct from other approaches.

Change of Religious Consciousness. Possible Stages and their Universal Significance

Different chronological ages lead people to make different religious judgements. Their relationship to an Ultimate obtains different qualities as well. Based on these qualities, religious judgements can be ordered developmentally, i.e., in stages. The question arises as to the universal validity of these stages. Necessary for development is an increasing differentiation in the religious interpretation of the lifeworld, (*Lebenswelt*)[1] and the integration

---

1. Cf. Habermas 1988. Paul Lakeland provides a helpful summary of the concept: "The lifeworld is the social and cultural background of the community and hence of the individual. It is everything that pertains to a society and that lies

9

of an increasingly mature and socially conditioned relation to an Ultimate. The implications are important: persons at different points of their religious development interpret significant questions of life (theodicy, creation, suffering and death, chance and fortune, the religious texts they read) differently, i.e., according to their specific point of development.

Children reason differently, process information differently, view the world differently, judge the origin and destination of human life differently from adults. If one takes these facts seriously, one has to draw a fundamental conclusion: Not only do fundamental differences exist between adults and children in the logico-mathematical, ontological,[2] moral, and social domains but also concerning the interpretation of human existence from a religious perspective. St. Paul knew this when he wrote in 1 Corinthians 13:11: "When I was a child, I spoke like a child, I thought like a child, I reasoned like a child; when I became a man, I put an end to childish ways" (NRSV). Development of religious judgement means that persons who construe personal and social experiences from a religious viewpoint do this in qualitatively more and more differentiated ways as they continue on their life journey.

In regard to content, this is reflected in the formation of a religiously grounded way of meaning-making, a religiously grounded political view, a religiously grounded cosmology, metaphysics, and ethics, and a religiously grounded commitment to other people. Structurally, this happens when, in a new situation, one's relationship to the Ultimate is reconstituted. The following narrative situation was presented to persons of different ages:

In a small town there lived a rich man. He was happily married, had four children, and owned a large house. He was very successful in his job as Superior Judge of the city. He prayed regularly and never forgot to thank God for his happy life. Also, he contributed generously to charitable causes and intervened personally on behalf of poor people. Although he was a just man, many persons in town feared the judge, for he was very strict. Certain circles in the city spoke ill of him and spread rumors and slander. Thus, without any wrongdoing, he lost his good reputation. After a certain period of time he was forced to resign from his position.

---

implicitly behind all acts of communication. . . . The lifeworld is both base and background to communicative praxis" (1990, p. 56).

Habermas states: "The lifeworld to which participants in communication belong is always present, but only in such a way that it forms the background for an actual scene. . . . [It is] a reservoir of taken-for-granteds, of unshaken convictions that participants in communication draw upon in cooperative process of interpretation" (1988, pp. 123f).

2. Distinctly different from "logical" development, i.e., the construal of formal reasoning-structures, "ontological" development designates the "psychogenesis" of those categories by means of which reality is conceptualized and interpreted. Cf. Piaget, 1930, p. 338; also Fetz, 1982, 1983; similarly Broughton, 1980b.

That was not all. Later, his daughter developed a type of paralysis which worsened by the day. The former judge could no longer afford the medical expenses for his daughter's treatment. He had to sell his beautiful house and use all the money to pay the doctor bills. Still, his daughter's condition did not improve.

At this point, we ask a number of question. A few are reprinted below:

The former judge reflects upon his misfortune and wonders about God's role therein. What is he supposed to think about God?

Were the events willed by God? Why or why not?

The former judge did not feel personally responsible for his dismissal from the court nor for his daughter's illness. Do you believe that God wanted to punish him for past injustices? Why or why not?

Does God punish people? Under what conditions? How? Is it not unfair for God to allow such suffering? Did God act unfairly or immorally in this situation?

If you believe that God was unjust, please explain why you think so? Why, then, does God permit the suffering of innocent people, e.g., in sickness, natural disaster, and war?

If God is almighty, can God not prevent suffering and offer help instead?

A child of five or six years of age would probably say that God was punishing the judge, that people ought to obey God's will, that God can still help the judge, that God can put all things back in order on earth, that God prevents injustices from happening, that God loves people, etc.

A twelve-year-old responds quite differently. Most likely, she would say that in order to be helped by God, the judge would have to pray or do something good. God wanted to test the judge's faith. The more the judge trusts in God, the more God would help him. God only punishes people who do not believe in God. Making a sacrifice or renouncing something would reconcile God and God would do God's best for the judge.

Quite different is the judgement of an adolescent at age fifteen. He thinks, for example, that the entire story is totally unrelated to God, that it was either a coincidence or the judge's own fault. God does not punish people. People need to decide for themselves what to do in such situations. God is much more mysterious. God is self-revealing only where life is created or when death occurs. If God exists at all, then there are sufficient other tasks for God to attend to.

A fourth example is an adult, age thirty-five, who expressed the view that the situation is entirely a human problem. God does not punish people.

However, the judge's mistreatment by other people has to do with the atheism of the world. Although humans have the choice to act abominably, as people did in the case of the judge, their actions then lead to the exclusion of God from the world. For God only wants the good, yet people must do it.

The distinctly different character of these four judgements is clearly visible. Each is qualitatively more complex and more integrated than the one preceding it. Thus, they reflect different stages of a developmental sequence. Table 1 provides an abbreviated summary of these stages which will be described in more detail in the following chapters:

Table 1: Summary of the Stages of Religious Judgment:

Stage 1: The Ultimate, regardless of its form and shape, protects or abandons, bestows health or illness, gives joy or despair. The Ultimate directly influences humans (and all other living creatures as well). The will of the Ultimate must be done, lest the relation with it will be broken.

Stage 2: It is possible to influence the will of the Ultimate by means of prayer, sacrifice, obedience to religious rules, etc. If one cares about this Ultimate and passes all tests given by it, then one receives its parental love and trusting care and becomes happy, healthy, and successful. Depending on one's own needs and use of free will, one can either influence the Ultimate or one can decline to do so.

Stage 3: Individuals presume to be fully responsible for their own lives as well as for the world and all that is in it. Freedom, meaning, hope—these are the categories on which decision making is based. The Ultimate constitutes an entity outside the human realm. It has its own domain of action, and it defines freedom, meaning, and hope completely differently from humans. Although this transcendent entity exists outside and away from individuals, it nevertheless represents the fundamental ordering of life and the world.

Stage 4: The relationship between a person and the Ultimate is now mediated indirectly. That means, individuals continue to see themselves as responsible for their fate and actions. Yet, they begin to ask and search for the conditions and contingencies which make this possible. These are represented by the Ultimate. It creates the conditions for freedom, responsibility, and hope which can be actualized only through the execution of a "Divine Plan," i.e., the actions of God on behalf of the world through us.

Stage 5: The Ultimate always and everywhere permeates interpersonal commitments while simultaneously transcending them. History and revelation testify to this with those moments when people begin to approach each other and cooperate with each other. Transcendence and immanence permeate one another and thereby establish the possibility of universal solidarity of all people. The "kingdom of God" becomes the "guardian" for those individuals committed to work on behalf of other people, who thereby make meaning and who cannot conceive of the Divine without concrete reference to human beings.

If we presume that such periods or stages of religious development exist and that, for an individual at a certain stage, the interpretive patterns of religious knowing are similar in various situations, then we can assume the following: (a) Children, adolescents, and adults rely on different patterns of religious interpretations of the world and ascribe qualitatively different religious valuations to their experiences; and (b) passing from one stage to another means undergoing major transformative changes. Indicators of such transformations are, for example, a new interpretation of traditional religious formulas, processes of demythologizing, or processes of reintegration where mythical qualities resurface in new symbols (e.g., friendship, closeness to God, etc.). Other indicators of such transformations are the reconstruction of an individual's worldview according to a newly adopted set of criteria—for example, scientific or artistic ones. Further indicators of stage transformations are a new perspective on freedom in the "practical-philosophical" domain or a new way of perceiving the Transcendent as the ground and source of total social commitment. Such a commitment, then, in turn, can provide a ground for answers to questions of ultimate meaning. Finally, as indicators for transformations we can also view all those crises in which something old is surrendered and something new is created. Such indicators alone, however, do not suffice. We must further clarify what we mean by stages and transformations.

Let us attempt a retrospective: A person who has achieved a particular religious consciousness—it is also possible to say, a particular religious identity[3]—can be presumed to have passed through a series of transformations. The substantive experiences, the particular core stimuli which ushered in each new stage, were biographical elements which contributed to the coming into consciousness of the current religious identity.

In other words, all the constitutive elements of the development of the religious personality, i.e., the ontogenesis of religious consciousness, are bio-

---

3. In this instance, we are using religious consciousness and religious identity synonymously. Although not quite accurate, it is nonetheless justified insofar as identity refers not to objective identity *(Sachidentität)* but to the structural aspects of the categories which are employed by persons for thinking and meaning-making. (Cf. Parsons, 1977, pp. 74f; Erikson, 1963, pp. 229f; Marcia, 1966. Furthermore, as Noam and Kegan suggest (1982, p. 422), identity refers to the constitutive activity of that overarching system "which construes the differentiation between self and other as such." Compare also Krappmann, 1973, Habermas, 1976, and Mette, 1983, pp. 97f.

graphical trajectories established in the matrix of an individual's life experiences, the expectations of others, with regard to society and history, and a
relationship with an Ultimate.[4] This development passes through a series of
discontinuous steps which are guided by the question as to how the Absolute
becomes part of and functions in this evolutionary process when persons
cognitively construe the various social situations in which they find themselves. This process does not take place in an unquestioning manner. Rather,
it is reflective. At each stage, the degree of reflectiveness possesses exact criteria, clear boundaries, and a structural definition.

The Relationship with an Ultimate (God) as the Central
Qualitative Criterion of Religious Consciousness

> A relational dimension is always implicit in our explanations
> of God's presence, support, and sustaining power in our lives.
> Thus, we are dealing here with subjective perspectives. By exam-
> ining individual instances we shall abstract the structural com-
> monalities of these individual perspectives. This is possible
> because religious reasoning contains similar elements in all per-
> sons in all cultures.

We have already indicated that growing into a "higher" form of religiosity means a reflective widening and deepening of one's relationship to an
Ultimate. This statement may lead to the erroneous conclusions that the development of the religious personality and the corresponding transformations
may lead to the collapsing of religious interpretations into situation-specific
rationality, that religiosity can be transcended via rationality, that religiosity
loses its grounding in reality, or that religiosity needs to be overcome.

To counter such false conclusions we would like to assert that, in a structural view of religious development, higher stages, in comparison to lower
stages, feature a different mix or balance of religiosity and rationality and that
the former *cannot* be dissolved into the latter. In this sense, rationality does
not only mean the unfettered cognitive mastery of one's lifeworld by means
of a free construction of one's experienced reality. Rationality does not only
mean critical and detached reflection on human realities. Rather, rationality

---

4. In this book, we are using the terms "the Absolute" "the Ultimate," and "the
Transcendent" interchangeably. All three presuppose and try to bring to expression a form of religiousness that is universally expressive and valid. The term "the
Ultimate" refers to a "final reality." These terms, therefore, are synonymous. The
term "the Absolute" refers to the conditions of possibility, i.e., to that which
always already exists, when we begin to relate to a final reality. The term "the
Transcendent" refers to that other reality which we can glimpse in acts of self-
transcendence.

refers to those processes demanded by grounding oneself and one's inter-pretation in an ultimate reality: the dual processes of accommodation and assimilation (by relying on the expressive means available to persons).

Processes similar to those underlying the changing construal of reality in the subject-object domain are at work when individuals wrestle or cope with worldviews, with contingencies, with questions concerning the origin and pos-sibility of religious meaning-making in the practice of everyday life. Regardless whether its substance is positive or negative, belief or doubt, theistic or atheistic, committed to one religion or another, the evolution of reli-gious meaning-making does not lead to enchantment, anxiety, detachment, etc., but to a more and more adequate integration of all these expressive ele-ments into one communicative reality: All of this expresses a person's rela-tional reality. One approaches the Ultimate by means of a repeated process of distancing oneself from it and then reappropriating it in an existentially new way. Thus, the increasing structural differentiation of religious meaning-making is coupled with a steadily improving integration of the relation to the Ultimate. Structural differentiation and integration must be equilibrated.

The responses given to our narrative about the judge tell us that the iden-tity and transformation of the religious personality involves persons' con-struals of their relations to the Ultimate. Many questions arising in this con-text are traditional ones: Certain contemporary theological schools have picked them up and dealt with them intensively under the rubric of "anthro-pology and theology" (cf. Pannenberg, 1972, 1983). For example, the con-cept of "correlation" was adopted from the social sciences and redefined theologically (cf. Schillebeeckx, 1971, Bitter, 1981, Ranke, 1981). It now refers to the connection between the presupposed Ultimate and concrete human situations. The correlation between the two poles connected in this way is more important than either pole singularly. Thus, theology and anthro-pology have become interdependent. And in this sense, religion builds upon the foundation laid by anthropology. To a degree, such an approach makes repetitions unavoidable. Its novelty, however, consists in its developmen-tal element, the view of a progression, and the issue of the generalizability of developmental structures. The responses to the judge-dilemma can easily be ordered structurally. For example, the answers of a five- or six-year-old can be perceived to mean that for him or her the Ultimate intervenes direct-ly in the world, that it assures people's welfare. God shows God's love through gifts, etc. However, when God is angry, God withholds love; when God is not angry, God becomes helpful. In other words, categories of love, trust, and freedom are directly mediated, physically visible, and accessible by means of their concrete manifestation. For the child, the Ultimate resides beyond human beings. Yet, it engineers that people are good, strong, agile, intelligent, etc. The other stages are very different from this.

However, if it is possible to abstract such characteristic categories from

each stage, then immediately the question about universal applicability arises. Presumably nowhere else except in the domain of coping with and interpreting the world in a religious fashion does this problem surface: Is the
developmental sequence of the underlying structures universally valid and are
the individual stages culturally invariant? Is it possible that, for instance, a
Tibetan, a Dominican, and an atheist exhibit similar religious deep-structures? Are there elements of religious consciousness that are universal? We
would like to postulate both: The deep-structure of religious identity as well
as the foundational developmental sequence are universal. There is, however,
the position of the so-called cultural relativists.[5] It states that the actual religious convictions of all peoples and cultures are fundamentally different,
that no transcultural system of religious content exists, and that hence no
criteria are available with which to judge different religious convictions. In
light of this position, then, is it still possible to postulate the universal uniformity of religious structures? Is it really possible to place these structures
in a universal sequential order? Insofar as religion does have significance and
meaning in a person's life, we make this assumption positively and we will
attempt to prove it theoretically as well as empirically. In the following section we would like to describe the various elements which constitute religious
consciousness and address the issue of universal validity. First, however,
we need to enumerate those conditions upon which they are contingent:

a) We are stressing the subjective aspect of religion, i.e., persons' actual
ways of reconstruing[6] and interpreting concrete situations in their lives in a
religious fashion. Our discussion centers not so much on traditional systems of faith and religious rites, but rather on the patterns of religious interpretations of experience.

Under the title, *Les formes élémentaires de la vie religieuse,* Emile
Durkheim (1912) summarized earlier studies in the history of religions.[7]
While Durkheim described the development and transformation of religious
systems from a sociological perspective, we are concerned with life-cycle
transformations. At first glance, life-cycle transformations appear possible
only as a collection of autobiographical experiences (from the point of view

---

5. Cf. Ginters, R.: *Relativismus in der Ethik,* Düsseldorf: Patmos, 1978, p. 10. We
   have merely attempted to adapt from Ginters the criteria of cultural relativism in
   regard to universal morality and to apply them to the religious judgement.
6. "Reconstruing" is a process of interpretation quite distinct from any form of
   "construing," for it does not imply the positing of an objective point of reference.
   In other words, using the term "reconstruing" avoids implying that the Ultimate
   (God, an Absolute, etc.) is a mere construction, or invention, of the religious subject.
7. Durkheim goes so far as to claim that individual religious thought is only a mir-
   ror image of those religious systems to which individuals belong: "It becomes
   clearly evident that these individual cults are not distinct and autonomous religious systems but merely aspects of the common religion of the whole church,
   of which the individuals are members" (English edition, 1915; 1965, p. 61).

of the development of religious identity). However, it will become evident that the application of the method of genetic structuralism provides the means to overcome idiosyncratic concepts. In contrast to Durkheim who sought to define the "religious phenomenon," we are concerned with the definition of the religious personality, i.e., with individuals' religiosity and their reflective processes upon that religiosity.

b) Undoubtedly there are persons living within the Judaeo-Christian tradition who process and interpret their experiences from a religious vantage point. For example, they may ask why God permits suffering, how it is possible to believe in God, what constitutes a relationship with God, what is the ultimate meaning underlying the secret of life's creation and destruction, whether something supernatural exists at all. They wonder what happens after death, whether there is a final judgement, ultimate justice, etc. They try to answer these questions in the form of a statement. Here one might object that this only proves the culture-dependent development toward a higher religious identity, that it follows a particular trajectory, and thereby cannot claim universal validity.

At this point, however, we must protest. We do indeed emphasize that, in our opinion, cognitive structures always refer to particular substantive conditions. Yet, it is exactly the hallmark of universal cognitive patterns of interpretation that they can be abstracted from particular contents while, at the same time, they are operative across various situations. Therefore, it is our opinion that the potential for universal validity which is present in every religion can be sponsored via subjective development until it, finally, represents the possibility of a higher form of religious identity. For that reason, we have introduced the concept of "mother-structure."

c) Another aspect must be added: Beyond the potential for universality, those elements for the description of persons' religious development which are constant and regular are primordial in nature. Constancy and regularity differ from particularity through an equivalency of functions. Regardless of their developmental origin or quality, cognitive structures serve (functionally) for the reconstruction of events from the same point of view. This does not say that various and different processes of religious socialization do not exist and that these processes do not vary from one religion to another. We merely assume that those regularities which have grown out of a fertile content-soil remain stable over a period of time. At the same time, these regularities are employed for the assimilation of and accommodation to new content.[8]

---

8. In this respect, Durkheim makes a rather sweeping remark: "Also, in whatever manner men have represented the novelties and contingencies revealed by experience, there is nothing in these representations which could serve to characterize religion. For religious conceptions have as their object, before everything else, to express and explain, not that which is exceptional and abnormal in things, but, on the contrary, that which is constant and regular (1915, p. 43).

d) It has already been pointed out that general and specifically religious socialization become crystallized in the ego-identity of the person. Ego-identity refers to something *holistic with specific qualifications*. Although this book's focus on the developmental processes of the dynamic self's religious cognition represents only limited research into the totality of what makes up ego-identity, it does not imply a curtailment of the investigation of religion as a separate domain of the socialization process. Rather, we see our approach as an integral part of attempts to describe the ontogenesis of the person. At issue is how human communication is experienced and reflectively processed in acts of success and failure vis-à-vis an Ultimate which transcends those acts. The development of the "religious personality" is grounded in the basic structure of communicative action which, in an unconditional and mutual recognition of equal freedom, constitutes the final center of interaction. However, this is only one side. The other side is guided more closely by the more subjective forms of religious interpretations of certain life situations by means of statements concerning contexts or connections which are experienced as religious, e.g., participation in the rituals of religious communities, the rejection of religious practices, meditation, prayer, etc. Communicative involvement with others and this second, more personal form of religiousness, provide the context in which the religious judgement surfaces. In other words, identity in the context of ontogenetic development of religious judgement always refers to an intersubjective identity (cf. Peukert, 1982). This real, basic structure of intersubjectivity must always be taken into account in the case of developmental stage transformations.

Let us now summarize what has been said so far: The answers people give to the story of the judge are very different in their quality. These answers always exhibit structural characteristics which reveal structures of development. Of great significance for these structures are autobiographical experiences. Presumably those experiences affect transitions from one stage to another. Compared to its antecedent, a new and higher structure features increased differentiation of certain characteristics—which will be introduced later—as well as a broadened integration of the relational dimension. Generally speaking, it can be stated that the development of the religious judgement is a part of the development of the personality. Two aspects are important for its description: (a) the ontological sensibility of persons, and (b) the relation persons have with what they consider to be their Ultimate Environment, i.e., the way a person relates to an Ultimate in concrete action-situations. The quality of this relationship can be developed more or less adequately and depends on the different interpretations of the relational categories. It is not possible to refute the claim of the developmental sequence to universal validity by simply calling our Judaeo-Christian data ethnocentric. Clearly, these data prove the universal validity claim only if we can prove that persons of the same religion rely on the same cognitive schemata even in different situations. And if we were to succeed in showing that this is the case even across religious boundaries, then our postulated universality would be well established.

Religious Judgement

> When persons (a) process their life experiences in a religious mode (e.g., in interpretations, conversation, prayer), (b) assimilate narrative texts (doctrine, proclamation, Bible) in a religious mode, or (c) participate in the life of religious communities (cultus, liturgy), then they actually employ that regulative meaning-making system which represents their relation to an Ultimate. In its totality, this system possesses many facets. It is a person's religious consciousness in operation. In its linguistic form, we call it religious judgement. A person's verbal articulation of this relationship may vary from situation to situation. Yet, the religious judgement of a person remains—for a certain period of time—the same.

In addition to the developmental concept of the religious personality we employ as another major concept that of the religious judgement. How can the structure of the religious judgement be determined? Which are the intellectual operations that, in the widest sense, can be designated as religious and, when transformed into a pattern, represent a person's religious judgement, and which can be grasped and investigated through language? We must add the following approach to the statements about the structure of persons' relations to an Ultimate made so far: If the construct "religious judgement" can be sharply distinguished from other forms of cognitive coping with reality, then it appears that the religious structure of knowing opens up a communicative reality which cannot attain a fully satisfactory cognitive equilibrium by means of other knowledge-structures. Taking this point of view, the religious judgement can be determined more exactly with the following frame of reference:

1. Religious judgement refers to those subjective realities which remain inadequately fathomed when they are investigated and described only with functional and strategic means of "objectifying knowing" [*Objektbewältigung*].
2. It refers to those subjective realities which have to do with meaning, meaning-making, and coping with contingencies.[9]

---

9. Contingency is always understood in its Aristotelian sense, i.e., something can be a certain way but does not have to be. The implications of this will be elaborated below.

3. It expresses the shape of the relation between persons and an Ultimate in situations in which "plausibilities," i.e., obvious structures of explanation and meaning, are not self-evident.

4. It represents the ongoing effort at creating security in a world in which securities, on the one hand, have to be achieved subjectively while, on the other hand, objectively they are doomed to fail.

Within this frame of reference, then, the following questions are to be answered: How can finite freedom be achieved vis-à-vis experiences of contingency? How can we conceive of the relational structure between autonomy and that which is beyond our grasp? How does the transcendent element manifest itself immanently? What is the origin of that measure of trust which makes possible the integration of new experiences? The answers to these fundamental questions in various life situations constitute the constant coordinates within which the logic of a religious stage theory must operate. The various "specifications" of finite, contingent freedom; of finite, contingent trust (faith); of finite, contingent hope; of finite, contingent sacredness, etc., assist in differentiating and integrating this stage theory. Put differently, the stage-determination of an individual stage is dependent on these elements' respective capacity for differentiation and integration. The elements themselves are related to each other in a way that is expressed in the respective structures of each of the stages (the elements will be described more carefully in the next section). The aforementioned capacity for differentiation and integration comes to expression in the mediation *[Vermittlung]* of the self to itself—and therein also to others—and to an Ultimate.[10]

Formulated in a different way, the religious judgement is the expression of a person's regulative system which, in certain situations, evaluates the individual's relation to the Ultimate. It is not necessary for this relation to be evaluated in each situation, although that is possible. It should not be maintained that this relationship surfaces only in limit- or contingency-situations, although such situations facilitate its surfacing. Thus, each person possesses a set of rules which are activated when the person enters into the aforementioned relationship with the Ultimate (God). In the act of their religious judgement, persons thus activate religious structures in order to integrate a certain contingent reality in a particular fashion which is clearly distinct from other modes of integration. (For example, I can describe the birth of a

---

10. We would like to stress again that we are not explicitly concerned with a substantive or even theological analysis of that which was characterized as "religious." Rather, the construct "religious judgement" is being analyzed strictly from the perspective of developmental psychology. In that context, the construct is understood functionally as a relational structure which represents a relation between persons and an Ultimate that is removed from concrete action. It comes to expression in the stage-specific modes of the cognitive processes.

child with elements of a structural sequence, such as conception, pregnancy, labor-pains, birth, etc. Simultaneously, however, I can activate dimensions or elements such as happiness, freedom, lack of control, transcendence, etc. In this way, the event is integrated differently compared with a structural sequence.) Preliminarily, we want to designate constitutive polar elements of that sort as follows: the holy vs. the profane, transcendence vs. immanence, freedom vs. dependency, hope vs. absurdity, trust vs. fear, functional transparency vs. opaqueness, eternity vs. ephemerality.[11] In the religious judgement of persons these elements are assembled into a certain interrelational structure in order to assimilate a situation in a comprehending, explanatory, and interpretive manner. Schibilsky's opinion (1978, p. 75) that religion has its significance beyond the realm of certainty and definitiveness must also apply to the aforementioned polar elements. They always have a creative and constructive positive pole, but they also have an objective negative pole. What we have called the certainty which must be established subjectively in the face of objective uncertainty and transitoriness is contained, in its opposite form, in each element and provides it with the necessary generative power. One of the properties of religious judgement is thus a process in which what is given is transcended toward an elusive horizon which can no longer be provided substantively. From there, subjects can reflect back upon themselves in their own facticity. In other words, the religious judgement makes it possible to cope with life situations when persons, who are living within concrete reality, are placed in relation to ultimate conditions and thereby engage their regulative system in a relational structuring-process. Thus, integrating an experienced reality means: approaching this reality in an interpretive fashion with one's own religious schematas and thereby revealing and extending one's regulative religious system.

An example shall concretize what we have said so far: A person discussing a problematic experience from the perspective of the relationship between self and the Transcendent explains what course of action she would take and why. In this reasoning process the aforementioned regulative system is activated. However, it is mediated via content, i.e., the person applies it without being conscious of the formal structure of this regulative system as such. For instance, such a rule could say:

The Ultimate is a Higher Being, God, but it can not influence human beings. People have to resolve their problems on their own. Human freedom is similar to

---

11. The structure of equilibration of these elements is described in more detail in the next section. [Translator's note: The translation of these polarities varies in different translations of earlier works by Fritz Oser. The terms selected here correspond to Oser's most recent and probably most accessible essay, "Stages of Religious Judgment: A Response to My Critics," in *Stages of Faith and Religious Development,* ed. Fowler, Nipkow, and Schweitzer (New York: Crossroads, 1991).

the freedom of the Ultimate. People can generate hope just as well as a personified Absolute is able to do (stage 3 judgement).

The following example demonstrates how the rule would be applied: In a life-
threatening situation a man makes a pledge to forgo a successful career and
to invest his energies instead on behalf of the poor in the Third World. A
respondent would apply the stage 3 rule in the following manner: "The crash
of the airplane happened because of mistakes made during maintenance.
This has nothing to do with God. God is unable to influence the maintenance crew."

It is now the task of the researcher to extract the aforementioned rule,
i.e., the structure (or form), from the content. By examining a series of
questions and answers concerning a concrete situation, the researcher
must identify the religious judgement of persons, i.e., their religious regulative system. This means that the researcher cannot utilize persons'
self-evaluations as far as positive or negative confessional statements
are concerned. Rather the researcher must observe how persons deal
with concrete problems; how persons, in concrete situations, construe
the connection between themselves and the totality of their reality; and
how persons establish an equilibrium among the aforementioned polar elements.

Thus, we follow an approach which sees persons as actualizing their relation to that which surrounds them ultimately [*das Umgreifende* (Jaspers)]
always in certain actual situations. Such situations include anthropological,
interpersonal, and transcendent dimensions—regardless of whether these
are actually recognized by persons or not. The relational reasoning is the
decisive element.[12]

The same process- and action-oriented, i.e., psychological-anthropolog-
ical concept of religion can be found in James Fowler's thinking when he
states:[13]

---

12. This has been clearly stated by Hasenhüttl when he says: "Relational reasoning
takes a view of process that is never complete nor ever satisfied with its achievements but rather points to the new possibilities implicit and emergent in new processes. This means that a concept of God that is verified by means of a critical
process instead of objective knowledge provides a social-critical function. It
does this by relativizing all objectives which are considered met and all results
which are deemed accomplished. In fact, it is impossible to supply an objectifiable
endpoint, because (a) none is given by the object as such, and (b) the reality-con-
stituting process itself reveals truth, thereby allowing persons to gain new insight
into themselves or to actualize themselves. Such a concept of God effects a radical openness for the new, for the transformation of social structures" (Hasenhüttl,
1979, pp. 130f).
13. In a footnote, Fowler defines this term as something which affects us from
beyond ourselves. It can be used theistically, monistically, or in other ways.

In a sense, faith [in our case, religious judgement] is a form of knowing, of construing or of interpreting that refers to the relation between persons or communities
and those centers of value and power which influence the lives of subjects in a
manner which cannot be controlled by them. Theologically speaking, faith is
that form of knowing or construing with which persons relate to a transcendent
entity (Fowler, 1974, p. 175).

Let us summarize: religious judgement refers to the possibility that persons, in their concrete realities, by means of their cognitive activity and by
means of their operations of reasoning, place themselves into a relation to ultimate conditions[14] and that they thereby engage their regulative system in a
relational structuring process. Integrating an experienced reality means to
engage this reality with one's own religious structures and thereby to reveal
and to extend one's regulative system. The actualization of this regulative system is an intensive and living process. Persons confronted with a religious
dilemma work intensively on a possible overcoming of the disequilibrium
given with the dilemma. Such an engagement involves, among other things,
explanations of present or subsequent consequences, time-analyses, correlational interpretations, valuations, preceding intellectual decision making and
reasoning, applications of meaning-making patterns to a situation (cf. Dietrich,
1978, p. 264), but—above all—a relational interpretation of this reality. The
perspective of the relationship between persons and their Ultimate stands
out from all the other perspectives until the best-possible integration of the
other dimensions in this reality is achieved—the ideal case being the integration according to the characteristics of stage 5 of religious judgement.

The Dimensions of Equilibrium and Disequilibrium of the Religious Judgement

When asked which substantive elements "belong" to the
description of the religious judgement, we introduce the following polarities: the sacred vs. the profane, the transcendent vs.
the immanent, freedom vs. dependency, hope vs. absurdity, trust
vs. anxiety, eternity vs. ephemerality, and functional transparency
vs. opaqueness (magic). Persons faced with a dilemma-situation
have to establish an equilibrium between these poles—e.g.,
between freedom and dependency—which is personally valid
and satisfactory for them. Here, then, we can observe stage differences. The lower stages emphasize more strongly the pole of

---

14. In this work we are using "the Ultimate," "the Absolute," and "the Unconditional"
in a way similar to Fowler's usage of the "Transcendent." The universal validity of religious judgement is thereby clearly distinct from all other forms of
judgement.

dependency, the middle stages reveal a "gap" between both poles which are viewed as opposites, while persons at the higher stages correlate freedom and dependency conjunctively. In other words, freedom becomes available only upon passing through dependency, or on the other side of dependency. The other elements are treated similarly. Various questions of our standardized dilemma-situations elicit the corresponding elements.

Every cultural domain that can be articulated in structural terms features its own economy of equilibration. For example, in the domain of "property ownership," a moral judgement could be described as the balancing of various distributive claims from the perspective of justice. A higher stage would imply a higher "external" reversibility of the competing claims. Similarly, the domain of religious judgement deals with the balancing of discrepant fundamental religious dimensions. We are attempting to delineate these polar dimensions by taking the point of view that different stages represent equilibria of different reversibility.

Thus, the religious judgement is the reconstruction of a certain reality between these poles whereby the equilibria of the different developmental stages are articulated each in a qualitatively different way. The "most complete" equilibrium is achieved at the highest stage.

How, then, did we arrive at these dimensions? Where did they originate? What is their function?

a) These dimensions emerge everywhere in the history of religion and we have encountered them repeatedly when surveying the literature in the field of psychology of religion.[15] Yet, we have obtained them from carefully mining the responses to our dilemma texts given by persons of various ages in our "pilot-study." They were not derived from a particular theory of religion. Rather they were gathered as comprehensive dimensions by assembling and grouping those content-elements which constitute the results of persons' religious coping with the world.

b) Although we had designed a developmental stage theory in advance, which was validated in cross-sectional studies, the dimensions which are determinative of the individual stages were established inductively.

c) The unified whole of all dimensions represents an interpretive means for assigning a person to a certain stage as well as for qualitative valuation of structural characteristics.

In the following we would like to supply for each of these dimensions some thoughts regarding the description and hermeneutic of the field of tension cre-

---

15. Grom (1981, p. 38) appeals exclusively to psychological criteria for "developmentally desirable religiosity." However, in our estimation, his criteria are not referring specifically to religiosity but rather seem to investigate certain dimensions in the domain of religious cognition.

ated by the polarities. Unfortunately, space limitations allow only for a sketchy exposition.

The first polarity is the sacred vs. the profane. According to Durkheim (1965, p. 52), the characteristic criteria for the sacred always precede any classification of elements, real or imagined. Religious membership, myths, dogmas, rituals, etc., determine this "sacred realm." God, spirits, even a rock, a tree, a well, a piece of wood, a house, etc., can be sacred. Words, expressions, gestures, formulas also belong to this realm. Durkheim believes that the sacred can be found in all religions. Buddhism, for example, creates sacred domains (e.g., the four noble truths and the paths leading to them), because it lacks gods.

Viewed psychologically, the sacred refers to acts which justify human behavior in light of an Ultimate. The sacred separates the Ultimate from the profane while, at the same time, mediating it. For Durkheim, nothing but completely heterogeneity can characterize the sacred in its relation to the profane. Therefore, the distinction between them is absolute.[16] And yet, the sacred is differentiated from the profane through the dimensions of absolute validity, unapproachability, and normativity.

Eliade (1955, pp. 21f) does a fine job describing the experience of non-homogeneity of space which, primordially, led to the separation of sacred and profane. By means of this experience an absolute reality opens up for people which contradicts the "nonreality" of the worldly. The sacred makes it possible to refer to a fixed point. In contrast to the uninterrupted uniformity of the profane, the sacred makes it possible to construct a center within the endless homogeneity of the profane. The transitional threshold, e.g., from the outside world into a church, affords the possibility to transcend the world; i.e., the new locale enables communication with an unexpected inner depth. The sacralization of a space or of a locale also means a repetition of cosmogony and the creation of a center which, on the one hand, provides security and sta-

---

16. "In all the history of human thought there exists no other example of things so profoundly differentiated or so radically opposed to one another. The traditional opposition of good and bad is nothing beside this; for the good and the bad are only two opposed species of the same class, namely morals, just as sickness and health are two different aspects of the same order of facts, i.e., life, while the sacred and the profane have always and everywhere been conceived by the human mind as two distinct classes, as two worlds between which there is nothing in common. The forces which play in one are not simply those which are met with in the other, but a little stronger; they are of a different sort. In different religions, this opposition has been conceived in different ways. Here, to separate these two sorts of things it has seemed sufficient to localize them in different parts of the physical universe; there the first have been put into an ideal and transcendental world while the material world is left in full possession of the others. But howsoever much the forms of the contrast may vary, the fact of the contrast is universal" (1965, pp. 53f).

bility while, on the other hand, dictates "to hallow," i.e., to transcend, life.[17]

In terms of developmental logic, the beginning of the sacred-profane distinction is the experience of the necessity of an absolute value, of a fixed point of reference in space. Later on, these dimensions separate out into two independent entities. They will come together again when, eventually, the sacred surfaces within, and transcends, the profane. However, Eliade is probably mistaken in believing that the desacralization of the world leads to tragedy. On the contrary, it (the desacralization) goes beyond all equilibria and finally comes to the point where it lets the sacred surface in the profane. Only the failure of this process, i.e., the loss of all sacredness, leads to tragedy. It is for that reason that children and adolescents are encouraged to go through a developmental process—from the unquestioning acceptance of the sacred to the separation of "the sacred" and "the profane," to the transformation of "the sacred" in the real—which enables them to appropriate "the sacred" symbolically as the condition for the possibility of rationally oriented meaning-making.

While the dimension "the sacred vs. the profane" provides a fixed point of reference, a center in the heterogeneity of experiences, the polarity "the transcendent vs. the immanent" rests upon a certain worldview. Psychologically, we are dealing here with the more or less abstract concept of "below and above." This is the difference between existing reality, on the one hand, and that which grounds this reality, on the other hand. If "the immanent" designates reality just as it exists, then "the concept of transcendence has the correlative function: defining reality as immanent means transcending it; defining the transcending means relating it to the immanent" (Simons, 1974, p. 154). Thus, the process of transcending has a twofold meaning: as a movement that goes to the bottom and investigates the ground; and as a movement, originating from the ground, which unlocks, changes, and improves reality. Both movements exhibit the feature of being qualified as well as qualifying and differentiating" (cf. Simons, 1974, p. 156).

Originally, on one side, we discover human helplessness in the face of contingency and alien, *unknown* powers, while, on the other side, we find conscious agency and *familiar* powers. On one side, we encounter the conditions for the human potential for thought and action. On the other side, we encounter persons' actual experiences and motivations. Thereby it is quite possible to personalize the Transcendent (God) in the same manner as subject-subject relations—i.e., communicative reality—surface in the interpersonal domain. Take the example of a person whose entire future is blocked because

---

17. In the chapter "Le sacré et le profane dans la monde moderne," Eliade says: "Quel que soit le contexte historique dans lequel il est plongé, l'home religious croit toujours qu'il existe une réalité aboslue, le sacré, qui transcende ce monde-ci, mais qui s'y manifeste et, de ce fait, le sanctifie et le rend réel" (1955, p. 171).

certain bodily injuries, sustained in an accident, limit this person's range of communicative and professional options. The person is able to explain the causality of the accident by reference to a chain of events. Yet, the person realizes that each key-event represents only one possibility—things could have gone quite differently. Thus, there have to be other influences upon the events in the chain: such as certain constellations, chance, an eternal plan, or God's intervention. These influences existed, then, at each key step of the way, in correlation to reality. The person is now faced with the task of creating an equilibrium which answers his or her questions sufficiently and plausibly. This occurs, on the one hand, by interpreting reality and, on the other hand, by relating and referring to the transcendent (if the existence of a personal divine being is assumed).

Psychologically, this means that persons produce stage-specific equilibria between the immanent and the transcendent, between "above" and "below." Stage 1 displays an active predominance of the "above," which is more powerful than the "below," and which guides the world and causes things to happen. This personified transcendence functions like something or someone treating people as puppets on a string. "Making things happen" thus reveals the sense of a so-called artificialism and is understood as a direct intervention of the transcendent into the immanent.[18] At the highest stage, the transcendent becomes evident in the immanence of human communication, and vice versa. When required by the religious interpretation of a situation, the progressively "higher" equilibria between the transcendent and the immanent also include religio-metaphysical images of the world. In different situations they explain, in fresh and different ways, basic views of the world as a whole. On the one hand, these views are concepts of the transcendent and of the immanent. On the other hand, these views of the world feature polarities, such as passivity vs. activity, asceticism vs. ownership, contemplation vs. a change-and-struggle-orientation. On the one hand, from a fatalistic perspective it is possible to perceive the equilibrium between absolute freedom and absolute dependency as reduced to a minimum. On the other hand, it is also possible to regard this equilibrium as a totally unrestricted possibility for meaning-making. Freedom and dependency, too, have to be equilibrated in concrete situations.

This sort of freedom has a social pole and a natural pole. Socially, freedom can be understood as limits on the claims of others by means of the regulative power of the law. In regard to nature, freedom is restricted by the possibilities inherent in phylogenetic development. Concepts of the exercise of freedom—e.g., by means of decision, consensus, engagement, etc.—are grounded transcendentally. Let us assume, for example, that a single encounter of two persons, which leads to marriage and family, is being interpreted

---

18. Cf. Piaget, 1930.

from a religious point of view. In this case, the task is the creation of an interpretive equilibrium between the poles of freedom, vis-à-vis the concept of a dependency on the preconditions of a historical constellation. The constituting of meaning for such an important action is an interpretive act or a relational act with the categories of absolute freedom vs. absolute dependence. Only in this act can the purpose of an action be interpreted meaningfully: i.e., as a somehow reversible equilibrium between fusion with the partner, autonomy from the partner, freedom for the sake of the partner, dependency upon the partner, and, finally, transcendental freedom and freedom from the transcendent.

> The knowledge of the meaning of our action does not derive . . . from any theoretical evidence. Rather it originates in our commitment to freedom, to freedom before God and with each other" (Krings, 1979, p. 53).

Viewed psychologically, at the lowest stage, freedom is exercised when persons actualize themselves cognitively and actually. (An eight-year-old child says: God decides everything, but I like it because I am doing well.) At a higher stage, freedom and dependency are interrelated. A decision is marked by the element of deciding "in favor of" something, and this deciding "in favor of" constitutes, for the pole of dependency, the communicative basis for freedom.

Finally, this polarity represents the ethical and the practical-philosophical part of the religious judgement. We are dealing with a type of freedom that forms the basis for all ethical thinking. A religious interpretation of a contingency-situation from this point of view poses the dramatic question of appropriate, humane, intelligent, just, etc., action.

The polar dimensions freedom vs. dependency are also of special relevance in the concept of religious development, because the autonomy of religious persons is grounded in them. This point is elaborated in the book, *Wieviel Religion braucht der Mensch?* (Oser, 1988). The concept of freedom is contained within the structure of the developmental sequence to the extent that persons are seen as helplessly dependent on an ultimate authority as well as in the shape and form with which this dependency is perceived. Neither apathy vis-à-vis this phenomenon nor the rejection of this feeling, but the integrative coordination of internal freedom within the contingencies of this world, with corresponding relational qualities, are decisive for becoming a deeply religious, an enlightened and liberated human being constituted by freedom.

The fourth dimensional polarity is expressed by the concepts "hope vs. absurdity." A religious judgement without these polar dimensions would be incomplete. Absurdity refers to the absence of assured, certain meaning and to the absence of an ultimately valid action-objective. Hope as *spes qua* describes the anticipation, sustained by intensity and certainty of various degrees, of a future reality. Hope as *spes quae* refers to something that is possible, forthcoming (e.g., eschatology, redemption, revolution, utopia, etc.). Any situation requires the striking of a balance between the two poles— a balance which exhibits a particularly high degree of psychological complexity and adequacy.

The meaning-dimension which comes to expression in the increasingly reversible equilibrium of the contrast between hope and absurdity holds

> that beyond the boundaries of the realm of defined action there remains a horizon of uncertainty, i.e., a domain which cannot be delimited by the regularities of definitions and determinations. Thus, this domain, while unavailable as a defined and definable entity, can still become a critical authority for all definition and interpretation-processes (Schibilsky, 1978, p. 75).

Of course, it is possible for this domain to be collapsed into action, into the sensational or the extraordinary. However, in order to be religiously relevant something else is needed. This addition often finds expression in doctrines of salvation which have the function of mediating meaning. However, they are unable to relieve individuals of that task which is demanded in every particular life-situation, the task of construing or reconstructing hope.

From a structural developmental and psychological point of view, the equilibrium at a lower stage would consist of portraying hope as completely embedded in the social context; any threat of falling out of it is experienced as "absurd." Even death and sickness obtain "meaning" by means of this absurd support. At a higher stage, hope, as communicatively grounded daily meaning-making activity, is an achievement that is constantly threatened. When assuming highest responsibilities for social conditions, for one's neighbor, the poor, the imprisoned, etc., persons interpret situations in such a way that the absurd becomes bearable through hope, that hope obtains its unconditional quality vis-à-vis the absurd, that hope is sustained by an Ultimate.

"Trust vs. anxiety" is the fifth pair of polar dimensions. If anxiety causes persons to react in a child-like manner, to make mistakes, to develop a communication-impediment, many observers are inclined to attribute such reactions to particular situations and not to the de facto nature of the person. Such an assumption echoes the view that anxiety is not necessarily a part of ordinary life. However, like experiences of positive living anxiety is a dimension which leaves its mark. Anxiety is important, because our religious judgement assists us in "structuring it" and coping with it.

Anxiety vs. trust aims not only at the affective and expressive components of religiosity, since each of the polarities mentioned has an affective-cognitive relational domain. Rather, it refers to the articulation of a person's relationship to a transcendent. In particular, it refers to the integration of death and life, sickness and everyday life, unjust actions and the communicative domain. In short, it refers to the resolution of the problem of theodicy. However, we must distinguish between anxiety and fear. There are numerous sorts of objects, events, conditions, and situations which are or can become fear-producing (cf. Izard, 1981, pp. 398f). One could say that at the beginning of all religiosity rests fear—or fear played at least an important role:[19] e.g., fear of spirits, fear of evil, etc. Thus, fear is also an element of this aspect. In religious writings, fear and anxiety as well as their overcoming are significant dimensions of change (cf. the Egyptian book of the dead and its descriptions of ways of liberation; or the theology of St. Paul who regards the victory of Christ over death as the victory over all anxiety). Fear arises also when objects are lacking which secure the social status quo. In such cases, fear can take the form of grief and worry. When such objects are available, fear is replaced by joy and trust.

Religiously processed, fear and anxiety function both as elements of coping with contingencies and as elements for the constitution of religious identity. Viewed psychologically, at the lower stages fear and anxiety react to externally induced stimuli, while at the higher stages they respond to internal regulation. At the lower stages, the nonfulfillment of a wished-for circumstance leads to fear or anxiety. At the higher stages, it is one's own failure vis-à-vis a communicative actualization of religiosity that leads to fear or anxiety which must be overcome. We discover different forms of equilibria at the different stages: At the lower stages the equilibrium is marked by its grounding in concrete actions, objects, or events. At the higher stages, the equilibrium is tied to the connection between either fear or trust and the degree of success or failure of communicative realizations and their creative connectedness to an Ultimate.

In the overview over the polar dimensions earlier we also mentioned the pair eternity vs. ephemerality.[20] Children have a different understanding than adults regarding that which disintegrates and that which remains. The emergence of a desire for continuation of one's life usually marks the construal of the concept of trans-temporality *[Überzeitlichkeit]*. Viewed from a psychological perspective, the conviction that that which has permanence is valu-

---

19. We refrain here from further discussing the distinction between fear and anxiety as elaborated mainly by existential philosophy. Generally, fear has a visible reference point (danger) while anxiety has more the quality of a psychic syndrome whereby a consciously perceived reference point is lacking.
20. Piaget's research on the dimensions "sequence of events," "simultaneity," "transivity of unequal and synchronous durations," "additive and associative composition of durations," "age," "inner duration," is significant for our work. However, these dimensions are more concerned with measuring and conceptualizing units of time rather than the equilibrium between "eternity" and "temporality" (cf. Piaget, 1970).

able and that that which is temporary is worthless takes center stage at a lower stage. At a higher stage, however, the timeless penetrates the temporal, the temporal reveals the eternal, and successful communication has a "timeless" dimension. For example, a meditative reconstruction of reality, the creation of cultic forms, or the concept of life after death—all symbolize aspects of the eternal. Also, the universal quality of principles of justice and creative works of art correspond to the concept that describes the integration of enduring values into ephemeral life. The polar dimensions ephemerality vs. eternity undergo an integration wherever a communicatively necessary act (e.g., attending to a dying person) obtains universal significance. Each stage's equilibrium is achieved in a completely different way from those at the other stages. The meaning-constitutive act inherent in the equilibriating act is connected to the way in which one is able to realize that which is communicatively valuable in that which is ephemeral. The history of religion provides examples of this dimension where techniques of inwardness are learned (e.g., the Egyptian and Tibetan books of death; meditation teachings, etc.). The time-dimension always penetrates the other polar dimensions in such a way that religiously interpreted dimensions acquire a temporal qualification which, then, reveals the various stages' equilibria. At the highest stage, the element of love, the knowledge of one's existence being a gift, lasts eternally while that which is eternally absolute acquires everywhere a momentary quality.

The next dimension mentioned was functional transparency vs. opaqueness (magic). "Opaqueness," in the magical sense, refers to a mysterious animatedness, to mysterious workings in nature, in certain objects, and in creatures—effects which can be influenced only through rites. A special form of processing the magical is represented by Animism. For children it means the animation of all objects including the uncanny (because it appears gigantic and overwhelming). Throughout human history, the animation of all things found its place in mythology.

> Parallel to science, mythology intends to provide human beings with a means for influencing and coping with the universe. Faced with a universe filled with uncertainties and riddles, mythology intervenes in order to anthropomorphize all sorts of elements and objects: the clouds in the sky, the sunlight, the storms over the oceans; all these non-human forms lose part of their terror when it is possible to correlate (their) purposes, sensibilities, and motivations to those experienced by ordinary individuals" (Grimal, 1967, p. 13).

Viewed psychologically, at the lower stages magic refers to animations that are presumed to be absolutely determined and steered. At the higher stages, aporias—such as the mystery of the possibility of human encounter and the mystery surrounding social arrangements—create a reluctance, a reverence, and a discovery of the limits of rationalization. An equilibrium at a higher stage signifies that any transparency of things always includes its limits and origins.[21]

We have not empirically verified the dimensions, "what is given vs. what is self-produced." Only in more recent projects have we begun to deal with this polarity, because we now have available a research-dilemma that can unlock this dimension. Commonly encountered themes or content-domains are "a call from above," "chance," "blessing and fortune," etc. The concept of receiving gifts as the result of chance is overcome by means of an interpretive process which says that chance and (free) gifts permeate every act and that any self-achievements are transcended therein. In other words, at the lower stages, good fortunes are interpreted as God's direct intervention, bad fortunes as the absence of God. At the higher stages, both types of fortune are transcended in an ongoing interpretation of human action against the backdrop of an a priori knowing of one's existence as a gift. The Ultimate as chance per se creates the conditions for "faith" or "groundedness."

In summary: the aforementioned dimensions determine the religious judgement of people in such a way that a higher stage facilitates a qualitatively "better," more adequate equilibrium between the conceptual pairs. It designates the cognitive work of reconstruction accomplished by persons when they "explain" an actual life-situation in which they are involved in a religious manner—i.e., with these dimensions. This reconstructive work corresponds to what we have designated as the daily effort of holistic meaning-making (of our reality). "The question of meaning limits the usage of the word 'meaning' to the classification of phenomena while claiming, however, thereby to be the highest and final expression of what can be comprehended" (Sauter, 1980, p. 7). The question of meaning becomes accessible methodologically when actions or events lack any kind of frame of reference or when an action or event fails outside of the ordinary sphere of meaning which constitutes my existence and my identity.

Thus, in the end, the process of constructing an equilibrium between the various polar dimensions constitutes the religious construction of reality. The grammar of this process lies not in content or substance but consists in the ability to interpret reality religiously by means of the aforementioned process of equilibration.

---

21. A special variant of this dimension is the supernatural vs. the natural. Swanson (1960), in his book, *The Birth of the Gods,* connects it to the development of the image of the human soul. He demonstrates, however, that its genesis is accompanied by many aspects. For Durkheim it is the God-concept which he himself introduces, although he himself also demonstrates the existence of religions without gods. This, then, is our reason for adding the polarity the supernatural vs. the natural to the universalizable categories: It surfaces in almost all of our interview transcripts. At the lower stages it coincides with the God who directs and governs; at the higher stages it coincides with what we have earlier called the Transcendent.

Like speech, this process follows certain rules. These rules find expression in the various stage characteristics and stage descriptions. Thus, they do not constitute a theory of religion but a theory of the nature of religious consciousness in human beings.

Structures of Religious Knowledge—Religious Deep-Structures

Knowing something quite well and still forgetting it is a common experience for many people. This has to do with the so-called *knowledge-structures* which persons have stored and which deteriorate over time. The situation is quite different in regard to the deep-structures of religious judgement: these are latently present patterns of religious consciousness which people use for coping with critical life-situations. They do not deteriorate but rather surface in persons' verbal contributions, e.g., in discussions. These deep-structures lie behind the linguistic reality. While knowledge-structures can be acquired rather quickly, a person's deep-structure cannot be altered easily.

First, an episode from the praxis of teaching: Fritz Oser, in a course on the didactics of religion, taught the subject "God is with people," *coram publico*, to a group of first-graders. During the introduction he mentioned the word "God." One child said: "God is love." A second child said: "God is like a good daddy." A third child said: "God forgives people." A fourth one: "God is everywhere with people," etc. In a sense, these introductory remarks began to form the outlines of a systematic doctrine of God, although it seemed a bit alien, coming out of the mouths of first-graders as it did.

Thus, Oser told the children a story. It talked about a man who never had any time. He was the director of a big factory. He was so busy that he didn't even have time for his children and his wife. Neither did he have time for God, nor could he think about his future or about other people. He was always too busy. One day he had a heart-attack and was hospitalized. Suddenly he had time. And he sensed how important it was that someone had time for him. He began to think about God and asked for strength.

At this point, the narrative would stop and the children would be asked whether, in their opinion, God ought to help the man.

The children's hands "flew up" and most of them thought: No, God is not obligated to help the man. It was his own fault. He deserved this. It would teach him a lesson, and, actually, he ought to be punished even more. One child said: "He should be beaten." And another said: "He ought to be locked up in the basement."

At this point, one of the attending teachers interrupted the children. Quite angrily, he yelled at them: "But earlier you all said that God is good, and now

. . ." He shrugged. Presumably, he was the teacher of the class.

Disregarding the fact that many instructors do not understand the religious thinking of children, disregarding the embarrassing loss of self-control in face of the children's picture of the world and its religious interpretation of communicative reality, this scene highlights another phenomenon: the difference between knowledge-structures (epistemic structures) and deep-structures for coping with reality.

In the scene described above, the children initially reproduced stored knowledge, which they had "childishly" acquired or stored by means of imitation or concept-construction. Later, however, after the narrative of the-man-who-never-had-time, the children used deep-structures of reality-interpretation in the sense of real assimilation and accommodation.

The difference between the two kinds of structures is exciting, for a person can possess a substantial amount of religious or theological knowledge while, nevertheless, being incapable of coping with critical life-situations. Such a person is unable to find a semantic application for this knowledge to a concrete reality. Obversely, it is possible to say that the religious judgement consists of those interpretive acts that are actually employed by persons in a religious examination of their reality (in the sense of searching for an equilibrium within the aforementioned polar dimensions).

When referring to the religious judgement and to stage differences involving this judgement, we are referring to deep-structures.[22] They represent valid forms of personality-organization and they make possible clear predictions about reasons for actions.

The Reduction of Religious Judgement to Coping with Contingencies

When persons deal with difficult, critical life-situations in a religious manner, they can be described as coping with these situations. This is commonly referred to as "they are dealing with it religiously," or they are coping with contingency. Of course, religion in not exhausted simply in coping with contingencies or in providing support for life. It also features a domain which

---

22. The relation between the two structural types is not clear. Aebli (1969), drawing on Berlyne, uses the term "epistemic structures" by showing—in comparison with deep-structures—that they easily deteriorate. From this results that, at each stage, knowledge-structures can be constructed in different measure. However, this hypothesis must still be tested. It is possible to deduce that, for instance, persons at stage 2 who possess a great deal of knowledge are different from persons at stage 2 with little religious knowledge. However, one could also state that, despite different contents and different ranges of knowledge concerning certain subject-matters, the structure remains the same.

comes to expression, for instance, in the concepts "love for one's neighbor" or "universal solidarity." In order to specify what we mean by "religious judgement" this section covers the concept of coping with contingency. We will point out the ambiguity inherent in this concept, but also its important and helpful role for situating and sharpening the concept of religious judgement within the framework of a critical theory of religion.

Whether we succumb to the temptation of infusing the stage-descriptions of the religious judgement with culture-specific dimensions depends on the degree of universalizability of our definition of religiosity. We believe that the before-mentioned polar dimensions are capable of describing the universal patterns of religious interpretation. However, as Lübbe (1980) and Peukert (1982) have done in their respective ways, it is also possible to designate religious judgement as a process of "coping with contingency." Since this concept holds a predominant position in the following elaborations, it is necessary to attend briefly to the ambiguity of the concept and to the meaning with which we employ it here.

In surveying the current discussion in the fields of sociology and psychology of religion, one can easily discover that the various approaches exhibit at least one common feature: the task and function of religion is defined as "coping with contingency."[23] Approaches in the field of structural functionalism, systems-theory, and symbolic interactionism regard religion as a form of coping with the problem of contingency. For Luhmann, religion deals with "the transformation of indeterminable complexity into determinable complexity" (Luhmann, 1977, p. 20). For Lübbe,

> our life is . . . contingent and can, therefore, be dealt with only religiously—that means: Our life is neither a product of our labor nor the result of our acquiescence to it at the end of a domination-free discourse. The religious practice of

---

23. This refers in all cases to the Aristotelian concept of contingency, i.e., something can be, but does not have to be, a certain way. For social scientists, however, this concept has a different connotation. It refers to the spacial, temporal, or thematical proximity of two entities (stimulus-response, response-stimulus, stimulus-stimulus). High levels of contingency mean a high degree of predicatability, noncontingency means total chance. If an action yields consequences that had been predicted with a high degree of probability, then this consequence is controllable and therefore contingent. The opposite kind of action leads to helplessness, especially in cases when no cause can be found for the noncontingent, and future noncontingencies are expected. The stress and anxiety syndromes accompanying noncontingency are areas of special social-scientific research. For our project it is important to clarify that, for social scientists, the concept of contingency means the opposite from traditional philosophical meanings.

coping with contingency has a stabilizing function in light of the absolute difference between that which we can control and that which we are unable to control. Furthermore, religion exercises this stabilizing function in the face of an
ongoing uncertainty regarding the location and nature of the boundaries (between
the two domains) (Lübbe, 1979, p. 18).

Thus, chance or contingency refers to that reality which "concerns an
action in a manner that is contrary to the (naturally-inherent) meaning of
the action" (Lübbe, 1980, p. 75). The religious practice of coping with contingency represents the effort "to cope with contingencies by attempting to
integrate them into the meaning of our actions" (Lübbe, 1980, p. 76). In
other words, the function of religion is "the practice of coping with contingencies which transcend the (inherent) meaning of actions (Lübbe, 1980,
p. 79).[24]

However, dealing with experiences of contingency can be extremely
ambivalent—this is an important point for religious judgement. W.
Pannenberg formulates this from a theological perspective:

When applied to the topic of religion, the concept "coping with contingency"
has a double meaning: on the one hand, it can simply designate the function of religion in the social system. This is possible without associating with its usage any
action designed to cope with contingency. On the other hand, this concept always
suggests (an association with) acting subjects—individuals or groups—coping with
the contingent conditions of their existence via religion. . . . However, religion can
fulfill this function in the social system only if it is something more than just
coping with contingency, namely a "representation of eternal truth." To that
extent, then, religious consciousness refers to a "meaning" which precedes any
actor. . . . However, it appears as if these "eternal truths" of religion should not be
perceived as results of human meaning-making. In that case, they would be seen
as the products of human action and, thus, negate the concept of religion. For it
is in, with, and through religion that persons see themselves from the perspective
of divine reality and divine action (Pannenberg, 1980, pp. 115f).

The view of religion as the praxis of coping with contingency is a para-
doxical one. As Peukert (1982) has argued convincingly, religion does play
an integrating and stabilizing function in an irrational social praxis. The
irrationality of that praxis shows up in a manner quite typical of modern
consciousness, namely, in the push to increase power and to extend the range
of authority and influence. Such a praxis only intensifies the problem of
ecological and social limit-experiences. It does not provide a resolution to the
identity crisis of the individual or of society. *"Religion, in its own irrationality, has to legitimize and—with levels of absurdity multiplied mani-
foldly—to sanction the irrationality of a social mechanism based upon
growth in power"* (Peukert, 1982, p. 84). When religion is understood as

24. In this instance, religion and religiosity are not distinguished.

the praxis of coping with contingency in this sense, it encourages the approval of something "that is because it is the way it is, and since it just happens to be. . . . One might joke that religion means that nothing can be done about it."[25]

In the face of this, Peukert suggests a concept of contingency, grounded in action-theory, that overcomes the resignative and regressive tendency and appears adequate as a foundation for the development of cognitive stages of religious judgement.

The starting point is the insight that, in any situation, persons not only have in principle the possibility to choose one course of action or another but also, in line with the mode of self-determination, can "choose to choose," i.e., they can "decide in favor of, or against, making a decision" (Peukert, 1982, p. 87). That is, they can pose to themselves the practical question of decision making "whether and how they want to go on living" (p. 87).

> If one wants to speak of the contingency of human existence, one obviously has to speak of the factual, temporally anticipated existence that is determined by the necessity of its facticity and, at the same time, by the action-possibilities which are opened up by this facticity and which require the taking of a certain position; this can be done consciously or can be refused" (Peukert, 1982, p. 87).

In this case, the afore-described contingency of human existence has to be conceived strictly intersubjectively; at least insofar as "the practical question is always also raised by others" (p. 88).

Thus, the problem of a religious coping with contingency has reached the point where human existence—understood as existence in which freedom is always mediated intersubjectively—finds its adequate interpretation:

> The original action-theoretical concept of contingency describes thus the necessity of temporally-finite freedom; i.e. (for persons), in interaction with others, to act free toward themselves, i.e., toward their own factual, temporally-anticipated existence. It is primarily a matter of contingencies of freedom while contingencies of factual situations are contained therein (p. 88).

According to this critical theory of religion, cognitive-religious functions of judgement are questions, disclosures, explanations, interpretations of occurrences which place religiously judging persons into a relation to another entity in which they are coping with contingency. Thereby these persons experience this relation as a connection with a Transcendent. Thus, religious judgement refers to the reasoning process—i.e., the way, shape, and form—with which people, as intersubjective beings of freedom, across the most important phases of their development constitute their identity through

---

25. Religion als in diesem Sinne verstandene Kontingenzbewältigungspraxis leitet zur Anerkennung dessen an, "was ist, weil es ist, wie es ist, und weil nun eben einmal etwas ist und nicht vielmehr nichts. . . ." Peukert, 1982, p. 83).

interactions in certain socio-historical situations, i.e., in such a way that this identity "is determined by an Absolute which cannot be reduced to this action or invented by it" (p. 10). If one can generally agree upon the point that "religious judgement" refers to a reasoning-process with which people interpret the relation between the human and the Transcendent across the essential developmental seasons, then this always implies the following normativitives:

1. Even the noncontingent dimensions enter into this process of religious questioning, explaining, interpreting, and disclosing;

2. The starting point for these religious interpretations is constituted by interactions—contingent ones and noncontingent ones;

3. Freedom which is conscious of itself, trust which is conscious of itself, temporality which is conscious of itself are not exhausted by the concept of contingency: Rather, they contain a religious explanation of all events that is of an interactive nature.

In sum, we can say that the concept of coping with contingency is perhaps insufficiently broad for the description of the religious judgement in light of "universal truth." Yet, such a reduction can be helpful because it manages to universalize the polar dimension mentioned by us. Thus it becomes possible to say that, according to the way it posits the problem, the religious judgement asks how finite freedom is initiated in the face of contingency-experiences, how the relational structure between autonomy, transcendence, hope, and the sacred, etc., ought to be conceived.

Previous Research on the Development of Religious Judgement

At the end of this chapter we would like to introduce those approaches in developmental psychology which have exerted an important influence on our own research. The work of Broughton, Döbert, Fowler, Goldman, and Kohlberg is of special significance.

Among previous research, three approaches deserve special mention: (a) the sociology of knowledge, (b) the field of concept research, and (c) the stage theory of Fowler (1974, 1976, 1981). This third domain includes Broughton's work on "the development of philosophical thinking" (1978, 1980a/b). These three research orientations differ significantly from our model. Whereas our work emerged directly from the paradigm of Piaget (1968) and Kohlberg (1971, 1974), the research orientations of the other models mentioned above are partly grounded in different theoretical backgrounds.

Concerning (a): The phenomenologically oriented sociology of knowledge, in the tradition of Peter Berger and Thomas Luckmann (1966) and

Alfred Schütz (1960), assumes that deficiencies in the encounter with the Other are processed religiously. This results in a transformation of thought to the degree that the basic questionability of the "thou" in its continuity and totality becomes experienceable, through the alien or other *[fremde]* consciousness, as a corollary to one's own consciousness. This process is mediated in the phenomenon of meaning-making (cf. Döbert, 1978, pp. 52f). This leads up to a concept of religiosity similar to the one formulated by V. Drehsen and H.J. Helle (1978, pp. 44f):

> Religiosity is that social force which meaningfully and plausibly interprets, though in manifold manner, the common problematic experiences of dependency, complexity, and discrepancy with respect to the possible solutions of freedom, continuity, and participation.

In this sense, religion mediates between the experience of the world and a certainty about the world. This mediation yields the capacity for transcendence which, in the process of meaning-making, makes it possible to go beyond the boundaries of space, of time, and of permanent conditions.

The problem of the sociology of religion as a sociology of knowledge lies in the fact that it is unable to reconstruct sufficiently the actual transcending-process of religious reasoning- and action-patterns. Precisely because it is a sociology of knowledge and therefore perceives religious processes mainly from the social perspective, it cannot sufficiently reproduce the actual religious, reflexively mediated action-process.

Concerning (b): Research studies on the development of religious concepts have been conducted by Goldman (1964), Elkind (1961, 1962, 1963), Rosenberg (1977), and others. In their view, concepts are images of an object or a person defined by certain characteristics. Goldman writes (1964, p. 15):

> Concepts of God are responses which tie together or link, or combine discrete sensory experiences such as father is strong, big, all-powerful, cares for me. God is like that and judges and cares for all children. Or God is a big daddy up in the sky.

In interviews with children, Rosenberg has unearthed their concepts of God, angels, priests, etc., by examining their prayer practices. B. Inhelder, from the Geneva School, investigated the development of the basic concepts of coincidence and probability in children (1978, pp. 98f). Also mentioned should be Piaget's work on the worldviews of children (1965) with questions about the origin of the stars, of the weather, the oceans, the trees, mountains, and the earth. From these data he developed phases of artificialistic explanations.

It might prove helpful to distinguish our approach from the research on the development of concepts. Unlike those studies, we are concerned with cognitive structures of coping with reality in the face of failures, deficiencies, good or bad luck, etc. In contrast to concept research, cognitive religious structures are means of judging, valuing, and meaning-making in the face of events which can be interpreted only insufficiently with the usual means of objectifying knowing *[Objektbewältigung]*. However, concepts do play a part in religious judgement. For example, we discovered the following statements of a twelve-year-old boy: "If something stupid happens to us, it is God's way of protecting us from a much greater calamity. This is God's plan." This statement would be assigned to stage 2 (at least to stage (2)1, a consolidation stage). The same boy imagines God as an old man with a white beard, which corresponds to the lowest, the intuitive stage of Goldman.[26]

However, the connection of certain concepts and religious judgement has to be carefully investigated with new empirical material.

Concerning (c): In previous religious research, Fowler's stage concept represents the third fundamental approach. It is closer to Loevinger's work on personality psychology than to cognitive psychology. Fowler's stages are described in the following:*

> In the pre-stage called undifferentiated faith the seeds of trust, courage, hope, and love are fused in an undifferentiated way and contend with sensed threats of abandonment, inconsistencies, and deprivations in an infant's environment. Though really a pre-stage and largely inaccessible to empirical research of the kind we pursue, the quality of mutuality and the strength of trust, autonomy, hope, and courage (or their opposites) developed in this phase underlie (or threaten to undermine) all that comes later in faith development.

> Stage 1: Intuitive-Projective faith is the fantasy-filled, imitative phase in which the child can be powerfully and permanently influenced by examples, moods, actions, and stories of the visible faith of primally related adults. The stage most typical of the child of three to seven, it is marked by a relative fluidity of thought patterns. The child is continually encountering novelties for which no stable operations of knowing have been formed. The imaginative processes underlying fantasy are unrestrained and uninhibited by logical thought. In league with forms of knowing dominated

---

*Translator's note: The stage descriptions in the original German edition of this volume came from a 1982 article in German. No published English version of that article exists. Thus, instead of retranslating the stage descriptions from that article back into English, I have chosen to offer summaries from *Stages of Faith* (Fowler, 1981, pp. 119-211).

26. Goldman's stages (1964, pp. 27f) are based on Piaget and are formulated as follows: stage 1: intuitive religious thinking; stage 2: concrete religious thinking; stage 3: abstract religious thinking. The only criteria to indicate general stage differences are logico-formal ones.

by perception, imagination in this stage is extremely productive of long-lasting images and feelings (positive or negative) that later, more stable and self-reflective valuing and thinking will have to order and sort out. This is that stage of first self-awareness. The "self-aware" child is egocentric in regard to the perspectives of others. Here we find first awareness of death and sex and the strong taboos by which cultures and families insulate those powerful areas.

Stage 2: Mythic-Literal faith is the stage in which the person begins to take on for him- or herself the stories, beliefs, and observances that symbolize belonging to his or her community. Beliefs are appropriated with literal interpretations, as are moral rules and attitudes. Symbols are taken as one-dimensional and literal in meaning. In this stage the rise of concrete operations leads to the curbing and ordering of the previous stage's imaginative composing of the world. The episodic quality of Intuitive-Projective faith gives way to a more linear, narrative construction of coherence and meaning. Story becomes the major way of giving unity and value to experience. This is the faith stage of the school child (though we sometimes find the structures dominant in adolescents and in adults). Marked by increased accuracy in taking the perspective of other persons, those in stage 2 compose a world based on reciprocal fairness and immanent justice based on reciprocity. The actors in their cosmic stories are anthropomorphic. They can be affected deeply and powerfully by symbolic and dramatic materials and can describe in endlessly detailed narrative what has occurred. They do not, however, step back from the flow of stories to formulate reflective, conceptual meanings. For this stage the meaning is both carried and "trapped" in the narrative.

Stage 3: In Synthetic-Conventional faith a person's experience of the world now extends beyond the family. A number of spheres demand attention: family, school or work, peers, street society, and media, and perhaps religion. Faith must provide a coherent orientation in the midst of that more complex and diverse range of involvements. Faith must synthesize values and information; it must provide a basis for identity and outlook. Stage 3 typically has its rise and ascendancy in adolescence, but for many adults it becomes a permanent place of equilibrium. It structures the ultimate environment in interpersonal terms. Its images of unifying value and power derive from the extension of qualities experienced in personal relationships. It is a "conformist" stage in the sense that it is acutely tuned to the expectations and judgements of significant others and as yet does not have a sure enough grasp on its own identity and autonomous judgement to construct and maintain an independent perspective. While beliefs and values are deeply felt, they typically are tacitly held—the person "dwells" in them and in the meaning world they mediate. But there has not been occasion to step outside them to reflect on or examine them explicitly or systematically. At stage 3 a person has an "ideology," a more or less consistent clustering of values and beliefs, but he or she has not yet objectified it for examination and in a sense is unaware of having it. Differences of outlook with others are experienced as differences in "kind" of person. Authority is located in the incumbents of traditional authority roles (if perceived as personally worthy) or in the consensus of a valued, face-to-face group.

Stage 4: Individuative-Reflective faith most appropriately takes form in young adulthood (but let us remember that many adults do not construct it and that for a significant group it emerges only in the mid-thirties or forties). This stage is marked by a double development. The self, previously sustained in its identity and faith compositions by an interpersonal circle of significant others, now claims an identity no longer defined by the composite of one's roles and meanings to others. To sustain that new identity it composes a meaning frame conscious of its own boundaries and inner connections and aware of itself as a "worldview." Self (identity) and outlook (worldview) are differentiated from those of others and become acknowledged factors in the reactions, interpretations, and judgements one makes on the actions of the self and others. It expresses its intuitions of coherence in an ultimate environment in terms of an explicit system of meanings. Stage 4 typically translates symbols into conceptual meanings. This is a "demythologizing" stage. It is likely to attend minimally to unconscious factors influencing its judgements and behavior.

Stage 5: Conjunctive faith involves the integration into self and outlook of much of what was suppressed or unrecognized in the interest of stage 4's self-certainty and conscious cognitive and affective adaptation to reality. This stage develops a "second naivete" (Ricoeur) in which symbolic power is reunited with conceptual meanings. Here there must also be a new reclaiming and reworking of one's past. There must be an opening to the voices of one's "deeper self." Importantly, this involves a critical recognition of one's social unconscious—the myths, ideal images, and prejudices built deeply into the self-system by virtue of one's nurture within a particular social class, religious tradition, ethnic group, or the like. Unusual before mid-life, stage 5 knows the sacrament of defeat and the reality of irrevocable commitments and acts. What at the previous stage struggled to clarify, in terms of the boundaries of self and outlook, this stage now makes porous and permeable. Alive to paradox and the truth in apparent contradictions, this stage strives to unify opposites in mind and experience.

It generates and maintains vulnerability to the strange truths of those who are "other." Ready for closeness to that which is different and threatening to self and outlook (including new depths of experience in spirituality and religious revelation), this stage's commitment to justice is freed from the confines of tribe, class, religious community, or nation. And with the seriousness that can arise when life is more than half over, this stage is ready to spend and be spent for the cause of conserving and cultivating the possibility of others' generating identity and meaning.

Stage 6 is exceedingly rare. The persons best described by it have generated faith compositions in which their felt sense of an ultimate environment is inclusive of all being. They have become incarnators and actualizers of the spirit of an inclusive and fulfilled human community. They are "contagious" in the sense that they create zones of liberation from the social, political, economic, and ideological shackles we place and endure on human futurity. Living with felt participation in a power that unifies and transforms the world, universalizers are often experienced as subversive of the structures (including religious structures) by which we sustain our individual and corporate survival, security, and significance. Many persons at this stage die at the hands of those whom they hope to change. Universalizers are often more honored and revered after death than during their lives. The rare persons who may be described by this stage have a special grace that makes them seem more lucid, more simple, and yet somehow more fully human than the rest of us. Their community is universal in extent. Particularities are cherished because they are vessels for the universal and thereby valuable apart from any utilitarian considerations. Life is both loved and held to loosely. Such persons are ready for fellowship with persons at any other stage and from any other faith tradition.

If one attempts to systematize the characteristics of these faith stages one will hardly succeed, because too much incidental information enters in. Thus information that may enter into one stage may be completely unrelated to the other stages. Also, the interplay among the conceptual, structural, and emotional dimensions of the relational and motivational aspects is a bit confusing, Furthermore, the stage designations appear not fully convincing. For example, why should a person at a higher stage not also be intuitive-projective (stage 2) when he or she reflects on this process in sufficient manner?

It becomes evident that we are taking a critical stance toward Fowler's approach. In addition to cognitive components, his theory also exhibits formal components which are correlated too closely with physical maturation. Consider, for example, the task of the young adult at stage 4 to take seriously his or her obligations, lifestyles, convictions, and attitudes. This reveals at least a partial confounding of age-variables and religious growth. This becomes problematic when a stage's cognitive elements do not necessarily have to correlate with age and universal context in terms of the logic of a subject matter. Kohlberg clearly demonstrated that stages of moral judgement, while longitudinally irreversible, can be judged situationally only in terms of *age-trends,* which, of course, vary.

Put differently: While we attempt to capture the generalized religious judgement, i.e., some type of cognitive pattern of religious knowing of reality, Fowler is more concerned with holistic faith. Even the generalized definition of his concept of faith—"faith has to do with making, maintenance, and transformation of human meaning" (Fowler, 1986, p. 15)—characterizes faith more as a category of ego-development with its emotive and unstable components. Fowler's approach refers more directly to a holistic act of faith, while, for us, the relation between persons and an Ultimate can be construed as a religious act by everyone, even by a nonbeliever. While we are addressing "religious" religiosity, Fowler aims at religiosity "determined by faith." To Fowler's statement (1986, p. 21): "Faith does involve constructions of the self and others in perspective taking; in moral analysis and judgement, and in the construction of self as related to others which we call ego," we would respond that, on the one hand, the religious judgement is construed communicatively as well but, on the other hand, obtains its specific quality from the polar dimensions described above.

There are other reasons why Fowler's stage-concept appears problematic to us: Instead of emphasizing the specifically religious, he presents a conglomerate of stage conceptions of different sources (logic, role-taking, moral judgement, form of world-coherence, locus of authority, symbolic interaction, etc.) which only in combination make it possible to experience the ways of the world based on faith. Furthermore, it is often difficult to follow the terminology, because so many different concepts have been integrated.

Nonetheless, this approach is extremely significant because it is the first one to build on the paradigm of structural developmentalism. Also, Fowler's applications of his theory to the praxis of congregational and spiritual life are very interesting. They are laid out in the book *Faith Development and Pastoral Care* (1987).

In this context, we must also mention Lawrence Kohlberg's writings on religious development. Fowler himself refers to and builds on Kohlberg. Our own approach, too, takes Kohlberg as a starting point. Therefore, we would like to summarize his various lines of thought.

1. Initially, Kohlberg got upset over religious answers to his moral questions. Still, as long as they fit his theoretical design (e.g., punishment/reward), he used them. If the answers didn't fit, he threw them in the trash can— reminiscent of Skinner throwing his "misbehaving" rats against the wall.

2. Later, however, Kohlberg developed a great sensitivity for religious phe-

nomena. And he asked whether the a priori of morality in general might not be discovered in the religious domain. Thus, he began to talk about a seventh stage.[27] This stage corresponded roughly to the philosophy of Spinoza in which the Ultimate is conceived as a totality that is inseparably connected with nature in the sense of pantheism. The basic question: "Why be moral? Why act justly in a universe that is largely unjust?" (Kohlberg, 1977, p. 250) led to the religious grounding of the stage-concept of morality. According to Kohlberg, the fundamental question can only be answered with a religious consciousness that has worked through the problems of doubt and hopelessness and provides the "resolution of despair" (p. 250). At its core, this seventh stage represents the individual's feeling "of being part of the totality of life and of adopting a cosmic perspective rather than a universal-humanistic perspective (stage 6)" (p. 250). Herewith, Kohlberg clearly reached the level of a transcendental grounding of his theory. It is understandable that, on the one hand, he did consider postulating a seventh stage. On the other hand, however, he did not formalize religious judgement at the other stages. Kohlberg states: "The faith required by universal moral principles I call stage 7, though at this point the term is only a metaphor. This faith orientation does not basically change the definition of universal principles of human justice found at stage 6, but integrates them with a perspective of life's ultimate meaning" (1974, p. 18). This refers to that religiously grounded attitude which rests a priori at the base of the universal principle.

3. The principle of stage 7 is elaborated best by Kohlberg and Power in their article, "Moral Development, Religious Thinking, and the Question of a Seventh Stage" (1981). They indicate that the contents of the seventh stage can have very different emphases. For example, it can feature a type of natural-law-based justice in the sense of Marcus Aurelius or agape in the sense of the religious commitment of Andrea Simpson. On the other hand, Whitehead's position, Spinoza's theology, or Teilhard de Chardin's conceptualization of a development toward a "divine milieu" as an evolution directed toward *omega,* are not really proof for a seventh stage. Rather, these are images of what stage 7 could be: "Knowing and loving God or nature as the ground of a system of laws knowable by reason is a support to our acceptance of human rational laws of justice, which are part of the whole" (p. 371).

4. In 1980, Power and Kohlberg published a paper which, for the first time, addresses the problem of religious content in the moral stages without

27. Personal conversations reveal that it was in the solitude of his remote cabin on Cape Cod that he had the idea to posit the a priori, i.e., the possibilities of a practical philosophy, at a seventh stage. Cf. L. Kohlberg: "Toward a Stage 7— Rational Science, Rational Ethics and Ultimate Faith." Cambridge: Working Paper, 1975.

reducing it to morality. They inquire into that which is specifically religious and they document empirically that the moral judgement is a necessary, though not sufficient, condition for the religious judgement. Further, they describe the connection between ego-development, the social atmosphere in schools, and religious judgement.[28] Yet more decisive is their description of a stage sequence which is clearly distinguished from Fowler's (cf. Kohlberg/Power, 1980, pp. 343-372).

Here, Kohlberg accepts the existence of an independent religious domain which cannot be reduced to stage 7 but rather appears at each stage with a different equilibrium of the various dimensions. He believes that it is possible to formulate our religious stages, for example, from the viewpoint of morality (freedom vs. dependency, justice vs. injustice). It might, however, also be possible to discover independent, specifically religious meaning-dimensions which resemble a religious mother-structure.[29] In regard to this, Zillessen (1982) comments that Kohlberg's reference to a seventh stage is insufficient, because with it he appeals to the old model of the natural and the supernatural:

Reflection is being transcended and completed via faith, which is threatened, however, with becoming merely a vague and undefinable feeling. It appears to me that it is more appropriate to view religion grounded in the dialectic of experience of and reflection on meaning, in the dialectic of reflection and meditation, discourse and play, control and ecstasy, self-determination and orientation, "speaking" and "listening." This sort of dialectic, then, appears as the condition for religious experience. The experience "of being part of the totality of life," will find expression and come into consciousness in the experience of the depth-dimension of all human and natural beings (p. 40).

---

28. At this point, we do not want to elaborate this connection any further, but list the stage scores of twenty-one persons of various ages who were tested for the development of their moral and their religious judgement. The results show that the development of the moral judgement precedes the development of the religious judgement. An appropriate description for this would be *décalage*.

Rel.Stage	Moral Stage	\	Rel. Stage	Moral Stage
1	1	:	4	4(3)
1	1	:	4	4
1	1	:	4	4.5 (Rel.)
2	2	:	4	4
2	2	:	4	4
2(3)	2(3)	:	4-5	5
3	3	:	4-5	5
3	3	:	5(4)	5
3	3	:	5(4)	5(4)
4	5	:	5	5

Source: Kohlberg and Power 1980, p. 360 (cf. Oser and Reich, 1990).
29. Cf. chapter two in this volume.

This experience, then, can be found at each stage in the form of religious judgement. However, Kohlberg had already accepted this by clearly distinguishing stage 7 from the religious judgement and its stage sequence: Stage 7 is a precondition for moral judgement, while the religious judgement actually represents, as a structural whole, the relation between an Ultimate and human beings in concrete life-situations.

To be counted among the works from a structural-developmental perspective are also those by John Broughton. In connection with his research on adolescents he has conceptualized stages in the development of philosophical thinking. In 1978 he presented a stage concept of "natural philosophy" which he validated in 1980 by means of a longitudinal study with adolescents. The basic elements of his research study are empirically gained images for the concepts "self," "reason," "body," on the one hand, and "knowledge," "truth," and "reality," on the other hand (Broughton, 1978, 1980a). Although Broughton's work may have a central importance for our research, we have not yet attempted any cross-validation of our stage-concept by means of his system. This task shall be assigned to future projects.

In sum: Our intention was not to submit a comprehensive presentation of developmental-psychological research in the domain of religious judgement. Rather, we were concerned with introducing those sources of related research which had a direct influence on our conceptualization. We mentioned the approach by Berger and Luckmann, concept research by Goldman and Elkind, and the works in developmental psychology by Fowler, Kohlberg, and Broughton. We have omitted research on the relation between psychoanalysis and religion. This is being discussed in another publication (cf. Bucher and Oser, 1988).

Chapter Two

The Structure of Religious Reasoning as Mother-Structure

Some people claim that religion is merely a marginal phenomenon in human existence. Moral and mathematical capacities, for instance, are much more important. In this chapter, we intend to show that the religious identity of people, including the religious judgement, constitutes an essential anthropological category which cannot be separated out. We try to convey this with the term "mother-structure." We conceive the religious mother-structure as an independent structure whose conditions and qualities will be described in the following. Our theoretical considerations will be illustrated by an example.

Disagreements about Definitions

The religious dimension of our actions and speech is an independent dimension which cannot be reduced to morality. The compulsion or inclination to dissolve anything religious into other categories and to deny the existence of a religious mother-structure always runs up against the notion that questions concerning the meaning of life, the future, or coping with fate and death concern everyone and that, at some point in time and in certain situations, every person must find answers to these questions. It is precisely in these answers that the structure of the religious judgement can be discerned.

If logical elements find entry into all the fundamental domains of reasoning, it would be reasonable to assume the existence of a single foundational cognitive structure and to explain all other domains as facets of this one basic structure.

In many conversations with Fritz Oser, Kohlberg has repeatedly voiced the convictions that religious structures are so-called "soft structures" while moral structures are "hard structures." Morality, he maintained, has a generalizable structure. There exists not a single society in which morality does not play a role. Religion, however, is something secondary. While religion may comprise and include morality, it does not belong to the generalizable domain of human experience. In his later writings, Kohlberg did come to assume the existence of a structure of religious judgement regardless of the fact that religiosity warrants the origin of any moral questioning (stage 7).

Nevertheless, we must inquire whether there exists a complete and independent domain which, after elimination of all logical, ontological, moral, social, and cultural forms and elements, is specifically religious. Shall the structures be formalized to such a degree that everything mentioned above falls into one and the same category, or is it possible to differentiate religiosity from other operative patterns of world-interpretation? In order to answer this question, we would like to analyze again the religious and moral structures and to introduce thereafter the concept of religious mother-structure.[1] The goal and purpose of this undertaking is to postulate the existence of a religious domain that cannot be reduced to anything else.

We take as our starting point the questioning, searching, comparing, perceiving human activity that can be called coping with contingency. Each person poses questions like: Whence do I come? Where am I going? What are the accidental dimensions of life? What surrounds and transcends me? What forces determine me? What is the meaning of life? What happens on the other side of death? What does religion proclaim? For this reason, we believe that the religious domain stands at the origin of human civilization and that it can be separated from many other domains. Morality deals with different questions; i.e., whether the distribution of material and intellectual goods occurs according to a certain reversibility, according to principles which are generalizable. The statement that coping with contingency (and thus religion and religious speech, actions, judgement) cannot be reduced to morality—although or especially because religious actions always already contain moral actions—depends on the various definitions of what one understands the one or the other to be. Furthermore, a transcendental-reductive analysis of the normative structure of morality can document that the obligational dimension of freedom implies the Ultimate which cannot be qualified in any way except religiously. This, then, makes it possible to speak justifiably of an independent domain of religiosity in regard to its function

---

1. Compare also our deliberations in connection with Kohlberg's theory in the previous chapter.

(cf. Krings, 1980, pp. 161-185; Krings/Simons, 1973, pp. 614-641; Böckle, 1980, pp. 48-80).[2]

On the other hand, it can also be shown that any kind of morality contains theoretical aporias, problems which point beyond the structure of the morality concept and sometimes even rupture the structure. This condition, then, makes it impossible to find a moral solution to these dilemmas. That freedom obtains its adequate substance only through another's freedom, i.e., in the execution of mutual, unconditional recognition of different forms of freedom, can also be understood as law in the sense of a moral claim or demand. The religious dimension is clearly reached only when intersubjective action—theologically speaking—begins with a promise that makes it possible to speak of freedom as liberated as well as liberating freedom. The religious dimension reaches an adequate level only when it can process the problem of guilt and—theologically speaking—justification, which is experienced in the difference between intentionality and concrete action or the ability to act. It must, however, process it in such a way that it yields an encouragement for all those acts which can only succeed when such an encouragement (absolute freedom, God, etc.) is assumed. Mechanisms of overwhelming pressure and strain, such as the tension between stress and resignation, the problem of death and of history's innocent victims, the problem of dead-end or failed actions, or *the* fundamental antinomy of moral action, i.e., that a true choice of love means withholding oneself from others, signal the central issue: These immanent aporias of every type of morality go beyond the mere "imperative" to an Ultimate Reality which establishes the imperative structure of obligations on the basis of an "indicative." The depth-dimension of the "indicativistic imperative" (theologically: grace/justification) was envisioned by Paul Tillich (1958) when he wrote in "The Lost Dimension in Religion":

> Being religious means asking passionately the question of the meaning of our existence and being willing to receive answers, even if the answers hurt. Such an idea of religion makes religion universally human, but it certainly differs from what is usually called religion. It does not describe religion as the belief in the existence of gods or one God, and as a set of activities and institutions for the sake of relating oneself to these beings in thought, devotion, and obedience. No one can deny that the religions which have appeared in history are religions in this sense. Nevertheless, religion in its innermost nature is more than religion in this narrower sense. It is the state of being concerned about one's own being and being universally.
>
> There are many people who are ultimately concerned in this way who feel far removed, however, from religion in the narrower sense, and therefore from every historical religion. It often happens that such people take the question of the

---

2. Compare also Kohlberg's assumption of a stage 7 in the previous chapter.

meaning of their life infinitely seriously and reject any historical religion just for this reason. They feel that the concrete religions fail to express their profound concern adequately. They are religious while rejecting the religions. It is this experience which forces us to distinguish the meaning of religion as living in the dimension of depth from particular expressions of one's ultimate concern in the symbols and institutions of a concrete religion. If we now turn to the concrete analysis of the religious situation of our time, it is obvious that our key must be the basic meaning of religion and not any particular religion, not even Christianity (p. 76).

The nature of religion, i.e., the aforementioned depth-dimension, surfaces in a different form at each of the developmental stages. As the ontogenesis of religious consciousness, however, the stage-like development and differentiation of this dimension is something independent which can be clearly distinguished from other structural domains.

The Concept of Mother-Structure

The previous section described the construct "religious judgement" only in regard to its formal relational structure. However, in order to grasp the legitimacy and the range of that which we call "religious judgement," it is necessary to determine more closely its general status. We intend to do this by means of the concept of "mother-structure," since it proves helpful in a heuristic sense for the fundamental developmental-psychological issue at hand.

It was Piaget who for the first time applied the concept of a so-called "mother-structure" to psychological structuralism (Piaget, 1968, pp. 23-28). However, he had adopted the idea of a so-called "mother-structure" from the work of the anonymous school of French mathematicians that signed itself "N. Bourbaki," which daringly set out the three basic or "mother" structures giving rise to all mathematics (Gardner, 1981, p. 172).

The method of the Bourbaki consisted in using isomorphisms to produce the most general structures to which mathematical elements of all sorts could be subordinated, regardless of their domain of origin and totally independent of their particular nature (Piaget, 1968, p. 24)

The uniqueness of mother-structures—this is the decisive factor for us—consists in the fact that they cannot be reduced to or developed out of one another and that all other (sub-) structures can be derived from them. In other words, mother-structures are fundamental cognitive structures behind which we can not go. Once these fundamental structures have been distinguished, it becomes possible to define sub-structures in two ways: by means of combination or by means of differentiation. Or, one might say, these methods reveal the transitional processes from strong structures to weaker ones. However, Piaget establishes also that the genesis of new structures ought to be viewed more strongly from the viewpoint of coordination of elements of the mother-structure rather than from the perspective of the mother-structure itself.

The Religious Mother-Structure

> The concept of mother-structure, as introduced by Piaget, can also be employed in the independent and original domain of religion. Meaning-making, hope, transcendence, freedom, trans-temporality [*Überzeitlichkeit*], etc., are elements of this structure. The religious mother-structure cannot be reduced any further, and it is being experienced by persons as a comprehensive depth-dimension. This means, judging persons experience congruency and wholeness, a sense of identity, when they manage to construe the various domains and dimensions of their lives as a unity.

In analogy to the mother-structures in the domain of mathematics it is possible to relate the concept of mother-structure to the construct of the cognitive-religious judgement. In that case, a cognitive-religious mother-structure ought to possess the following quality or accomplish the following function: 1) as a fundamental structure it ought to possess an irreducible core, which 2) facilitates a specifically religiously qualified coping with reality with a quality that goes beyond content, and which 3) proves to be resistant to enlightenment and to secularization when examined from a historical perspective.

Thus, religious mother-structures, when made conscious, must be "experienceable" for anybody. In other words, any person has the potential to activate, by means of religiously laden experiences, the religious mother-structure as a specific reasoning pattern. This implies that the religious mother-structures are universal.

What, then, is the particular *religious* quality by means of which the religious mother-structure can be identified as religious mother-structure? The religious quality refers to something

> that is located above or below everyday reality and the common perception thereof. At the same time, it points forward to the future, thereby making it possible that life continues. Another essential element of the religious quality is the fact that the meaning-making element is coupled with either a detachment or distancing from, or with a doubling of, the ordinary meaning-making process so that the religious appears as beyond or over against it as the provider of meaning or maker of meaning of an absolutely different sort. This new way of meaning-making can

exert a normative and orientating function on the level of everyday experience. Finally, an essential ingredient of the religious quality appears to be the fact that it makes possible some form of processing of those questions which confront persons in certain situations of their existence" (Waardenburg, 1980, pp. 30f).

Thus, the religious mother-structure contains a very specific reasoning potential which moves on the very specific level of the *question of meaning* by bringing to expression, in its capacity as final authority, not only the human need for orientation and guidance, but also, in the question about absolute meaning, the fundamental human need for justification (cf. Sauter, 1980, p. 80).

The religious mother-structure, according to its own, inner quality, does not only thematize a relation to persons' existence, actions, and selfhood— for "religion is not an immediate self-actualization, but that process with which people enter into a relationship with an Ultimate Reality which transcends all empirical determinants" (Rendtorff, 1980, p. 199). Also, there becomes apparent the unique double meaning which is contained in the religious-metaphysical mother-structure. On the one hand, the religiously qualified meaning-question, as "question about the whole picture," aims at the commonality of all of reality. On the other hand, however, it aims at the ground which makes this unity possible. The major theme of the fundamental religious structure consists, therefore, in the "conceptualization of a totality which distinguishes its ground from itself" (Pröpper, 1976, p. 136). This specific rationalization-concept of "totality" and the meaning-making ground finally makes possible and animates a logic of religious development with its various forms of structural levels.

The religious mother-structure represents, therefore, a unique form of knowing of concrete situations with the aid of the seven polar dimensions. This form of knowing cannot be reduced further, and it does not refer to morality. Rather it must be understood as the constitution of the self in the context of communicative engagement vis-à-vis an Ultimate, as a universal and universalizing "depth-dimension" of human life. The operations belonging to these mother-structures are of the relational type, e.g., in prayer a person affects the Ultimate. Relational operations are not any more abstract than the foundations of mathematical reasoning. But they are of a different sort. The statement "God reaches out to human beings" constitutes an operation which does not exist in any other form.

The question concerning meaning and salvation, the problem of the conditions for true living, is articulated in the mother-structure also as the image of wholeness and unity. For

persons feel safe and secure—i.e., partaking of "salvation"—when they succeed in experiencing the various domains and dimensions of their lives as unified, as whole. Such a fundamental experience, however, never occurs by itself but always in the experience of ferment—i.e., in the absence and anticipation [*Ausständigkeit*] of that wholeness.

This absence and anticipation is experienced as resistance, i.e., the integration does not happen as something self-evident, normal, expectable but as something that can be accomplished only through the sublation [*Aufhebung*] of its opposites. This fundamental experience of dichotomy fuels all activities of the theoretical and practical intellect: religion, myth, philosophy, science, politics, the arts, etc.

The question concerning salvation, posed as the question concerning integration, constitutes the most contagious element of human existence. But exactly at the point where the question concerning the wholeness of human life is raised we also face the original antinomy of reasoning: the indeterminability of that which is absent and anticipated in this life implies at the same time openness and possibility, yet also a final resistance. A final integration can only be achieved in death. However, death also questions human wholeness most radically. This final resistance, then, confronts human beings in the most direct way with the problem of the failure of the question concerning wholeness (Schupp, 1975, p. 83).

The question about absolute groundings and meaning, the question concerning unity in general, expresses in the religious mother-structure a nonreducible, final implication about human self-constitution which may be viewed as a specific quality of the religious-cognitive coping with reality. The religious mother-structure, in fulfilling not only a human need for orientation and a frame of reference but also for justification, "addresses the meaning of reality in general as well as the absolute meaning of the being who is able to inquire into it. The religious mother-structure addresses the meaning of being and existence in their facticity" (Pröpper, 1976, p. 135). The question concerning absolute meaning and a rationally grounded justification is provoked by a person's own fundamental experience of his or her own facticity and contingency. This has probably been formulated most succinctly by the later Schelling:

If I want to go to the limit of all reasoning, then I must consider the possibility of finding nothingness everywhere. The final question is always: Why does anything come into existence rather than remaining in nothingness? [*Warum ist überhaupt etwas und nicht nichts?*] This question cannot be answered with mere abstractions about true being (1954, p. 242).

Objectified Religious Mother-Structures

The independent and irreducible religious mother-structure does not underlie only the verbal speech of persons. The same phenomenon can be shown just as well in written texts. Religious narratives contain a hidden mother-structure which can be extracted, for instance, with the methods of hermeneutical analysis. We will demonstrate this in the following using the example of the legend of Simon, the peasant.

We would like to reserve the concept of mother-structure for the cognitive representation of "religious reality," i.e., the *process of the irreducible implications [das nicht hintergehbare Implikat]* of human knowing and self-constitution. This process has been demonstrated repeatedly in the religious literature. The following example itself, however, is not a religious mother-structure. We believe that the process of making and receiving meaning explained earlier is a good example for the equilibration among the various polar elements. The cognitive act lies hidden in the mother-structure. For the mother-structure assimilates reality by means of the elements which are at its disposal a priori and by means of their interrelation.

Our example, the ancient Russian legend about Simon, the peasant, goes like this: "Simon was a devout peasant with many children and even more servants and maids, all of whom frequented the living room of the house. He was sad that he had so little opportunity for being alone to talk with God or to encounter God. Therefore, he left the house and his farm in order to embark on a search for God. Suddenly, he sensed that God was very near; he felt drawn toward a door on which the name of God was written in fiery letters. When his trembling hands opened the door, he found himself amidst his children and servants in his old living room."[3]

For the understanding of this little text it is helpful to grasp its underlying religious pattern of action (structure). It consists of several important elements which are related to each other in reversible fashion, i.e., they can be comprehended from beginning to end or vice versa. We will attempt to describe these elements:

ELEMENT 1.

It contains the human search for meaning, peace, happiness, the Ultimate. This is a fundamental dimension shared by all people; it is an existential dimension.

ELEMENT 2.

Persons leave their matrices of everyday obligations and embark on a search outside of themselves.

ELEMENT 3.

The Absolute takes the initiative vis-à-vis human beings. It cannot be

---

3. This is, of course, an example from the Judaeo-Christian tradition. However, the mother-structure is not identical with the narrative but rather contained within it. The example is not universalizable, the structure contained in it is. Along the same line, it is impossible to say that Kohlberg's Heinz-dilemma is universalizable. For some elements of the narrative, e.g., a pharmacist, cancer drugs, etc., do not exist, for instance, in the culture of Brazilian aborigines. Nevertheless, the structure contained within the story is universalizable.

appropriated by force at a particular place or time. As far as humans are concerned, everything is always already present, though hidden, because it has been given already.

ELEMENT 4

People experience the Ultimate in their immediate environment. The Divine's approaching of the world is also an approaching of people; thus it is a liberating interaction. Human beings become human beings in finding meaning; in this case, they find it in a relation to the Ultimate or, better yet, in the relation of the Ultimate to human beings.

The text possesses a certain disposition for action which can be designated as a religious mother-structure. While being original, this process is also transferable to many other situations which "provide meaning in a religious fashion."

However, religious mother-structures always contain a potential for transformation. In the aforementioned example this becomes evident clearly in the fact that the man embarks on the journey seeking fundamental surprises. The search is fruitless, for the discovery does not only depend on the search but also on the process of seeing and knowing: the "sacred," which he seeks outside of his "profane" everyday domain, reveals itself precisely within this domain. And this sort of knowing is always coupled with the question, how does one construe such a situation in the face of an Ultimate: But this constitutes exactly what we have designated as religious judgement.

Chapter Three

Stages of Religious Judgement

This central chapter presents the stages of religious judgement. It introduces and explains the decisive concepts of developmental psychology (content, structure, developmental sequence, stage characteristics). Finally, the stages of religious judgement are described from various points of view. The image of the double-helix is employed to conceptualize stage development.

The essence of this chapter consists in the depiction of the developmental logic of the stages of religious judgement. What changes from one stage to the next? It is not a substantive change, i.e., a change in content, but a change in the way the elements which determine the religious judgement are interrelated. The different ways in which the elements are coordinated at each stage are significant in a different manner at each stage.

Design for a Stage Hierarchy

The stage hierarchy which we present in this chapter was not simply abstracted from interview transcripts. First, we developed a theoretical design, then we validated and corrected this theory with the data. It will become evident that the development of *intelligence* rests mainly on subject-object relations, the development of *morality* on the subject-subject relations, and *religious* development on the relation person—person—Ultimate.

A stage system is a theory. It predicts the course of development. The empirical generalization is based on the assumption that different persons with the same stage pattern use similar structural reasoning. This makes explanations possible which subsume that which needs to be explained under law-like regularity.

It is easier to design such a theory than to validate it. For that we need elements of experience, of intuition, from other systems. However, above all it is necessary to see that it is logically possible to differentiate patterns of religious reasoning which possess a higher degree of organization and a greater equilibration from those patterns which possess these characteristics to a lesser degree. Whoever undertakes such a venture is usually dependent on two things: first, he or she must know what shall be designated as the highest or most complex religious judgement and what the pertinent criteria are; here theological and philosophical models can perform—heuristically—a certain service. Second, one should be able to draw on other developmental stage hierarchies which possess a certain affinity to the theory of religious judgement, such as moral judgement (cf. Kohlberg, 1974), social perspective taking (cf. Selman, 1980; Keller, 1976) or communicative competence (cf. Döbert/Nunner-Winkler, 1975), etc. It is also possible to employ individual examples (case studies) as experiential background and assume that certain persons possess a high capacity for religious judgement. The lower stages of the religious judgement are reflected, among other things, in Piaget's early investigations into the animism of punishment [*Strafanimismus*]. Or they can be recognized in the direct observation of children, for example, in educational contexts.

In 1978, we attempted to sketch such a stage sequence by forging theoretical conceptualizations and individual responses to certain dilemmas into a preliminary stage hierarchy (for an abbreviated version, cf. Oser, 1979, pp. 221-249). Subsequently, this model was repeatedly tested, revised, and validated with many examples, until we arrived at the research project presented in this book. This project, then, necessitated a substantial revision of the original stage concept.

What, then, is the difference between the new stage concept of religious development presented here and Kohlberg's moral stages or Piaget's level of intelligence or Selman's stages of social perspective taking? Piaget relates his theory, his genetic epistemology, primarily to the tension between subject and object which he overcomes with the functionalistic a priori. Kohlberg and Selman do things differently: Their starting-point for the cognitive-social basis in the domain of moral norms is the equilibrium between subject and subject. Our religious structures deal with the much broader spectrum of the relation between person and person and an Ultimate. The following table intends to clarify this:

INTELLECTUAL DEVELOPMENT	SOCIAL DEVELOPMENT	RELIGIOUS DEVELOPMENT
subject—object relation	subject—subject relation	subject—Ultimate—subject relation

It is important to understand that these domains are interrelated, i.e., the third set of relations for one and the same reality is meaningless without the other two. Yet, it is possible to isolate structurally the reasoning patterns for each relational domain. For these cognitive patterns are relational matrices of formal elements which reappear in the same shape and manner across different realities. The hierarchy which we designed refers to the third of the cognitive patterns, religious development, which, however, includes the other two relational systems.

The Structure-Content Distinction

> Central to understanding the present (structural) approach is the comprehension of the difference between structure and content. The religious judgement is defined as a structure. A pure structure is present when it is abstracted from any sort of concrete content (formalization). A structure, however, is obtained from certain concrete contents, and it can be applied to any new content.

The cognitive structure of religious reasoning of an individual stage is a basic pattern which is valid across a certain age-spectrum. It consists of elements and their interrelations. It is trans-situational, which means that it is employed in similar fashion in various situations. Figure 1 attempts to present this graphically:

Figure 1: The Trans-situational Quality of the Stage Pattern

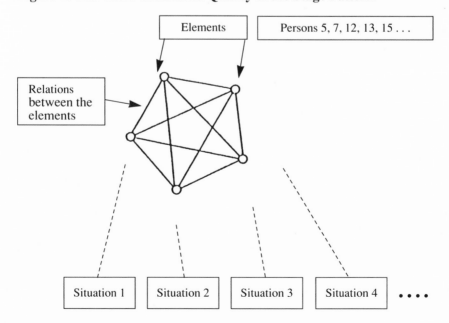

This figure conveys that a person's pattern of religious cognition is operationalized in different situations and that a certain group of persons exhibits a structurally isomorphous pattern, even if the members experience and evaluate the contents in various ways. Put differently: Across highly different contents, persons maintain the same religious judgement. This structure of reasoning, in the form of a set of rules, is applied to certain content-statements in order to assign a stage to the person.[1] Content-statements are culturally dependent. They consist, for example, of the words and ways of religious practices. They form the basic religious knowledge of a certain culture. We believe that processes of religious enlightenment, as mentioned by Lübbe (1980, pp. 65f) concern, for the most part, religious content. Such processes are:

FIRST, the translation of transmitted religious doctrines from the language of the discipline of theology into statements which can exist without dissonance in the system of our contemporary, or even in the continuously evolving, cognitive worldview.

SECOND, the functionalistic characterization of religion by means of practical achievements which we evaluate according to their utility and not, like doctrines, according to our reasons for holding them to be true.

THIRD, the historization (*Historisierung*) of religious teachings and institutions insofar as they, in their transmitted form, relate to the unalterable functions of religion in a contingent manner.

It is from such content-determinations that the *structural* religious dimensions must be distinguished. They determine the religious judgement. We have designated them as cognitive religious structures, as elements which are connected by means of a certain type of relationships. The structures are the truly formal element, although it is impossible—as in the domain of logical structures—to achieve absolute formality. This formality consists main-

---

1. For the domain of moral judgement, the structure-content problem was intensively treated by Nisan (1981). For him, "moral content" means the internalized behavioral instruction concerning right or wrong. "The learning of norms is a one-time event in the sense that the child regards them as objective data, i.e., data of prescriptive nature and not incidental commands. In contrast to knowledge of a foreign culture, children believe that the norms of their own culture exactly match what is objectively right or wrong. This is the result not only of direct mediation but also of a process of deduction which leads children to conclude that prohibited actions are bad, while socially desirable ones are good" (Nisan, 1981, pp. 5f). We can make similar assumptions about the construal of religious reality; cf. the concept of "domain-specificity" [*Bereichsspezifität*], Seiler, 1973.

ly of those characteristics which can be gained from judgements through inductive work. They concern the coherence and inner organization of the structure. This shall be illustrated with an example: Let us assume that someone, possessed by mortal fear, makes a solemn promise, i.e., that he will employ his professional medical skills in a Third-World nation. Subsequently, he is offered a good position in Europe. Now he is uncertain how to decide. Children between seven and eight years of age reacted to this situation with the following, and other, responses:

> Student: "He must keep the promise." (Why?) "Because God says so."
> Student: "Otherwise, God gets angry." (Why ought one keep a promise?) "Because if one does not, God might do something." (Like what?) "God will make me stumble or fall off my bicycle."
> Student: "He simply has to keep the promise." (Why?) "Otherwise, he would be dead now. Something else might have happened."
> Student: "He must go, because he told God he would. If he doesn't go, he would have lied to God." (Why must one not lie to God?) "Because that makes him sad." (Must one not lie to other people either?) "No, God does not like that." (What does God do when we lie to him?) "He will no longer help us."

The common characteristics are: recognition of an absolute authority, keeping rules without questioning them, attention to the punishment-reward pattern. These elements are connected with each other by means of the coordination of the possible resolutions to the story (keeping the promise vs. not keeping it, making substitutions, etc.) on the one hand, and by means of the externalization of an immediate ground (causality), on the other hand.

Although different children use different words, different proportional forms, different images of God or the Divine, the structural givens can be reduced to a few characteristics. These characteristics determine the pertinent stage. The relation between content and structure can be defined in such a way that the structures can be elicited from the contents, while, vice versa, that what is cognitively transferable can be applied, as structure, to new contents, thereby making it possible for these contents to be integrated. The structures are coupled with those fundamental capacities which, on the one hand, make it possible to assimilate religious contents, and, on the other hand, to accommodate the structures themselves to new situations, thereby producing new religious interpretations.

However, the relation between structure and content must also be viewed in such a way that, due to a lack of possible formalizations, the structures in the religious domain can never be entirely purified of content-aspects.

Similarly, structures of religious judgement are always applicable in contexts which have produced these structures. At the same time there is the claim that these structures are universal, because they illuminate similar phenomena in similar ways. Thus we face, on one side, cultural contextualization and, on the other side, universal transformability. Part of the cultural contextualization are the so-called "social representations."[2] By way of the meaning-making activities of the members of a culture, social representations take shape in stories, legends, myths, theological models, didactic poems, etc. These are (a) assimilated by persons according to their respective cognitive religious structures (e.g., a child at stage 1, an adult at stage 4; and (b) these social representations cannot fully relieve individuals of interpreting their own situations themselves. This is decreasingly possible with ascending development.

Still, these social representations perform an important task. Among other things, they warrant the continuation of a certain dimension of reasoning (in this case, religious reasoning). Simultaneously, they ground the individual subject in general action patterns. In addition, theological and philosophical concepts belong to the social representations as well. These may serve to prescribe how persons ought to interpret their mortality, death, the surprise element of love, poverty and loneliness, illness, bad fortune, or chance. However, individuals perform such explanations generally on the basis of their variously developed semiotic or interpretive patterns. Therefore we assumed that structural similarities do exist in these reconstructive processes which, despite differences in content situations and their linguistic articulation, manifest themselves as religious structures of cognition. Nonetheless, such concepts perform an important function: They achieve the highest possible rationalizations of holistic religious life which make possible universal solutions to the same questions and always new integrations of old content dealing with salvation.

However, we must not answer the following question too quickly: Is it not models of theology or various objectifications of religious culture like stories, legends, myths, parables, etc., that determine how individuals, as part of their personality, ought to interpret the relation between themselves and the final things, i.e., an Ultimate, in concrete situations? Basically, legends, myths, etc., are more like etiological groundings of characteristics of cultural behavior patterns, while theological models or ontologies are meta-descriptions which are often too difficult to apply in the limit-situations of life. What individuals actually do is more the outcome of a subjective ontological reconstruction of reality or of a subjective communicative construction

---

2. Social representations are characterized by two major psychological processes: (1) "Objectification" signifies the transformation of unfamiliar abstract concepts into familiar, concrete experiences; and (2) "anchoring" refers to the categorizing of new or strange ideas under familiar concepts so that they become cultural beliefs; cf. Billig, 1988.

of meaning whereby the resulting differences are dependent on the religious language employed. The linguistic differences (content) are coupled with differences in regard to the aforementioned stage hierarchy, the religious structures of cognition.

Therefore, a system of religious development must always be viewed against the background of those processes which facilitate or hamper the development of the personality so that, among other things, it becomes possible to decide "whether a religion contributes to the resolution of the identity-crisis by means of a transformation of consciousness onto a new stage, or whether it fosters regression to behavioral patterns which were already considered obsolete" (Peukert, 1982, p. 77).

Finally, the structure-content problem is related to the issue of religious identity described in the first chapter. This identity is warranted via structure and content. In Western culture it is always realized in a post-Enlightenment society. Therefore, it is senseless to describe religiosity as an unenlightened submissiveness or to dismiss religious content as "medieval" and primitive while praising the structural dimension as enlightened. The experience of the holy, a faith in a personal God, the cultic dimension, etc., these contents of religious phenomena are reconstructions without any positive or negative sanctioning in contemporary society, or without institutional support for their validity (cf. Lübbe, 1980, pp. 60f). The magical has already transferred its power into the symbolism of communicative forms of expression. Religious praxis occurs as self-empowerment of people by themselves and for themselves. On the one hand, religious contents and the corresponding structures are, in one way or another, formed by and dependent on historical-social formation. On the other hand, they determine, in correspondence with the existing structural stage, the prevailing structures of plausibility. Thus, when we say that religious identity, in an occidental society like ours, develops along a post-Enlightenment path, we do not mean to deny the universality of these stages of development. We simply mean to say that the religious processes of reconstructions occur in a particular culture and epoch which is shaped by the historic achievement of the Enlightenment and by the Christian religion. The resulting ambiguity for a concept of religion cannot fully be resolved.

The Stage Characteristics of the Religious Judgement

The religious development of persons does not happen slowly and steadily, but in steps. The passage from one step to the next is complicated and constitutes, in any case, a discontinuity. This sort of movement is usually designated as phases or stages. The formal qualities which describe the individual stages are: qualitative differentiation, sequentiality, holism, and the incorporation of lower stages into higher ones.

The core element of any psychological theory of development, as established by Piaget and elaborated by Kohlberg, is the concept of "developmental stage" or "cognitive stage." Within genetic structuralism there is widespread agreement about the necessary conditions that must be met in order to apply the designation "stages of cognitive development." Four characteristics must be distinguished (cf. Kohlberg, 1974, pp. 17f). These are 1) qualitative differentiation, 2) irreversible sequentiality, 3) structural wholeness at each stage, and 4) hierarchical differentiation and (re-)integration.

In the following, we will discuss the aforementioned four stage characteristics in the context of the development of the religious judgement. Generally, it can be assumed that the domain of religious judgement does exhibit a developmental tendency in the direction of an intersubjectively mediated subject-subject distinction, i.e., a course of development characterized by increasing autonomy. Thus, in the case of religious judgement we can clearly identify developmental-psychological criteria such as increasing independence from external stimuli, a raised level of abstraction, a widening differentiation, and a general heightened objectivity of the perception of reality (cf. Döbert/Nunner-Winkler, 1975, p. 22).

Now, let us address the first criterion "qualitative difference." It means that at each stage, in the context of a concrete situation, the question about absolute meaning and about an Ultimate favors and activates a particular problem-solving potential. Each stage is distinguished by a determinable structural web. One must take care, however, that the qualitative differences in the forms of reasoning or in the solutions to the same problem at different age-levels are not confused with increased knowledge of religious concepts or with internalizations of religious convictions, since each stage represents a "structured whole." For "a certain stage-reaction to a task does not simply represent a specific reaction which is determined by knowledge or familiarity with said task or similar tasks. Rather, it represents a fundamental cognitive organization" (Kohlberg, 1974, p.17). In this case, qualitative difference means that at each stage the previously mentioned seven elements are interrelated according to a prevailing principle (e.g., *do-ut-des*). This principle of reasoning which is unique at each stage constitutes the "essence" of each developmental stage; it gives each stage a particular shape and color which distinguishes it from the other stages.

Second, we said that the individual, self-contained patterns of reasoning form an invariant sequence, i.e., development follows an immanent logic of structural transformation. Although we presently lack longitudinal data concerning this characteristic, the data from our cross-sectional and intervention studies do reveal a clear trend that confirms this element of developmental psychology. The immanent logic of structural transformation inherent in the stages of religious judgement surfaces in the increasing autonomy and differentiation of the perception of the relation between persons and the Ultimate;

this relationship is not at all regressive. Thus, the stage sequence cannot be changed nor can a stage be omitted, since each stage of the sequence derives its qualitative difference from and builds upon the preceding one. These stages, then, must be regarded as hierarchically ordered.

Earlier stages are integrated into later stages. Temporally earlier forms of cognition are preserved through the transformations. However, one can recognize the common disposition among persons to select the highest available degree of problem-solving strategies.

We already referred to the third and fourth criteria: When someone resolves a religious conflict in a fashion described with stage 2, then, someday, it will be *inevitably* necessary for this person to resolve the same conflict according to the mode of stage 3, i.e., in a more autonomous, more differentiated, and—in comparison to stage 2—in a reinterpreted fashion. Wherever such a necessity does not exist (anymore), development has ceased. For that reason, the skipping of a stage is impossible. For in the sense of continuous development it is not possible to undergo a process of integrations that exhibits a gap, because in such a process it is impossible to arrange the elements of earlier stages into a cognitive equilibrium.

A few final remarks in regard to the essential characteristics of the stage model: The advantages which generally result from the theory of a stage-logic prove helpful especially for the domain of religious judgement! They can be characterized as follows:

> Psychological personality theories with a developmental orientation exhibit all the advantages of systematic typologies: When important dimensions are being grasped, they define for a given field of research the domain of possible objects. Compared to purely formal typologies, developmental logics accomplish more insofar as they—because the forms of the individual dimensions amalgamate into structured wholes—are not affected by the consideration of additional dimensions in such a way that totally new types arise—what happens is that only the description of a stage becomes richer" (Döbert/Nunner-Winkler, 1975, pp. 22f).

Higher-level Coordination: or the Dichotomy of Having and Being as Means for the Description of Developmental-Psychological Progressions

Why is a higher stage of religious development more differentiated, more complex, etc., than a lower one? In order to aid us in answering this question we are introducing the two developmental-psychological concepts "externalization" (decentration) and "internalization." They enable us to explain plausibly the transformational process from one stage to the next by reference to its internal principle.

Externalization means that persons can hold up their own

judgement for examination, which makes it possible to coordinate this judgement with other judgements. Internalization means that a new step, an advance is being made, a new stage is being achieved.

Describing stages of developmental psychology is difficult because one must make intelligible why a higher stage is more differentiated, more complex, more adequate, more integrated, etc., than a lower one. Whoever wants to describe stages must have means available that assist in capturing the qualitatively more advanced personality structure. Normally, this happens by integrating a new element into the existing structure, thus conferring on that structure a different psychological valence.

Noam and Kegan (1982)* suggested a way for describing the developmental gains more from the point of view of psychological transformation instead of from the logical point of view:

> Our contribution deals with two concepts which are of central importance for psychoanalytical ego-psychology and object-relations theory, for which we will attempt to work out a social-cognitivistic reading: namely with the idea of psychological boundaries and the process of externalization related to it, especially through the process of projective identification. These concepts are of decisive importance not only for the psychoanalytical school of thought but also for the perspective of social cognition. Our attempt endeavors to prove that, essentially, these concepts are not truly "psychoanalytical" or "cognitivistic" concepts, but rather, in a broader sense, concepts of developmental psychology, which make possible the integration of both perspectives (pp. 423f).

The two concepts "externalization" and "internalization" are central. Each equilibrium between the two constitutes a temporary resolution of the tension between the lifelong yearnings for inclusion and affiliation, on the one hand, and autonomy and separation, on the other hand. This means precisely that, at a given stage, persons externalize a particular important dimension so that they are able to relate this dimension to other similar ones (coordination). At the same time, however, these persons also integrate a completely new dimension in such a way that they are still unable to objectify it; i.e., they are "dependent" on or "embedded" in it. Kegan and Noam describe this "dependency" or "embeddedness" with the phrase "I *am*" (e.g., at stage 2, I *am* my needs, just as others *are* their needs). When Kegan and Noam describe the process of externalizing or differentiating a dimension and, therewith, the process of moving the dimension from subject to object and integrating it, they use the phrase "I *have*" (e.g., at stage 3, I have a certain need and I am able to externalize it in such a way that I can coordinate it freely

---

*Translator's note: The following quote is translated from the German. For an English-language publication by the authors see Noam and Kegan, 1989.

with the needs of another individual or the needs of a group).[3] Thus, when a particular dimension or an element of a structure is newly internalized, the initial identification is assured by subjectifying this dimension, i.e., it can neither be released from its "knowing-function" nor externalized by possible critical distance. What, at one stage, is the newly internalized, structure-transforming element, becomes, at the next stage, externalized in the sense that persons have it available like an object. The process of a dimension moving from subject to object makes possible a coordination at a higher level. Metaphorically speaking, persons hold up the objects in front of them and set them in relation to each other. A dimension that exists at one stage without being reversible becomes reversible at the next stage, in the sense of social exchangeability. This sort of decentration constitutes the fundamental principle for stage transitions in general. Formulated according to the "dichotomy of having-and-being": For subjects it becomes necessary to let go of the "being" quality of stage 2 and to transpose it into the "having" quality of stage 3 in the form of a reflexive process of self-distantiation.

In order to view the development or the stage-hierarchy of religious judgement within this framework, it becomes necessary to analyze structurally the interpretive process of subjects who define their relationship to a religious Ultimate in concrete situations. For persons who are interacting with the Ultimate use these decentrations to form meanings which not only explain their real-life situations causally but also transform them.

Stage Descriptions from the Perspective of Decentration

In the following we are describing the stages of religious development in more detail. In order to illuminate the developmental process according to its inner, structural workings our description is from the standpoint of decentration.

This enables us also to describe the various stage transitions more precisely. For clarity's sake we are supplementing the description of each stage with a schematic sketch and a significant example. To give a better initial overview we will first present another brief summary of the five stages of religious judgement.[4]

Now we would like to apply the "having/being dichotomy" to the description of various patterns of reasoning which are developmentally conditioned (religious judgement in stages). We hope this will enable us to sketch out clearly the stage sequence. The title for each stage serves only to provide a

---

3. Possibly Noam and Kegan are building upon Piaget's concept of "reflective abstraction" (cf. Inhelder, Garcia, and Vonéche, 1977, pp. 307f).
4. Cf. Bucher; 1986.

STAGE 5: Intersubjective Religious Orientation

Complete mediation of Being and world. Universality. Unconditional religiosity. Subject occupies a totally religious standpoint, feels no need to be grounded in a plan of salvation or a religious community, etc. Rather subjects experience unconditional and proleptic acceptance. Various forms: unconditional intersubjectivity, *unio mystica, boddhi*, divine illumination, etc.

STAGE 4: Mediated Autonomy and Salvation-Plan Orientation

The Ultimate is mediated again via immanence, either as constitutive ground of possibility or as a cypher for the "self." Manifold forms of religiosity, always presuming and no longer questioning ego-autonomy: nature-worship, contemplation, social activism to make God real. However, subjects reject the claim of being able to accomplish all things on their own, they surrender again to an Ultimate. "Images of God" exist, if at all, as symbols only, otherwise as universal principles.

STAGE 3: Absolute Autonomy Orientation (Deism)

The Ultimate is being pushed out of the world, transcendence and immanence are separated. Persons are solipsistically autonomous, responsible for the world and their own lives. Frequent rejection of religious and ecclesial authority: "Here I stand, I can do no other!" Formulation of ego-identity, distancing from parental and educational forces.

STAGE 2: "Do Ut Des" Orientation

The Ultimate is still viewed as external and omnipotent, capable of punishing or rewarding. However, now the Ultimate can be influenced. Humans can undertake preventive actions. Limited automony. First form of rationalization.

STAGE 1: Absolute Heteronomy Orientation (Deus Ex Machina)

The Ultimate interferes actively and unmediated in the world. Persons merely react. Pressure of expectation. Artificialism. Punctiliousness.

---

metaphor for the complexities at hand. For each full stage we will provide a representative example, something we call a "core-example."[5] The one used in the following relates to the Paul-dilemma. It portrays the situation where, in an environment of fear and emergency, a young medical doctor makes a promise (a solemn vow) to God: that is, if he is rescued he will forgo a

---

5. "Core-examples" are reduced orientation-systems for brief interpretations. They provide an initial general impression of an interview which has to be interpreted. We would like to supply such "core-examples." Since we already described the stage pattern, i.e., the regulative system for each stage, it will be possible to discern the religious, cognitive structure in those examples.

career in this country and instead put his knowledge and skill into service for persons in a country of the Third World. He is rescued and soon thereafter receives a great offer to become the leading physician in one of the nation's finest clinics. What shall he do? Upon reflecting briefly, he decides against leaving the country. A short time later he gets involved in an accident caused by him.

Stage 0: Perspective of the Dichotomy Between Interior and Exterior

Children are still incapable of distinguishing between different forces outside of themselves. They only know that they are being influenced from the outside. They can differentiate between doing something themselves and being influenced by or being dependent upon others. (When parents speak of God, God can, on one occasion, be something indeterminable and, on another occasion, an uncle or an unknown guest. From a cognitive point of view, this is a *prereligious* attitude. Explanations of events are functionally always visible. (Q.: Why is this happening? A.: Because he or she did it.) Adults can be influenced only by means of articulating needs (e.g., crying). The child understands: either I affect something or someone, or something or someone will affect me. Therefore, it is possible to say that children at this stage *are* entirely embedded in interiority or exteriority. They do not yet *have* different forms of exteriority that can be connected causally.

Stage 1: The Perspective of *Deus ex Machina*

Children assume that everything is guided, led, and steered by external forces. Yet, for the first time, they clearly separate the forces of the Ultimate from the influences of adults and educators. The Ultimate is active, humans are reactive. This reactive posture is perceived as a pressure of expectation. The great advance from stage 0 to stage 1 consists in the children transferring those patterned behaviors, which they have learned from parents and educators, onto the still undetermined Ultimate and its effects. Although children still *are* their reactions to certain behaviors, they do *have* an Ultimate[6] (in terms of content, most children in our cultural sphere speak of God) which they are able to separate clearly from other domains of influence. On the one hand, all of life, all actions *are* guided, created, led *without mediation*. On the other

---

6. We are employing the term and concept of "Ultimate" because it is more easily generalizable across different cultures and their corresponding religions than the terms and concepts "God," "Divinity," "Supernatural." These three concepts are related to specific forms of the structures of religious judgement; therefore they will appear in the pertinent "core-examples" and parenthetical remarks. When we use Ultimate or Unconditional we mean to say that persons can conceive of things above and beyond that which they encounter in the world. Whether it is possible for a stage description to be so formal as to be totally "unstained" by any content elements seems hardly likely.

hand, there exists this Ultimate Power which is distinguishable from other forces. In other words, the active Ultimate (i.e., active as person, spirit, God, power) constitutes the first externalization. Simultaneously, however, there occurs the internalization that persons have reactions to this creating and guiding Ultimate. Humans are executive vehicles for the Ultimate ("God knows what to do;" "God acts this way, because that is how God acts.").

Core-Example for the Paul-Dilemma (Stage 1)

Question 7a: Is this accident related to the fact that Paul did not keep his promise to God? Why or why not?
> *Answer:* "Yes." *Why?* "God simply punished him." *Why does God punish people?* "He punishes them when they don't obey him." *Why must we obey God?* "If we don't obey him, he punishes us." *What is God telling us with his punishment?* "That he doesn't like what we have done." (girl, age 7)

Figure 2: Matrix of Influence in the System of Reasoning at Stage 1

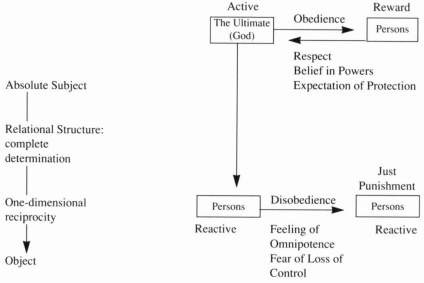

Stage Transition 1-2

A stage transition becomes necessary when ontological problems can no longer be solved with the first stage. For example, suddenly a child no longer believes that the Ultimate (God) *makes* the weather but that it depends on cloud constellations and the wind. In addition, the child comes to believe that persons can do something to change the constellation, e.g., keeping the Divinity happy. This constitutes an increase in complexity. On the one hand, the child questions the one-way street of the Ultimate's influence and actions. On the other hand, the subjectivity of the child begins to surface. New conditions are being introduced: When people conform to certain rules, perform certain rituals, are good to poor people, pray in a particular manner, etc., then the desired effect takes place. This brings to an end the image of the Divine affecting things and persons much like a puppeteer manipulates his or her puppets or marionettes. Although the child still feels that she is somehow influenced by an outside force, she begins to waver between the negation of an Absolute influence and a new conception postulating a connection between human action and Ultimate or Divine action or reaction.

For example: a mother reports that her eight-year-old son always prayed for everything, including good weather for an excursion at school. The things that he prayed for always seemed to have occurred. Thus he interpreted this as his prayer being "answered." One day, however, despite his prayers, exactly the opposite happened, resulting in a big crisis for the boy. Now, after resolving that crisis, he knows that not everything asked for in prayer comes true. However, he still believes that prayer is necessary to keep God happy. The crisis is an example for the transition from stage 1 to stage 2.

Stage 2: The Perspective of "Do Ut Des"

The advance over against stage 1 consists mainly in the fact that persons can now objectify consequences and thereby are able to coordinate them with the power of an Ultimate Being outside of them. Now there are means available for influencing the transcendent Absolute (Fate, spirits, God). This influence can be of various sorts: It can reduce punishment, it can achieve favors, or have a preventively calming character. (Seafarers during the Graeco-Roman period made sacrifices to the gods in order to obtain favorable winds.) Religious or animistic actions motivated by fear serve primarily for obtaining favors (wealth, health, a long life). Obversely, incidents of bad luck are viewed as actions by the Ultimate in direct correspondence with the quality of sacrifices, renunciations, and prayers, etc.

At this stage, persons *are* the counterpart to an Ultimate Other. Now persons *have* selves of their own, just as the Ultimate may also have a self. Both must be distinguished. Persons can talk, bargain, interact with the Ultimate and even placate it. Now, persons *have* the means available to them and therewith control over positive or negative consequences. They can coordinate the meaning of events or actions in such a way that being good and following the rules stands in a linear relation with fortune, welfare, sickness, death, salvation, and disaster. The advance over the previous stage consists in the ability to articulate one's self and in the possibility to resist and object to the pressure of expectations. The relationship between the self and the Ultimate, as the Absolute Subject, is bi-polar and reciprocal.

Core-Example for Stage 2

Question 7a: Is this accident related to the fact that Paul did not keep his promise to God? Why or why not?

Answer: "I say it is, because afterward God was angry. Paul did promise that instead of getting married he would help poor children. This is supposed to teach him a lesson, so he won't do it again. Perhaps he won't learn his lesson at first, but when something happens to him for a second time. . . perhaps when he has a son who is very little and dies, perhaps then he will catch on." *What ought he do?* "He ought to pray to God, he ought to apologize earnestly. Praying ought to be done in the evening. . . . I just pray to God and ask him not to let anything happen to me during the night." (girl, age 9)

Figure 3: The Matrix of Influence in the System of Reasoning at Stage 2 (The directional arrows indicate the "self-articulation" of the individual.)

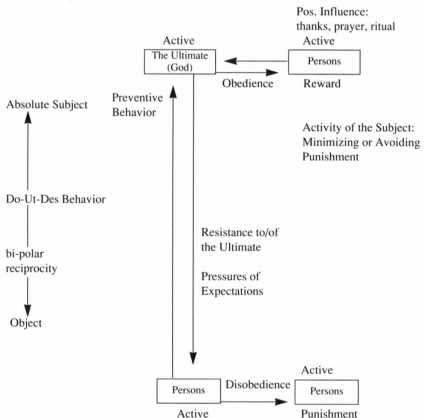

Stage Transition 2-3

The transition to stage 3 also represents a major shock which negates the previous patterns of reasoning and simultaneously initiates the acceptance of new elements and dimensions. Young persons believe that certain things are unchangeable and not even their greatest effort can make a difference (e.g., a student realizes that an infant may die without anyone being responsible; Job doesn't understand why he is being punished in the face of having lived righteously). Thus, persons begin to negate that they might be able to influence the Ultimate. They begin to take as much personal responsibility as possible, i.e., they begin to distinguish between those things which they can execute and take responsibility for and those which they can appropriately ascribe to an Ultimate. The transition surfaces in the struggle between the rejection of "consistent" religion (e.g., the new "youth religions") which places a divinity above everyone and everything else, above the world and above human beings. An example: A young man fulfills all his religious obligations. He is successful in his career. One day, he discovers that he does well on examinations even without prayer or religious engagement. Uncertainty befalls him. He feels "exploited." From that point on, he intends to take all responsibilities onto himself, even for those actions that involve risk. Initially, however, he will not succeed. In any case, he must try living without God, without a supernatural being.

Stage 3: The Perspective of Absolute Autonomy and Deism

Persons at stage 3 are able to separate completely the domain of the Ultimate from their own. They attribute to themselves a great deal of responsibility for planning and decision-making activities. Yet, they fully separate out the Ultimate (Fate, Absolute Being, Spirit, God) and relegate it to an independent sphere of influence. This results in something akin to a "two kingdom theory." Now it is possible either to postulate consciously an atheistic worldview or to profess an extreme religious conviction. To the degree that the self of the person at stage 3 becomes "interpersonal" it becomes possible to distinguish between the domains of one's own competence and domains attributed to a Higher Entity (this is evident in a strong awareness of the distinction between God and humans, the sacred vs. the profane).

At this stage, the person *is* a decision-making, responsible, determined self, just as the Ultimate *is* its own domain of decision making (solipsistic ego-structure). Influencing the Ultimate is no longer important, because it has its own sphere of responsibility. Another advance over stage 2 consists in the fact that now persons *have* decision-making competencies of their own which can be coordinated with the decision-making competencies of the Ultimate. Insofar as subjects are embedded in the context of meaning-making of their own actions and their causal effects, the subjects have the possibility to differentiate themselves from the Ultimate which appears as a contra-factual entity. We are dealing here with a religious judgement which is not simply identical with the immediate system of meaning. What is stressed is the activity of meaning-making. To the degree that the mastery of their own sphere of decision making is emphasized, persons at stage 3 delimit their sphere over against the influence of the Other, the More Powerful.

Core-Example for Stage 3

Question 7a: Is this accident related to the fact that Paul did not keep his promise to God? Why or why not?

> *Answer:* "I cannot imagine it. Suppose he had chosen another path, like keeping his promise, going into the Third World. He may just as well have died of malaria or something like that. That scenario is just as conceivable as not keeping his promise and having an automobile accident. I just don't see any causal connections with that higher power, these connections just aren't there. If you do postulate a higher power, if you claim that it exists, then the first thing that I wonder about is the missing logical connections: you did this, now you are being punished for it; that no longer works. There is no more distinction between good and evil. God does not keep score and does not punish. I believe that this guy, Paul, brought punishment on himself via some sort of unconscious mechanism. But that the process was engineered by some higher power, that I do not believe." (Protestant male, age 23)

Stage Transition 3-4

During this phase, persons begin to deny the stage 3 concept of human self-determination and autonomy ("In the end, everything has to come from somewhere"). Although all responsibility still rests with people, a consciousness begins to emerge that sees a mediated relationship between the Ultimate and human beings. A breakthrough occurs to the degree that persons begin to perceive the simultaneity of transcendent and immanent forces and slowly begin to construct a new model for the mediation of the two dimensions. The crisis of this transition is being articulated in the negation of extremes. Persons have to learn to view different things simultaneously.

It is no longer possible to resolve problems by neatly dividing each polarity into its individual entities. (A young adult says: God's kingdom is present only when I know that all of my actions are related to the Ultimate.") The breakthrough from stage 3 to stage 4 is such a crisis because, at least initially, persons consider it a regression when reflections about the final grounding of existence, communication, world-events, etc., can no longer be related solely to their own decision-making competence. An example: A young woman, who would like to see her responsibilities completely independent of God, meets a highly success-

Figure 4: Matrix of Influence and System of Reasoning at Stage 3

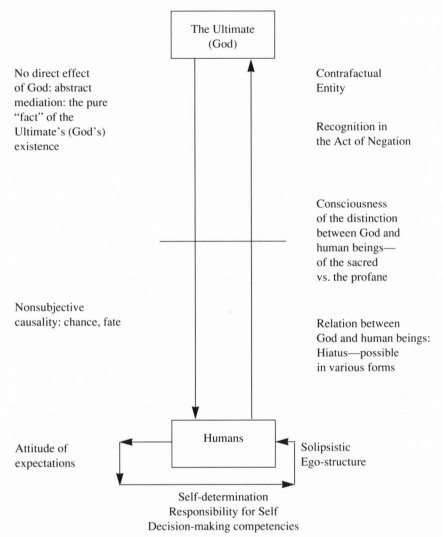

The Ultimate
(God)

No direct effect
of God: abstract
mediation: the pure
"fact" of the
Ultimate's (God's)
existence

Contrafactual
Entity

Recognition in
the Act of Negation

Consciousness
of the distinction
between God and
human beings—
of the sacred
vs. the profane

Nonsubjective
causality: chance, fate

Relation between
God and human beings:
Hiatus—possible
in various forms

Humans

Attitude of
expectations

Solipsistic
Ego-structure

Self-determination
Responsibility for Self
Decision-making competencies

ful female politician during a lecture-series. The politician explains that, for her, all her reasoning and actions are finally embedded in the concept that the possibility of free decision making is grounded in a power which has been given to persons as a gift from someone or somewhere else. This precipitates a crisis for the young woman, for, on the one hand, she admires the politician while, on the other hand, she is upset about her childish attitude. At the same time, however, she begins to realize that essential problems of her life cannot be solved sufficiently with her stage 3 concept. However, at this point she does not yet perceive an acceptable alternative solution.

Stage 4: The Perspective of Religious
Autonomy and the Plan of Salvation

The essence of judgement at stage 4 consists in a new possibility of mediating between the decision-making autonomy of the subject and of an assumed Ultimate. Although imagined as transcendent, the Ultimate becomes immanent in the sense that it is identified as the condition for all decision making and actions. The world is no longer determined by the Ultimate, in the sense of stage 1. Rather the earthly is seen as the "likeness" of the Divine, in the sense that it becomes the guarantor for the possibility of human accomplishments. One possible expression of this concept is to say that the Ultimate appears symbolically in nature, culture, and human capacities for love. (Or, put in the language of the philosophy of religion: God does not actively intervene in history: rather, as the ground of the world and of human existence God constitutes the condition for human action.) Persons begin to assemble a new semiotics for perceiving the preconditions which make possible human communication. (Wonderment about new-born life, for example, is always also an inquiring wonderment about the possibility of life in general.)

The advance over stage 3 consists in the fact that persons now *have* a decision-making self which they can bring into a correlationally mediated relation with the Ultimate. Subjects view themselves in a decisive role, while being located in a universal plan that constitutes the conditions of life (plan of salvation, cosmic evolution, divine providence, kingdom of God).

However, this stage has a limitation insofar as it is fixated on this plan. A person *is* a plan. Persons structure their freedom almost rigidly in accordance with it. In this sense, a person *is* fixated on freedom. The religious self is still representative of "freedom from" but not yet "freedom for." The symbolic, i.e., the immanent presence of the Ultimate, cannot yet be externalized in such a way that it can be coordinated with human interaction by means of an absolute surfacing of the Ultimate in such interaction. In other words, decisive for the structure of stage 4 is that neither the plan of salvation nor the Ultimate negate the autonomy which had been internalized at stage 3; rather the plan and the Ultimate make autonomy possible.

Core-Example for Stage 4

Question 7a: Is this accident related to the fact that Paul did not keep his promise to God? Why or why not?

> *Answer:* "I don't think so. I can't quite resolve the problem of the accident, but personally I do not believe that

those who are bad or evil are being punished by God. That is so much like the Old Testament; but the Old Testament also knows of many who were bad or evil and yet are doing well. It shows that often precisely those who keep God's commandments have no success while those who disobey are successful."

Then the accident is not a punishment from God for the nonfulfillment of the promise?

"Not at all. That would be a funny sort of God who becomes manifest only in the negative stuff. Here we reach a problem which we cannot resolve—it is the big problem of theodicy. As far as I am concerned, God does not personally or directly interfere in human affairs. Though I do believe that God is everywhere, and that therefore certain insignificant events have somehow to do with him, this does not happen in a direct manner. Take this accident: it is self-induced, for God leaves us space for our own actions and their consequences, just as God leaves space for the laws and effects of nature. Natural disasters are not so much of a big problem for me, because I believe that God fashioned creation in such a way that it keeps evolving; God created certain laws—take earthquakes, for instance, they have been part of evolution from time immemorial. In that case, creation possesses an independent dynamic, which can indeed cause the death of human beings. But it is in the small affairs of everyday life where God is present for me—especially in the unfortunate events; that's where I make the connection with God. But these theories of punishment which posit that this automobile accident is a punishment from God—that I cannot accept. As far as I am concerned, God is present at this accident—especially when people are hurting, for God is on the side of the suffering. For me, God is a God of love and thus also a powerless God who allows us to act without correcting us all the time. If you say that God causes an automobile accident, then we are talking about a God who acts as a puppeteer."

Let us assume that Paul does not accept the position as physician, yet also decides to give one-tenth of his income to charity. Does this justify his decision?

"Yes, if you presuppose that he made the wrong choice. He should have gone the other way, and now he has to try everything to make amends. For that reason, I would say, no. However, if he comes to be convinced that a genuine devotion to God can also occur at his current place of employment, then his tithe can be part of his service. However, if his giving is motivated by a guilty conscience, then it is an invalid solution. He wants to dedicate his entire life to God. This is evident, for instance, in his working hard all day and in his family life, which is another domain for him to encounter God. I do think it is meaningful to give 10 percent away, perhaps with contacts to another physician in the Third World—as long as it is not regarded simply as compensation for the promise he made." (Roman Catholic male, age 32)

Figure 5: Matrix of Influence and System of Reasoning at Stage 4

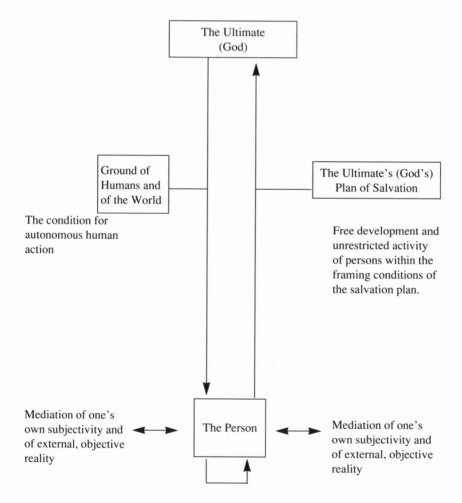

Stage 5: The Perspective of Religious
Autonomy by Means of Intersubjectivity

At this stage, the relation between the self and the Ultimate is perceived as being mediated intersubjectively. Like at stage 4, the question "why does something exist?" leads to the assumption that an Ultimate constitutes the possibility for human action. But now it is no longer possible to tie the ground of life and of the world to a predetermined plan without coupling this plan with human freedom and self-determination. The relation between the Ultimate and the human being is no longer directed by some sort of positive law (plan of salvation, the will of God), but the locus of the Ultimate is transferred as *norma normans* into the domain of human communication. The experience of salvation or damnation is now tied back to an intersubjective basis, i.e., it is interpreted as loyalty or disloyalty to that Ultimate dimension in interactive actions. In the context of real, practical, and transcendental freedom, this sort of cognitive model defines the human essence of the person strictly as freedom. The Ultimate is viewed as absolute freedom which makes possible and meaningfully warrants finite freedom. Noncontingent, unconditional intersubjectivity becomes the significant locus for the manifestation of the Transcendent: because the Transcendent appears as the possibility for finite freedom, others, in their own freedom, become the true goal of, and provide the meaning for, all action. We are speaking here of religious subjects who have passed through the stage of selfhood (as mediated by stages 3 and 4) and are finally being constituted through others in the encounter and in love via the Ultimate.

In contrast to stage 4, persons now *have* a plan, i.e., they are authors of their own life-histories and they have the possibility, at any point, to write them differently. Persons at this stage finally explain all major decisions with reference to the "knowledge" that the Ultimate can surface in no other way than in the unconditional dimension of intersubjective action. And this, then, implies a responsibility, derived from and intended for freedom, that takes an active role in the stewardship and shaping of this world.[7]

At stage 3, freedom *from* the Ultimate was dominant; at stage 4 it was freedom *by means of* the Ultimate. Now, at stage 5 freedom is viewed always for others and is postulated for them. The Ultimate, God, comes into existence whenever this freedom is conferred and realized intersubjectively. (For this stage no "core-example" is available.)

Remarks About Stage 6

During the course of our study we have frequently asked ourselves what the highest possible structure of reasoning of religious consciousness could

---

7. Speaking in terms of content this model presupposes a form of autonomy and responsibility which at no time places blame for our communicative circumstances on a divine being, for there always exists the possibility of investing oneself for the betterment of things. In those instances of human grief one can always sense the failure of those interactive possibilities; the grieving itself is viewed as suffering manifestation of the divine being: God grieves with human beings.

Figure 6: Matrix of Influence and System of Reasoning at Stage 5

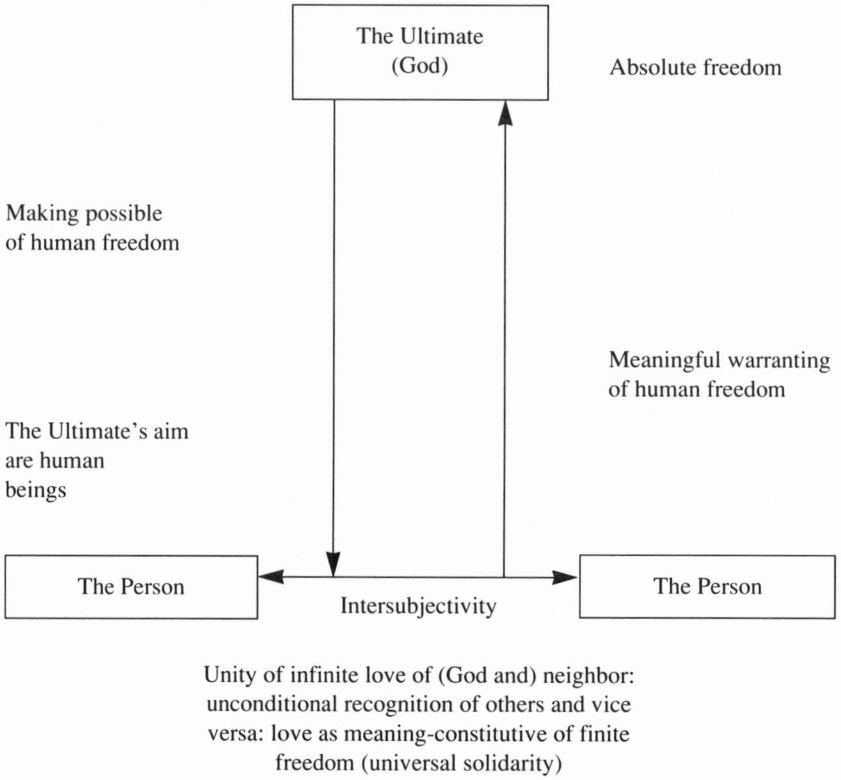

The Ultimate
(God)

Absolute freedom

Making possible
of human freedom

Meaningful warranting
of human freedom

The Ultimate's aim
are human
beings

The Person

Intersubjectivity

The Person

Unity of infinite love of (God and) neighbor:
unconditional recognition of others and vice
versa: love as meaning-constitutive of finite
freedom (universal solidarity)

be. On the one hand, this question was significant in regard to demonstrating and legitimizing the independence of the religious dimension and its distinctiveness over against other dimensions of cognitive development, especially moral development. On the other hand, the most differentiated pattern of reasoning has legitimizing, orientation-giving, and normative functions in regard to the less complex structures. Thus, we attempted initially to construct such a highest stage deductively from theological and philosophical models (cf. Oser, 1979, p. 234). However, the subsequent empirical studies yielded no data that corresponded to this highest scheme of consciousness. However, after we had fashioned and reformulated stages 1-5 according to our empirical material, we postulated and formulated a possible stage 6 based on the immanent developmental logic underlying the first five stages (cf. Gmünder, 1979, p. 633; cf. also Peukert, 1982, note 38, p. 102). Until this stage can be verified empirically, its character is suggestive and theoretical.

However, a linguistic and conceptual elaboration of this position appeared not to be without some difficulty. Therefore, we attempted to make the basic structure conceptually intelligible by employing various descriptions. Due to the lack of empirical data the description may be related a bit too closely to our cultural sphere.

Globally speaking one could say the stage 6 orientation tends toward universal communication and solidarity. What was valid for stage 5 must be decisively qualified.

At the center of the reasoning structure of stage 6 rests a communicative praxis with claim to universal validity, intending universal solidarity (communicative praxis with the Ultimate, mediated through interindividual actions). Again, one's own autonomous freedom is viewed as constituted intersubjectively, though always from the perspective of universal communication and solidarity and, at the same time, in consideration of that which grounds, mediates, and makes possible this freedom. At stage 5 there still exists the possibility of interpreting the unconditional freedom of others legalistically; this, however, finally results in an aporia.

The highest possible mediation is achieved only when one can presuppose a promise which makes it possible to let guilt, injustice, death, suffering, etc., take their course while totally trusting in the acceptance by the Ultimate— also, and particularly, in failure and pain. (Pannenberg speaks of God as the "reality which determines everything" becoming revealed as love and absolute freedom.) It is a finite freedom, which understands itself as liberated and liberating freedom, it is "the experience of unconditional acceptance which I can never produce by myself but only receive communicatively" (Fuchs, 1982, p. 168). Decisive for this stage is a consistent attending to the indicative structure: the indicative simply precedes the imperative. This happens in such a way that the categorical indicative not only does not curtail or hide the always existing human situation of conflict but rather does integrate it fully. Only from that perspective it becomes fully plausible that God can be experienced as the possibility and fulfillment of absolute meaning—mediated through finite freedom in fragmentary actions of powerlessness and love.

This is a position which knows

> that what we want to designate, without any sentimentality, as love and as the overcoming of suffering can never and will never reach fulfillment. In this sense of actually achieving the ideal fulfillment it is doomed to failure. Yet this failure does not condemn it to meaninglessness since its validity does not depend on a so-called total success but rather on making a real contribution to the realization of true life (Schupp, 1975, p. 28).

Only at this stage does the difference between human beings and the Ultimate finally become fully conscious in its true essence. It is the awareness of that qualitative difference which not only recognizes "that 'I am,' that I claim my freedom for the knowing and shaping of the world, but also that I am *supposed to be* and that I am *allowed to be*. In short: that *I am accepted, totally and unconditionally*" (Pröpper, 1976, pp. 138f)[8]

The Double Helix of Stage Development

Religious development as a hierarchy of stages is best expressed using the image of the double helix: each time a new stage is integrated there occurs at the same time a differentiation of the previous stage. If one stage is more subject-related, then the next one aims at the communicative counterpart. If one side of the helix represents reality, then the other one represents the relation of that reality to the Ultimate. Thus, we are always dealing with two decisive dimensions: one inward-directed, the other directed outward.

The stage hierarchy as described by us resembles a double helix. Each plateau represents a qualitative change and a transformation from lower to higher. Put differently: according to this scheme, religious development proceeds in such a fashion that, at each stage, there occurs both an integration and a differentiation; at each transitional stage something is negated while at the same time something positive is constructed. At each stage, a person *is* a certain characteristic, which he or she then *has* at the next stage. First this characteristic is integrated, then it is differentiated. At the lower stage, this characteristic can only be grasped but not *coordinated* with other characteristics. That can only happen at the next stage. For that reason we have attempted to explain the developmental differences in our stage descriptions with *complementary* characteristics. We even tried this approach in characterizing the individual structure of religious judgement. This proved valuable also in making transparent our structural and holistic claims as such.

---

8. In their terminology, theologians are able to describe the structure of stage 6 in multiple ways. They may say something like: God is that love in which we live. God is the one who created, the one who sustains and fulfills and who makes it possible for humans to be creative as well. Or as the overcoming of the final fear one could formulate in accordance with the Pauline dialectic of "with fears and yet without fear;" in being with others one is fully (with) oneself, although one is separated. (For this reason, we may perhaps designate this position at its core as mystical.) Or, following a formulation of H. Marcel, one could say: loving a human being means: you will not die—also and especially with regard to the innocent victims of history (solidarity without amnesia). Or also in the formulation of Peukert: God appears as the saving "reality which is approximated by any communicative action that is in solidarity with the dead in such a way that it asserts this reality for others and thereby for the actors themselves" (1976, p. 315).

Figure 7 depicts a representation of this process of integration and differentiation. In the transitions from one plateau to the next, the spiral lines represent the complementary processes. Their opposition expresses the positions of "having" and "being." In different words: the lines signify that the externalization of the one aspect frees a person for the internalization of the respective other.

Figure 7: The Double Helix of Religious Development. The loops represent, on the one hand, the transitions to decentration and, on the other hand, the transitions to a new integration (sketch by Arthur Lotti).

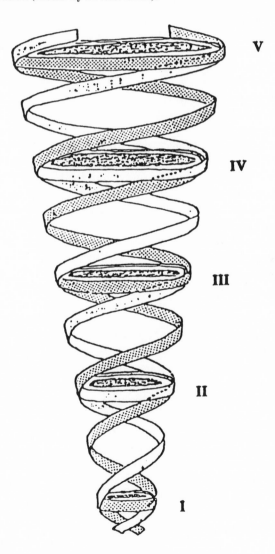

The following remarks are in order: Developmental approaches from the perspective of discontinuity generally tend to overemphasize one dimension of a particular stage. Accordingly, Eckensberger and Reinshagen (1980, pp. 108f) believe Kohlberg's moral stages 1 and 4 to be centered more on objective phenomena, while stages 2 and 4 1/2 represent more of a concentration on subjective phenomena. Stages 3 and 5, they believe, are decentrated and integrative.

Albeit in somewhat different fashion, we find a similar structure with Turiel (1978, p. 59). He demonstrates that, at the age of six and seven, conventions represent a sort of uniformity or a sort of lawfulness demanding obedience. These conventions, then, are denied and rejected at age eight and nine. At age ten and eleven, however, conventions are regarded as positive elements of a system of rules. A renewed rejection occurs at age twelve to thirteen. Between age fourteen and sixteen, conventions are interpreted as something which is mediated through the social system. The next two years, age seventeen and eighteen, sees another negation of them. Finally, between eighteen and twenty-five, conventions come to represent the coordinating elements of social interaction.

In our opinion, these are typical, one-sided views of the discontinuity-approach. They imply the neglect of the counter-dimension. Noam and Kegan (1982) reduced this one-sidedness. From the perspective of personality development, they suggest that the so-called self-other relation at stages 1, 3, and 5 favors inclusion and integration while stages 2 and 4 favor differentiation. Therefore, they speak only of a developmental helix for the relation between self and other. We go one step further and suggest that inclusion and integration equally imply a differentiation, and vice versa. Therefore, the term double-helix of development.

Based on that image we assume that it is wrong, for example, to emphasize at a certain stage the negation of one dimension, for this negation always occurs in tandem with the simultaneous adoption of a new dimension. The new one is always construed to the same degree that the old one is being negated, until, finally, a new equilibrium is achieved. Expressed differently: When we say that in those stages, which Turiel posits along the ages of eight to nine, twelve to thirteen, and fourteen to sixteen, something is being negated we must also say that at each stage, something else is being accepted and constructed; this, however, constitutes a newly emerging dimension which must be sponsored. When Eckensberger suggests that stages 1 and 4 are concentrated more on objective phenomena (punishment, law, etc.) this merely means that the subjective element of these stages is not recognized adequately. Even if we reduce the structural stage hierarchies to one aspect, autonomy vs. dependency, each stage would still need to contain this aspect in a transformed form according to the hierarchical developmental logic. To the same degree that one pole is being negated, the other pole can evolve a new quality until an equilibrium is reestablished. Looking at Figure 8, we observe that the newly emerging quality at each of the stages does not favor differentiation over integration or vice versa. Both are present at each stage, though intermixed with other qualities. At stage 1, the Ultimate is completely identical with the person because of his or her total dependency. At stage 2, the person begins to emerge from the stage 1 union; he or she gains independence and begins to influence the Ultimate. Stage 3 features the complete separation of the person from the Ultimate. Stage 4 sees a reintegration of the two in the sense that the Ultimate and existence are not conceived of as objects but rather as condition and ground of possible existence. Stage 5, finally, shifts the Ultimate, the ground of being and existence, into the realm of communicative action. Stages 1 and 2 appear as stages of dependency, stages 3 and 4 seem like stages of separation, and stage 5 looks like a stage of communicative integration. However, this is a correct observation only insofar as one chooses to examine and evaluate this issue from the perspective of stage 5. If one considers each stage individually, one discovers the dynamics of separation and integration, differentiation and inclusion, externalization and integration in all of them. Yet, the highest stage is the most autonomous one. At this stage, separation is most intense and freedom is most real. The highest stage features the best equilibrium.

The internal logic of this development, thus, features the establishment of an increasing integration of a person's relation to the Ultimate. These, then, are the steps of a certain type of logic, which every individual must slowly take in his or her life: 1) "The Ultimate affects everything . . ."; 2) "the Ultimate affects everything, if we . . ."; 3) "the Ultimate and human beings act independently of each other"; 4) "human beings are able to act, because of the a priori existence of the Ultimate"; 5) "human beings act through the actions of the Ultimate which itself is contingent upon the acts of human beings." In order to be able to reconstruct this developmental logic, the dynamics of continual decentration and integration are indispensable.

Regulation by Means of Higher Reversibility of Cognitive Religious Structures

Another important element in the development of religious consciousness in the sense of the double helix is the element of higher reversibility. Higher reversibility refers to increasingly more differentiated, more independent, and more intense communicative relations in the constellation subject-subject-Ultimate. Higher reversibility refers also to the increasingly more flexible capacity for processing concrete religious content. For the sake of clarity, we will introduce the distinction between temporary and

**Figure 8: Representations of Stage Development from the
Perspective of Autonomy vs. Dependency**

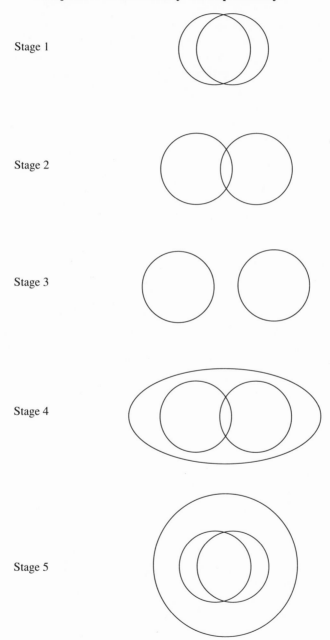

Stage 1

Stage 2

Stage 3

Stage 4

Stage 5

permanent religiosity. Thereafter, we will describe each stage
from the perspective of higher reversibility.

Our presentation up to this point needs to be expanded. A mere description of the stages is insufficient. Also, we believe that the double helix
exhibits features of structural differentiation in addition to those of inclusion
and decentration. The following section presupposes that the structure of a
developmentally higher religious stage is more capable than the structure
of a lower stage to assimilate religious content such as worship, proclamation, or revelation. We are dealing here with a form of higher *reversibility,*
which we intend to explicate below.

But, let us first embark on a brief excursus to examine a distinction which
enables us to describe more accurately the concept of higher reversibility. This
is the distinction between persons who perceive religiosity as a temporary
event and those persons who regard religiosity as a permanent part of their
identity. The former generally find themselves in situations where they can
no longer control events and the concept of "chance" becomes important.
Suddenly, religiosity is actualized. It makes possible the reconstruction of
these events from the standpoint of the sudden insight that individuals represent only a small part of the reality that surrounds them. In that role they
make a small contribution to the process of meaning-making. Or religiosity
is viewed as the sudden intrusion of the Ultimate into the "quiet" life of the
person, or as the sudden sensitization of the subject for that part of our total
ecology in which we participate or which we cannot explain. On the other
hand, however, there are persons for whom religion constitutes something permanent, for example in the question concerning the conditions of the possibility of human existence. Rahner (1968) uses in this context the concept
of pre-apprehension (*Vorgriff*). He writes:

> This transcending apprehension of further possibilities, through which
> the form is possessed in a concretion in sensibility is apprehended as lim-
> ited and so is abstracted, we call "pre-apprehension" (*Vorgriff*).

> So our task will be to determine the breadth of the horizon comprehended
> a priori, which horizon, apprehended as such in the pre-apprehension, offers
> the possibility of experiencing the forms of sensibility as limited, of dif-
> ferentiating them from the ground of their limitedness, the sensible "this,"
> and thus of creating for knowing the possibility of a complete return (142).

Finally, ontologically "religiously" extended, he says:

> Insofar as man enters into the world by turning to the phantasm, the rev-
> elation of being as such and in it the knowledge of God's existence has

already been achieved, but even then this God who is beyond the world is always hidden from us (p. 408).

The pre-apprehension is the permanent introduction of the religious dimension in correlation to the reality which surrounds us. How is it possible that people can love one another, that they are capable of causal explanations, that they perceive nature to be ordered according to simple logical laws? Pre-apprehension subsumes all events forever under the viewpoint of religious a priori. It provides a meaningful explanation of existence.

At an intermediate stage between those who introduce religion temporarily and those who understand it as permanent pre-apprehension, there are some people who separate religion and the world. Listen, for example, to A. Einstein:

> I do not believe that the basic concepts of the theory of relativity can claim a different kind of relation to the religious domain than any other scientific knowledge can. As I see it, this relation involves the fact that profound connections and conditions in the objective world can be grasped with logically simple concepts. However, as far as the theory of relativity is concerned, this is the case to an especially complete degree.

> The religious feeling which is evoked by the experience of logically grasping profound connections and conditions is of a somewhat different sort than the feeling commonly designated as religious. It is more a feeling of being in awe of reason as such as it is manifest in the conditions and connections in the objective world. This, however, does not lead one to take the step of forming a divine person in our image—a person who places expectations upon us and is interested in our individual existence.

> Therefore I view morality as a purely human matter—although as the most important matter in our human domain (1981, p. 66).

The three positions can be summarized as follows: It is just as probable that temporary religiosity can be found at stages 1 and 2 as it is probable that the second position, the position of the pre-apprehension (as condition for the possibility of religion), can be encountered at stages 4 and 5. The third position (cf. the Einstein quote) is most likely to surface at stage 3.

What we have said up to this point indicates what we mean by higher reversibility: the higher the religious judgement, the higher also the correlation between reality and the Ultimate.

In order to explicate the concept of "higher reversibility" in more detail, we are introducing an example which is altered according to the hierarchical sequence of stages. It is a simple example. It deals with children who discover that there are other children in the world who did not, or do not, have parents, or whose parents have deserted them, or whose parents have died. The children pose the question how God can be so unjust to allow this to happen. Let us, then, examine the explanations of persons at the various stages of religious development.

Stage 0: Children at this stage are unable to distinguish between events which are the result of human failure and those explanations that include nonhuman elements. Typical answers are:
"That is just the way they did it."
"That is the way it is. They are poor."
"Somebody did it."
"God did it, etc."

This inability to differentiate between human and nonhuman causality of events is the starting-point for our explication of the concept of higher reversibility.

Stage 1: Higher reversibility means a clear differentiation between human and nonhuman. The method for this distinction is the assumption of a hidden or revealed intentionality. The discovery of this intentionality is the liberating, distancing element.
"It is the parents' fault, they did not want to stay together. Now the children have to suffer."
"Perhaps God wanted this to happen."
"It is a punishment from God. This is how God deals with some people."
Why can we speak here of higher reversibility? The intentional element (e.g., he wanted to show them a direction) makes it possible to take an internal step back from the facts of the situation. There exists a direct cause/effect relationship in the way the domain of events is structured and described. For instance, "Because God was angry, God sent a war." "Because the people were bad, God sent a famine." "Because he served God well, God made him a famous king."
An equilibrium is achieved by discovering the reasons behind events and circumstances. This discovery provides people with a new sense of freedom. This new-found capacity of discerning reasons behind events and circumstances also translates for people into a new hope. The equilibrium between immanence and transcendence rests in the knowledge that events have noticeable reasons. Such reasons are immediately recognizable. Usually, they are located on the level of human shortcomings or they rest with a divine or ulti-

mate will or are due to a "supernatural" deficiency:

"Perhaps the father no longer loved the mother and the children."

"Maybe the father no longer believes in God."

"Maybe they did something bad. *Who, the children?* No, the parents."

"Perhaps God has forgotten them."

"Maybe God does not really like these people; but I don't really believe that, that does not have to be the case."

Stage 2: The child at stage 2 is no longer satisfied with a response patterned according to stage 1 for knowing the reason, i.e., the intentionality behind events is not meaningful to the child. When the stage 2 child externalizes causal statements, when she distances herself from them, she senses their bareness, their nakedness, their incompleteness. Higher reversibility means that the reason behind an event must be embedded in a means-ends scheme. An example can be a preventive pattern, or the concept of "give-so-that-you-can-get" (do ut des).

These were the responses of a girl, age 12:

"Perhaps God wants the children to have a different father; for he might love them more than their own dad would have."

"God considers this a better solution. For otherwise the dad might have killed his own children one day."

"Maybe God wants to teach them a lesson, and this can only be understood fully at a later time."

(In contrast to children at stage 1, this girl indicates that she has occasionally reflected on this question.) These answers indicate that the immediately perceivable reason (stage 1) is insufficient. There is "another" reason, more comprehensive, and not immediately available. This requires a new form of intellectual pre-apprehension in order to intuit why a certain event may have occurred.

"Perhaps God wants for the children to have a different father; for that one might love them more than their own dad would have." What is assumed to be the hidden reason surfaces occasionally in the responses. Furthermore, the reconstruction of such a "fact," i.e., the existence of a removed, *hidden* meaning which we don't know, implies that Fate, the Ultimate, that what surrounds us, can be "influenced" in such a way that this veiled meaning must break through.

Higher reversibility means that persons at stage 2 base their interpretation of factual reality not just on an immediate reason but that they are capable of distancing themselves further from events and experiences. As already mentioned, they *outright* presuppose the existence of a veiled reason which is revealed through the course of events. Thus all events, even the tragic ones, obtain a hidden meaning, and persons at this stage bring this angle of vision to their interpretation of reality. The fact that it is possible to influence the invisible "powers" is merely the result of persons' capacities to distance themselves from events to that degree that they perceive the hidden reality as always "having had in mind" a meaningful intention. Higher reversibility means to interpret situations always from the point of view of this hidden intention.

Stage 3: Let us examine now the form higher reversibility takes at stage 3. Persons at this stage are no longer content with explanations of events that refer to hidden intentions or veiled purposes. This is precisely the point of their critique.

Persons at stage 3 are primarily concerned with uncovering events to such a degree that they can be assigned to the sphere of responsibility of sovereign "individuals" and that the Ultimate is allocated its own sphere of existence, independent of and separate from this world. A sixteen-year-old boy remarks: "That people die, that parents separate and leave behind `divorce-orphans,' all that is a matter of human responsibility. God cannot be held responsible for that."

Or:

"It is ridiculous to ascribe a hidden ground or motive to everything that goes wrong in this world. People have to forge their own destinies."

Or:

"The divine has nothing to do with the misery caused by the parents' separation. One ought to pray to God without asking God to do something for the couple or the children. In a situation like this, we, the people, need to pitch in and take action."

At this stage, persons take an additional internal step back behind the "veiled reason" of stage 2. They transpose that hidden motive into the domain of human action. For that reason it becomes necessary to separate the divine from the human. Higher reversibility means that the pre-apprehension, with which persons approach all situations they have to interpret, locates all causalities in the realm of human decisions and responsibilities. Also, this sort of a priori declares that the "divine develops an independence" which is expressed either in the negation or in a solemn adoration of this "divinity."

The following three manifestations of stage 3 are to be understood as different types of one and the same pattern of religious cognition:

1) the separation of the sphere of human responsibility and the

sphere ascribed to the Ultimate into two parts of equal value;

2) the one-sided emphasis of the independent human will and the negation of the Ultimate;

3) the stressing of an independent domain of the Ultimate and of religious, symbol-oriented forms of action which are completely removed from all things that are "important in earthly terms."

But let us return once more to the concept of higher reversibility. At this stage, not only are the hidden, yet nonetheless meaningful intentions (stage 2) separable from the domain of action, but persons are capable of dealing with the "hiddenness" because they are able to stand back from and objectify this concept. Now the untouchable, distant form of existence of the Transcendent is not claimed for human purposes. The gulf between immanence and transcendence cannot be bridged. The same is true for the gulf between the other polar dimensions. This also constitutes a limitation. Yet, each situation that needs to be interpreted is approached from the perspective of the pre-apprehension which recognizes the impossibility of bridging the gulf. And this exhausts the equilibrium of stage 3.

Stage 4: The structural a priori of stage 3 are not sufficient for a person at stage 4. We must take account again of a higher reversibility. It consists of negotiating a new balance between immanence and transcendence. Human beings do not have their origin in themselves. They did not create themselves. The separation between human responsibility and the "domain of the Ultimate" is therefore experienced as constraining freedom. Here, the pre-apprehension is the recognition that the ground for the possibility of human action has always been existent in the form of the primordially human and, simultaneously, ultimate quality of people. In other words, part of human existence is understood as human potential, and a second part is understood in terms of the Ultimate taken as a condition for the possibility of human freedom, interactional understanding, and action possibility. For the first time, persons can combine both perspectives in a genuine religious perspective, because they distance themselves from, and objectify, both dimensions. Their pre-apprehension consists in the assumption that the ground for the possibility of human action is a *permanent gift* that surrounds and transcends them, that this gift is the presence of the Ultimate. Reversibility consists in subjects' abilities for drawing correlational conclusions between reality (i.e., the here and now) and the Ultimate, and vice versa. Possible manifestations of such reflections are concepts like "the human being as God's vessel" or as

"God's instrument or tool." The new equilibrium thus consists in the immediate mediation of immanence and transcendence (and of the other polar dimensions) by means of recognizing the preconditions for human life, action, suffering, and death. This is complemented with the image of a plan according to which the world always has moved toward, and eventually will develop into, something good. Nonetheless, one insight of stage 3 remains, i.e., the awareness that the demand for engaging in a certain form of historical existence in obedience to a final and higher being does not constitute a demand made by the Ultimate but by humans.

Stage 5: Subjects at this stage are able to objectify the correlationally mediated interpretation of existence which represents the religious judgement of stage 4. In other words, the connection between humans and the Ultimate of stage 4 is objectified. The locus of that connection is human love and communication. A going beyond all objects and ciphers, true transcending can only be discovered in the immanence of human, strategy-free communication (cf. Jaspers, 1967, p. 428). Thus, transcendence becomes visible in the reconstruction of reality from the perspective of helping, loving, and committed action. Speaking theologically: God became human *among human beings:*

> There are moments when thinking about God actually separates us from God. In true love we do not love the unfortunate ones in God but God in us loves the unfortunate ones. And if we ourselves are in misfortune, then God in us loves those who wish us well. Compassion and gratefulness originate from God, and when they are being exchanged through a glance between human eyes, then God is present exactly at that point where the glances meet. The unfortunate one and the other one love one another because their love originates with God and not because their love is directed toward God; they love one another simply because their love is for one another. This is impossible, and therefore it can happen only because of God" (Simone Weil).

The highest possible form of reversibility is, therefore, the interpretation of human conditions in light of the presence or absence of communicative love. Take, for example, the following possible response to our aforementioned question:

"By adopting such children and in counseling such parents, we provide for them the possibility of development. It is only in such acts that the divine can become evident."

The reversibility of this highest stage consists in the pre-apprehension which implies a stable and continuous anthropological religiosity, i.e., the discernment of being and transcendence is transferred into the domain of human interaction. "Always being a neighbor for the other" is not part of a formula but the whole. Put different-ly: "God reaches out to human beings," or "God's concern are human beings."

Only if we understand the pre-apprehension of each stage, the a priori of each stage, can we appreciate the cognitive religious stages as important elements of personality which cannot easily be altered. Stages are not different "types" of the construction of meaning. Rather, they are fundamental struc-tures of personality. As such they assimilate and accommodate reality with the respective pre-apprehension and with great flexibility. For that reason, higher reversibility refers to an increasingly more differentiated, more lib-erated, and more intensive communicative relationship between subject—sub-ject—the Ultimate.

If higher reversibility can be described in clear fashion, then the follow-ing summary statements can be made regarding the processes of transfor-mation:

1) We assume the existence of a basic universal structure of develop-ment which cannot be described with theories of probability or similar mod-els. Individuals are at certain stages, in certain domains: the next stage pos-sesses a qualitatively different structure, although it integrates the previous one.

2) It is possible that individuals do not bring the structure of their stage to bear, for example, because they are not religiously sensitive, because reli-gious role-taking appears impossible, because certain defensive mechanisms prevent it, because the situation lacks sufficient relevance; or because there is not enough time to apply the interpretive structures since a decision must be made before the reasoning process can be completed. This is designated as the discrepancy between competence and performance.

3) We assume that cultural development can hamper or sponsor the con-struction of the individual stages while, simultaneously, shaping the con-tent of the stages. A certain content may be inappropriate at a certain time and may therefore fail to yield religious reasoning. One thousand years ago it was hardly necessary to reflect ontologically on the destruction of nature, because nature seemed inexhaustible and sufficiently resilient against interference. Rather, then, the danger emanating from nature functioned as the decisive impulse for reflection.

4) We believe that the social praxis of meaning-making either sponsors or hampers the religious structures. Moments which count as moments of meaning-interpretation are those which interpret everyday life communica-tively by means of judgements and actions, i.e., the linguistic, ritualistic, and relational interpretation of experience. In its intersubjective form, such an interpretation is contained in the religious rites, actions, prayers, as well as in the linguistic interpretation of the pressure exerted on reality by glob-

al events and their limit-situations. This means that structures take shape differently in different cultures or civilizations. They differ in their function of coping with the inexplicable circumstances which are transcended in a variety of particular ways. Still, in our opinion the religious structures are universal.

5) We believe that higher reversibility of religious judgement is socially desirable.

Chapter Four

Measuring Religious Judgement

In this chapter we are introducing the method of the so-called clinical interview employed to ascertain the stages of religious judgement. The centerpiece of this method is the "Paul-dilemma." From among a number of possible dilemmas, the "Paul-dilemma" has proved to be most valuable. Almost all persons react to this example, provide answers, entangle themselves in justifications and rationalizations, and consciously take a position. The questions pertaining to this dilemma must be viewed in connection with the fundamental dimensions of religious judgement. The question-clusters, then, form the core for the subsequent analysis. In order that readers may perform their own assessment we have supplied for each stage and for each of the seven types of questions exemplary answers by different persons. Interpreting these responses against the backdrop of a stage theory ought to lead to the determination of a stage of religious judgement.

Methodological Introduction: The Semi-Clinical Interview

What procedures might be employed to stimulate and to measure religious judgement in a methodologically controlled fashion? This central and difficult question will have been answered when it becomes possible to employ a method which in fact leads persons to express their religious judgement. The method of the so-called "semi-clinical interview" fulfills this expectation. It makes it possible to confront persons with a complex issue laden with religious dimensions and to elicit from them reasoned action-decisions. Thereby—and this is decisive—a great measure of openness and flexibility in regard to the possible responses remains. Thus it is feasible to obtain the most competent response of a person, which is most likely to correlate with the person's actual religious deep-structure.

If we want to obtain the religious judgements of different people, we must know how to evoke such a judgement. As we already pointed out in the introduction and in the chapter on religious judgement, religious judgement is actualized in connection with the religious interpretation of personal experiences or in situations of coping with contingency in light of an Ultimate. For that reason, persons who would be ideal for the research of religious judgement are those who actually and concretely experience such contingency situations. Yet even in this ideal case there would be no guarantee that these persons' religious reasoning is valid and that they reveal their pattern of religious judgement. For example, it is possible that they activate different defense mechanisms, that they repress the problem, that they deal with the issue superficially on a confessional meta-level by applying learned explanations. Vice versa, it is possible that they apply their religious deep-structures especially in situations which do not necessarily constitute contingency situations. Our task, therefore, consists in finding a way which makes it possible to present persons with problem-laden domains of reality in such a fashion that their engagement with them will actually lead to the expression of their religious judgement.

In order to investigate how persons activate their system of religious reasoning we have decided to employ the method of the so-called "semi-clinical interview." The utilization of this method in the domain of developmental psychology goes back mainly to Piaget (and Kohlberg). According to this method,

the interviewee is (a) confronted with a certain task or a certain problem and (b) required to decide on a course of action. A special characteristic of this method is (c) the follow-up on the responses with theory-guided and hypotheses-oriented questions aiming at the reasoning behind the decisions made by the interviewee, i.e., his or her proposed solution for the problem. Decision and reasoning together form the judgement. We are dealing here with a continuous process of hypothesis formation and testing which places serious, almost impossible, demands on the interviewer: on the one hand, the interviewer must provide the interviewee with sufficient opportunities to explicate his or her thought process without any influence or interference. On the other hand, the interviewer must always have available definite working hypotheses which must be clarified with the interviewee. Nonetheless, Piaget believes that only this method makes it possible to observe persons' intellectual processes (L.H. Eckensberger et al., 1980, p. 338).

The advantages mentioned suggest that for the investigation of the religious judgement, too, the qualitative clinical method appears preferable over against quantitative measuring and standardized tests. This decision is supported by the unique problem domain of the religious judgement as well as the assumptions of the paradigm of developmental psychology. Piaget writes:

> The clinical method of investigation is part of the experiment to the extent that the clinician poses problems for him- or herself, formulates hypotheses, alters the existing conditions, and finally tests each of these hypotheses via the reactions which are elicited in the course of the interview. However, the clinical method of investigation consists also of direct observation to the extent that, by guiding the interviewee, the good clinician allows him- or herself to be guided as well. Thereby the interviewer includes the entire intellectual context instead of becoming a victim of "the systematic errors," as is often the case with so-called pure experiments (Vinh-Bang, 1978, pp. 86f).

The semi-clinical interview, as we employ it, generally consists of (a) standardized questions (concerning content), and (b) nonstandardized questions, in the sense of the competence-performance-tension, which follow up on responses to the standardized questions.[1] Thus, we differentiate between given, standardized interview questions and those which depend on the responses of the interviewee, whereby the nonstandardized questions are supposed to support the standardized ones in two ways.

First, they are supposed to assist in steering the interview along those lines which are relevant for the investigation of the religious judgement. These, then, are questions which directly relate to the dilemma situation. For example: "Do you believe that this decision has any consequences for Paul's future life?" It frequently happens that interviewees avoid or evade these questions by either generating descriptions of similar situations, by referring to other situations, or by listing a variety of possible answers, without committing themselves to any one answer. In that case, the nonstandardized questions are supposed to return the interview to the topic with which the investigation is concerned. For example, an answer to the aforementioned question like, "It all depends on how deeply he believes in God," obviously does not constitute the personal judgement of the interviewee, for he or she really did not say anything relevant. An appropriate follow-up question would be: "If you were in his shoes, what would you think?"

Second, the nonstandarized questions are supposed to assure a certain level of reflection in the interviewees' responses. The underlying concern is to assist the respondent in approximating as closely as possible the highest

---

1. We call our interviews "semi-clinical" because, in addition to employing semi-standardized questions, the measuring process is "semi-blind," i.e., the rater knows our theory but not the age, social status, name, etc., of the interviewee.

level for their response-competence. The term, response-competence, denotes here the fullest reasoning capacity of a person. This can be contrasted with response-performance.

Response-performance comprises those answers which are activated in certain situations and which do not necessarily build upon the highest reasoning capacity of a respondent. Consequently, performance cannot be used as a value to draw new conclusions about underlying cognitive structures. That can be achieved by relying on competence. Decisive for determining the competence-structure is the grounding of a response. Accordingly, we try in our interviews to follow up on every answer with "why?" or "why not?" The follow-up question, aiming at the reasoning underlying a response, becomes especially important in the case of additional probing questions. However, the interviewer needs to know when to stop what initially seemed like a meaningful and necessary response insisting on an answer to a why-question—perhaps, because the respondent is unable to supply a reason, or because of repetitiveness—and when to employ additional questions (cf. L. H. Eckensberger et al, 1980, pp. 340f). As a rule, the interviewer is not satisfied with the first answer given by the interviewee, since it is generally impossible to assess whether the response accurately reflects the interviewee's competence-level. Again, it is becoming evident that the interviewer must not only know the stage-specific and stage-distinguishing characteristics but furthermore must also have a detailed grasp of the theory of the development of religious judgement.

In short, the nonstandardized questions are supposed to reinforce the effectiveness of the standardized questions. Concretely, this mostly serves to encourage interviewees to provide the reasoning for their answers, the clarification of unclear statements, the uplifting and probing of contradictions in the answers of the interviewees. For example: "Do you believe that this accident is related to the fact that Paul did not keep his promise to God?" Answer: "No." Standardized questions concerning the interviewee's reasoning: "Why not?" Answer: "Because God has nothing to do with accidents, illnesses, etc., in this world." Nonstandardized questions concerning the reasoning of the interviewee: "Could you elaborate a bit further why God does not interfere in this world in such a manner?" Answer: "Because people are responsible for their own actions and because God is always concerned with our well-being." The semi-standardized interview thus provides for the interviewee a great degree of flexibility concerning the range of possible answers. Although certain questions are formulated in advance and are given to all interviewees, the interviewer can, at any time, change the sequence of questions and probe the argument of the respondent by employing additional questions.

To summarize, the following elements are constitutive of the semi-clinical method: 1) confronting interviewees with a certain dilemma task, 2) the necessity for a content-based decision for action, 3) providing the reasoning for the action-decision, 4) eliciting further reasoning by means of follow-up questions, or 5) eliciting further reasoning by means of nonstandardized additional questions. Although our decision to rely on this method has not always been understood, it is still possible to designate it as a critical method, for it allows a degree of differentiation which is much needed for our research-domain of religious judgement.

This method receives its critical edge from its systematic questioning of the interviewees' responses; not in order to measure the consistency of a conviction, but in order to interpret the underlying logic and to get at the typical structure of a certain developmental stage and not just its functional achievements or its spontaneous meaning" (Vinh-Bang, 1978, p. 91).

The Religious Dilemma

The centerpiece of the clinical method is the so-called religious dilemma. It proves to be excellently suitable for the activation of the religious regulative system. Dilemmas place persons into conflict-situations. Persons have to make fundamental decisions between two principled action-alternatives. Persons who are discussing such dilemmas suggest how they would act and they provide reasons for their decisions. The specific aim of the religious dilemma-situation is the activation of a so-called mother-structure.

In the case of the semi-standardized interview on religious judgement, the problem is posed by presenting the interviewee with so-called religious dilemmas. Generally speaking, these dilemmas contain a conflict between two "values," e.g., immanence vs. transcendence. The specific conflict-situations of the dilemmas obtain their uniqueness from the fact that, regardless of the solution proposed by the respondents, their cognitive disequilibrium continues. In principle, dilemmas resist a satisfactory solution. Thus we are faced with a dilemma whenever two opposing alternatives suggest themselves. If I select alternative A, then I must truncate possibility B. If I reject alternative A, then I must adopt alternative B.

The uniqueness of the religious dilemma consists in thrusting respondents into a religiously relevant situation of conflict or contingency where they are faced with the task of having to create an equilibrium between finite claims to meaning and the question about absolute meaning, i.e., the unity of the whole. Finite meaningfulness reaches its limit when subjects experiencing contingency are no longer able to integrate the meaning of the whole into their own personal meaning-structure. In this context, a religiously relevant situation of contingency is defined as possessing in its content a so-called mother-structure. As a religious structure it always consists of the seven contrasting dimensions, or elements thereof: the sacred vs. the profane, transcendence vs. immanence, hope vs. absurdity, eternity vs. ephemerality, freedom vs. dependency, trust vs. anxiety, and functional transparency vs. opaqueness. These seven dimensions are always latently present in some sort of unresolved state in every religious mother-structure or dilemma. When the concrete dilemma-situation limits interviewees in their decision-making range they are forced to give religious explanations. The "resolution" and the integration of an experienced reality, i.e., the overcoming of the religious disequilibrium, occurs when the interviewee, in a subjective fashion, begins to connect the seven contrasting dimensions which are latently present in the religious mother-structure. When subjects, in concrete dilemma-like contingency-situations, relate to ultimate conditions according to their cognitive possibilities or their religious competence they perform a relational structuring of their regulative systems. In this process of relational structuring, the seven dimensions of the objective structure are transformed into subjective dimensions or elements insofar as they are being connected in a particular manner. The preference and activation of certain dimensions by the subject represents the respective subject's system that regulates his or her religious reasoning. In other words, the dimensions inherent in the dilemma are being activated via the decision-making process of the subject. Thus, we can speak of a decision-making element. This element constitutes the dilemma as dilemma and activates in the subject, in representative fashion, the specifically religious conditions or the cognitive-religious structure. In this way, the religious dilemma activates a dialectical process: Forced by the decision-making element to apply their religious scheme to the experienced limit-situation, subjects, through their subjective structuring process, awaken to new life the latently existing, basic religious elements. At the same time, the subjects' unique way of connecting the elements reveals their regulative system of religious reasoning.

An additional important aspect of the religious dilemma's uniqueness consists in the fact that individuals faced with contingency-situations supply religious judgements only when religious elements are already present in events described in the dilemma's content or when the semi-standardized questions aim at the religious reality. For that reason it is necessary to build into the dilemmas formulations of religious content, e.g., "in this situation he thinks of God and begins to pray." This sort of prestructuring of the content proved to be necessary so that persons would actually initiate religious attributions. Were we to omit this the religious dimension would have to be relegated solely to the standardized questions. In that event, however, the individual would not be sufficiently prepared to deal with "religious questions" at all. On the other hand, there is the danger that with the direct introduction of religious elements into the dilemma-situation there occurs a prestructuring which no longer provides the respondents with sufficient latitude to formulate completely free answers. In our assessment, the prestructuring only affects the content of our dilemmas, not the structure.

The Paul-Dilemma

In the following section we are introducing in detail a religious dilemma that has performed extremely well. It is the so-called Paul-dilemma which, as our standard interview, has been employed in all our various research projects.

As a religious dilemma, the Paul-dilemma contains a mother-structure. This is evident, among other things, from the reactions of persons who designate themselves as believing: They accept the description of the situation and begin to deal with it. Furthermore, many of the research subjects have emphasized the parallelism between the hypothetical conflict-situation and their own lives; many have made similar promises in their own childhood or youth. Although during the course of their reasoning many respondents, for a variety of reasons, objected to the way the promise was attributed to Paul (and also stated that they would never make such a statement), they did on the whole confirm the dilemma's affinity to their own lives. How then can we describe the "grammar of the story," the deep-structure which underlies the Paul-dilemma? It is possible to discern the following chain of events: 1) Paul's happy life; 2) the crisis situation; 3) Paul's reaction in the face of an emergency; 4) his promise in response to this reaction; 5) the positive resolution of the crisis (Paul is saved); 6) the tension between keeping or breaking the promise; 7) the decision.

Figure 9 illustrates the chain of events.

The Text of the Paul-Dilemma:

Paul, a young physician, has recently passed his board exams. He has asked his girlfriend to marry him. Before the wedding, he goes on a trip to England paid for by his parents as a reward for having successfully completed his education. Paul embarks on his journey. Shortly after take-off, the plane's captain announces that one engine is malfunctioning and that the other one is working unreliably. The plane is losing altitude. Emergency procedures are initiated immediately: Oxygen masks and life preservers are being handed out. At first, the passengers are crying and yelling. Then, there is a deadly silence. The plane races toward the ground at a great speed. Paul's entire life flashes past his eyes. He knows it's all over. In this situation, he remembers God and begins to pray. He promises that, if he was somehow saved, he would

Figure 9: Schematic Structure of the Paul-Dilemma

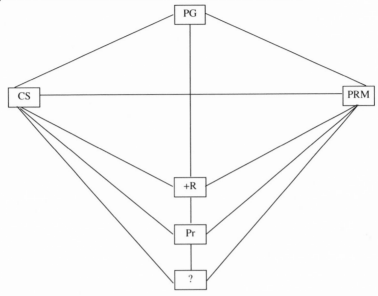

CS = crisis situation
PG = relating the situation to the origin of religiosity (prayer to God)
PRM = the promise that is given in response to the prayer (PG)
+R = positive resolution of the crisis (Paul is saved)
Pr = pressure in regard to keeping or not keeping a promise
? = the initial decision-making elements of the interviewee

invest his life in helping people in the Third World. He would also renounce the marriage to his girlfriend, should she refuse to accompany him. He promises to forgo a high income and social status. The plane crashes in a field—yet, through a miracle, Paul survives! Upon his return home, he is offered an excellent position at a private clinic. Because of his qualifications, he has been selected from among ninety applicants. However, Paul recalls the promise he made to God. Now, he does not know what to do.

    The standardized questions are:
1a) Should Paul keep his promise? Why or why not?
1b) Should anyone keep a promise to God? Why or why not?
1c) Do you believe that one has duties to God at all? Why or why not?
2)   What is your response to this statement: "It is God's will that he should go to the Third World (i.e., that he keeps his promise).
    In the aforementioned story two demands oppose each other: first, Paul's girlfriend and the job offered to him; second, God and Paul's promise to God.

3a) Which of these two demands do you consider to be more significant? Or: How do you experience the relation between the two?

3b) What is more significant in this world: God or human beings?
(If the answer is "human beings," the follow-up question is: "What role does God play in the world?" If the answer is "God," the follow-up question is: "What role do human beings play in this world?"

Let us suppose Paul tells his (religious) parents about his experience and the difficult situation in which he finds himself. They implore him to obey God by all means and to keep his promise.

4) Should Paul follow the advice of his parents? Why or why not? Paul feels obligated to a religious community (church, temple, etc.) in which he is highly active. The spiritual attitude and precepts of this community require that the call and the will of God must be accepted by human beings, i.e, Paul should keep his promise unconditionally.

5a) What does this demand mean for Paul? As a believing person, must he let his decision making be informed by the principles and demands of a religious community? Why or why not?

5b) Must anyone let his or her decision making be informed by the principles and demands of a religious community? Why or why not?

5c) What sort of duties does one have to a religious community in general? Why?

5d) Are persons entitled to claim their personal freedom over against the claims of a religious community? Why or why not?

Let us assume that after many sleepless nights and a time of uncertainty and despair, Paul does not keep his promise and, instead, accepts the promising position at the private clinic.

6) Do you think that this decision will have any consequences for Paul's future life? Why or why not?

Shortly afterward, Paul gets into a serious car accident for which he is at fault.

7a) Does this accident have any connection to the fact that Paul did not keep his promise to God? Why or why not?

7b) Do you think that God punishes Paul for not keeping his promise? Why or why not?

7c) If this is so, does God intervene in this world in all instances? If not, does God manifest Godself at all in this world? In what way?

Suppose Paul accepts the fine position as a physician and decides to donate a tenth of his income to charitable causes.

8) Do you think that with this course of action Paul does justice to the original promise? Why or why not?

Additional standardized questions on the Paul-dilemma:

1) Until now, we have attempted to resolve a hypothetical religious dilemma. Now, I would like to ask you to be so kind as to reflect on, and to

describe, a religious dilemma that you have personally experienced.

1a) What was your personal decision?

1b) How did you know that this was a good/bad decision?

1c) Has your decision making (your judgement) concerning religious questions changed during the last few years, or can you remember changes from your youth?

2a) How would you describe these changes?

2b) How did this change come about? Or: Why weren't there any changes?

(Unfortunately, we are unable to include in this volume any results concerning these additional questions because these questions were developed during the course of our first research project. Thus, at this point, we have very little data on hand. However, research results will be included in future publications.)

Supported by the grammar of the story, the Paul-dilemma contains the seven contrasting dimensions. The decision-making situation—i.e., "Should he keep his promise to God? Why or why not?—initiates the problem-solving process in the sense of the subjective structuring of the mother-structure underlying and inherent in the Paul-dilemma.

According to our theory, the decision-making element in the Paul-dilemma undergoes the following: Since Piaget (1968) maintained that to "perceive" an object means to act upon it, this means that persons faced with the aforementioned dilemma, begin to act upon it. For this they employ those patterns (systems of transformations) which they have already established in their interactions with other people. Precisely because respondents reflect their structures via their internal operations, their existing structures are revealed. For "to perceive reality means to construe systems of transformation which correspond to reality in more or less adequate fashion" (Piaget, 1973). "In more or less adequate fashion" refers to stages of different quality, adequacy, and flexibility. The inner structure which is revealed in this process is nothing else than the constructive process of problem solving, whereby the existing structuring patterns come to reveal the process itself, while at the same time they themselves are revealed through this process.

B. Inhelder remarks on this matter: "The progress made by the child in the discovery of his universe results from the overcoming of the conflict created by the confrontation of different procedures destined to resolve problems of a physical or linguistic nature" (Inhelder, 1980, p. 204). We would say "religious nature," since the presented dilemmas contain religious mother-structures.

The Types of Questions Employed in the Paul-Dilemma

Now we would like to mention another unique quality of our dilemma-construction: The questions which immediately follow upon the presentation of the dilemma-story can be distinguished according to different categories. The individual questions are designed to address the seven fundamental dimensions. On the one hand, these types of questions are constructed by means of the content of a certain dilemma-story; on the other hand, their construction is supposed to follow a basic dialectical principle (cf. Figure 10).

The total number of the individual questions pertaining to the Paul-dilemma is sixteen. They can be clustered in seven groups of questions. Each group represents a particular kind of question which is distinguished from other types through aim and orientation of its particular content. In other words, each group of questions poses quesions in regard to the religious coping with a particular reality (the Paul-dilemma). The content of the questions in each cluster is structured differently.

The purpose of these standardized questions is to activate the seven fundamental religious dimensions in the interviewee. The responses to these questions are supposed to yield the respondents' personal structures of religious judgement which consist of a subjective and specific way of connecting and emphasizing the fundamental religious dimensions.

Each individual question addresses *all* of the aforementioned contrasting dimensions; nonetheless, each question-type accentuates one of the polar dimensions.

The seven question-types of the Paul-dilemma exhibit the following, content-determined structure:

1) Question-type 1 comprises question 1a:

This type of question intends to spell out the general structure of the relations between the finite subject and the transworldly transcendence. It is a question concerning the nature, the obligation, and the dynamics of this relation. The emphasis is located on the activity of the subject in correspondence to the challenge, "freedom vs. dependency."

2) Question-type 2 comprises questions 1b and 1c:

This type addresses the poles, "opaqueness (magic) vs. functional transparency." Some sort of action is necessary so that the effect of the Ultimate can be channeled into a certain "direction." Of course, opaqueness (magic) is portrayed as part of the divine which is mediated via human activity.

3) Question-type 3 comprises question 2:

This question-type places the emphasis more on that transcendent reality which subjects experience as "the Other" or "their counterpart." In the face of finite human contingency, this question addresses the transcendent reality that is removed from the sphere of human action. It is the question about causality and about the manifestation of transcendent reality in this world. It amplifies the duality of "transcendence vs. immanence."

4) Question-type 4 comprises questions 3a and 3b:

These questions address the polarity "the sacred vs. the profane." Human beings encounter the sacred and locate it in their lives. Although the content-description of the sacred seems to have a tendency toward the Judaeo-Christian version, i.e., equating the sacred with God, these questions, nevertheless, are capable of revealing general relational structures. (The question-type perhaps most clearly indicates how all dimensional pairs surface in each question while only one is stressed.)

5) Question-type 5 includes questions 4, 5a through 5d:

These stimuli concerning one's groundedness in communities emphasize the dimensional pair "hope vs. absurdity." In community, individuals are supported by norms which are determinative for the community; they afford the members support, security, religious-social identity.[2]

6) Question-type 6 includes questions 7a, 7b, and 8:

The questions of this type attempt to elicit more general responses which put into words, in an area of religiously relevant content (theodicy), the structure of the relation between the human and the Transcendent in a concretely limited domain of religious perception: "anxiety vs. trust" are accentuated. At issue is how the consequences of a certain decision are determinative of future life, which possibly can be ruined.

7) Questions 6 and 7c belong to question-type 7:

The polarity "eternity vs. ephemerality" surfaces in the discussion of future consequences and in potential eschatological images. That which is imagined as temporal has an evaluation function, for any decision made is supposed to be a decision in favor of a better, more secure, more hope-filled lasting state of affairs.

We want to stress again that each question "touches on" and activates each dimensional pair because the dimensional pairs are connected. The emphasis on one dimensional pair merely means that this one is stressed. The interviewer may attempt to employ additional questions either to emphasize, underline, or elicit the preferred dimensional pair or others.

The construction of question-types results, on the one hand, from the immanent logic of the various dilemmas and, on the other hand, from a con-

---

2. Nonetheless, this question-type constitutes a special case to the degree to which it does not directly elicit the structure of a psychological judgement, nor the foundational religious dimensions. Since, in regard to content, the topic of this question-type concerns issues of institutionalization and socialization, this question-type belongs to a different theoretical level. It tries to assess to what degree given patterns of interpretation have been and are being internalized. Thus, this question-type is not immediately relevant for the investigation. It was added, however, since it functions as an indicator, as an interpretation aid, and since it supplies additional material and may furnish important pointers for the analysis of the interviewee's other answers.

struction-principle constitutive for the structure of the religious judgement.

The question-types are intended to be constructed according to a basic dialectical principle, i.e., a dialectic which tosses the religiously judging subject to and fro, especially in the process of forming a judgement. This logic can be illustrated with a dialectical three-step process:

1) Human actions in the face of a transcendent challenge: The emphasis is on the active human side (thesis).

2) The "actions" of a transcendent reality. The emphasis is on the active side of the Ultimate (antithesis).

3) The mediation of the action-domains of the human being and the Transdencent (synthesis).

In the Paul-dilemma, this comes to expression in the question-types 1,2,3. Question-type 5 provides no principally new aim. Rather, it attempts, through the content of a different religiously relevant domain inherent in the dilemma itself, to verify and to specify earlier answers.

Figure 10 provides a schematic representation of the dialectical process.

**Figure 10: The Basic Dialectical Principle in the Construction of the
        Process of Religious Judgement.**

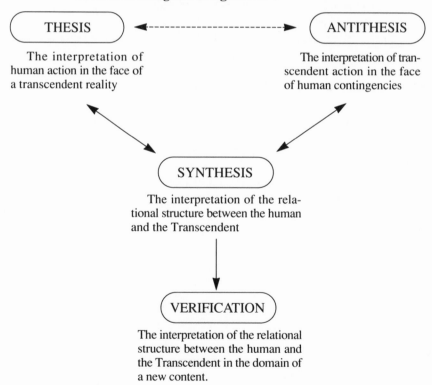

THESIS

The interpretation of
human action in the face of
a transcendent reality

ANTITHESIS

The interpretation of transcendent action in the face
of human contingencies

SYNTHESIS

The interpretation of the relational structure between the human
and the Transcendent

VERIFICATION

The interpretation of the relational
structure between the human and
the Transcendent in the domain of
a new content.

The Measuring Process

This section describes how the data gathered with the method introduced above are analyzed. Since the method employed here involves certain presuppositions and requires interviewers to be highly flexible and sensitive, we would like to explicate in detail the required general presuppositions as well as the practical procedures. Also, we will present the basis on which interviews are coded and ascribed a certain stage.

Presuppositions

The aim of the coding process is to examine the statements, gathered by means of the dilemma discussion, according to their structural qualities. This means eliciting the cognitive structure of the interviewee's religious reasoning and ascribing it to one of the five stages of religious judgement. The coding process[3] constitutes a highly demanding process which cannot and should not be compared to simple "tasks of ascription." Thorough training in the coding procedures is a necessity.

Presuppositions for the practical coding procedures:

1) Raters must be familiar with the entire field of structural developmental theory. They must be very clear about the fact that this is a theory which is qualitatively different from the traditional psychometric approach. When searching for structures of religious reasoning, a mechanistic approach is insufficient for reaching the desired goal. Rather, the fundamental concepts of structural developmental theory—such as structure, content, stage, invariant sequence, hierarchical integration, etc.—must be understood.

2) Instead of the customary focus on content, raters must learn and practice how to recognize structures of reasoning "underneath" an argument. Raters must be fully aware of the fundamental distinction between structure and content.

Practical Procedures

PHASE I:

Reading of the entire interview transcript. Goal: a rough preliminary assessment of the entire interview material. In addition, during this phase, three preliminary tasks are to be executed:

1) The rater is to eliminate those responses which contain no reasoning pertaining to action-decisions, e.g., meta-theoretical statements, the enumeration of various options without a personal decision, thematically irrelevant discourses. Furthermore, stereotypical answers of any sort are to be excluded as well.

---

3. For the process of specifically recognizing and assessing a particular stage we will use the term "coding process."

2) The rater is to designate those core statements and key sentences which, in his or her opinion, are relevant for the structure of the religious judgement of the interviewee.

3) Based on his or her knowledge of the stage model, the rater is to make an intuitive stage assessment.

PHASE II:

This phase sees the concrete evaluation of the interview material on a response-by-response basis.

1) The detailed assessment of individual responses always occurs in the framework of their respective question-types. A question-type comprises all the questions whose content aims at the same or a related issue. Each individual question-type, which can include one or more single statements, is independently coded and assigned to a stage.

2) In case there is uncertainty on the part of the rater concerning the correspondence between a particular stage's structure and an interviewee's concrete response, the rater examines whether the response to be coded should be ascribed to one of the neighboring stages (-1 or +1). If this procedure still does not produce a clear assessment, the response is assigned a "guess-score." This is indicated by placing a G in front of the stage number.[4]

Stage Calculations

The stage assessments of all relevant structural statements are calculated into a global score for each dilemma-story (global score = calculated stage from all individual scores of the question-types). The procedure is as follows:

1) Pure global stages:

Eighty percent or more of the relevant structural statements of an interviewee are at the same stage, e.g., stage 2. The remainder is distributed evenly above and below.

2) Transitional stages:

Seventy-five percent of all responses are at the same stage, e.g., stage 2, while 25 percent of the responses belong to the next-highest stage. Final score: stage 2(3) or 2.33. Or 50 percent of the responses belong to stage 2 and 50 percent to stage 3. Final score: stage 2/3 or 2.5.

3) Consolidation stage

Twenty-five percent of all responses belong to one stage, e.g. stage 2, while 75 percent belong to stage 3. Final score: stage 3(2) or 2.66.

The mixed stages 2 and 3 are relatively frequent due to the rarity of the jugements that are entirely stage-consistent. Furthermore, the global stages are converted into "Religious Maturity Scores" (RMS), similar to Kohlberg's

4. Compare the different coding instructions of the different versions of Kohlberg's three-volume coding manual from the years 1971-1983.

procedures with the "Moral Maturity Score" (MMS).

Let us demonstrate this process with an example. We assume that we are using five question-types from an interview-transcript. The partial scores (P) of respondent X are:

P1 = stage 3 (unambiguous)
P2 = stage 2/3 (unambuguous)
P3 = stage 3 (ambiguous)
P4 = stage 3 (unambiguous)
P5 = stage 2 (unambiguous)

The calculations proceed as follows:

	P1	P2	P3	P4	P5	:	sums	RMS		
Stages 3:	4p	2p	2p	4p		:	12	36	(3X12)	
2:		2p			4p	:	6	12	(2X6)	p: points
							18	48		

RMS: 48X100 = 267 corresp. 3(2)
————————
      18

Calculating Interrater-Reliability

When calculating interrater-reliability we presume that two scores disagree when the score of one rater differs from that of the other by more than one-third of a stage. Thus, for instance, we view the two scores 2 and 2(3) (difference = 0.33) as still in agreement, while, for instance, the scores 2 and 2/3 (difference = 0.5) signal a disagreement.

The following table briefly illustrates the procedure for determining the interrater-reliability:

Interview	Rater I	Rater II	Difference	Agreement
	Stage	Stage		
1	1	1	0	yes
2	2(1) = 1.67	1/2 = 1.5	0.17	yes
3	3	3/4 = 3.5	0.5	no
4	2(3) = 2.33	3(2) = 2.67	0.33	yes
5	4	3	1	no

The percentage of agreement is calculated according to the formula

$$\text{Percent } (\%) = \frac{\text{number of discovered agreements}}{\text{number of possible agreements}} \quad \text{X } 100$$

The above example yields an agreement of 3/5 = 60 percent. That means that in 60 percent of all assessments the rater agreed within a third-stage (which, of course, would be insufficient).

It is important to see that the response-analysis of religious interaction-texts possesses a so-called "inner context" (cf. Overmann et al., 1979, p. 422). These are the "permanent" structural features, which must be correlated with the stage descriptions by extracting them from specific content. The coding or rating process is primarily the interpretation of a reasoned reality against the backdrop of presumed objective structural descriptions. In addition to the stage description and the "special cases" there are examples which paradigmatically illuminate the rules of the coding system, thereby facilitating the interpretation process. It would be erroneous to believe that these examples represent absolute coding-patterns. Rather they only contain those criteria which can be employed in relating a response to those structural features known to be typical for a particular stage. It would be equally wrong to believe that the numerical designation of a stage, e.g., 4, represents a ranking. Rather it designates a higher degree of complexity than, for instance, 3. More important, however, is the fact that these numbers designate something highly complex which we attempt to express in different stage descriptions.

For that reason the calculation of an RMS in order to facilitate a complicated statistical analytical process is problematic. This is the case, because the qualitative discontinuity-measures have been transformed linearly. We nevertheless selected this procedure knowing that it is secondary compared to the global, interpretive approach. We will treat all results of inferential- and correlation-statistical analyses with the utmost care. This, however, cannot camouflage the problem that the social sciences have not yet developed adequate analytical methods for the comprehension of analytically and structurally complex relations.

Stage-Specific Examples of Religious Judgement

The following examples are intended to illustrate concretely for all stages what the previous sections elaborated in a more or less abstract fashion. Once again, the Paul-dilemma will serve as the basis. These examples not only illuminate the inner structure of each individual stage but they also make immediately accessible the overall developmental logic of the religious judgement.

The following examples stem from various research studies which were conducted in the course of the entire research project. Not all question-types of the dilemma are represented. We have selected only those clusters of questions which are immediately important for the stage structure. For each question, the answers of three different persons are supplied. For each stage we have attempted to provide the answers of the same person for all questions of a dilemma so that the consistency of the structural judgement becomes clear even with varying content responses. However, due to personal reasons of the interviewee or technical reasons related to the interview process it is possible that we do not have responses available to all of the questions posed. In that case, we will draw on the responses from other interviewees. Such responses are especially marked with an asterisk (*). When necessary, we have also reproduced all follow-up questions which serve to clarify answers given to the standard questions. Furthermore, please note that yes/no answers (e.g., "should Paul keep his promise or not?") are irrelevant for determining the stage of a response.

(The questions are reproduced here in their original wording; obviously, they have been simplified for children. Sometimes they have been rephrased and posed twice in order to achieve optimal comprehension. "In" stands for "interviewee.)

STAGE 1

• *Question 1a: Should Paul keep his promise to God?*
            Why or why not?

▶ *Responses:*

In1: Girl, age 8

"Paul should go to Africa—because he told God that he would go to Africa and not stay at home. It would be nicer if he did what he told God—he would not be a nice guy, if he would not keep his promise to God—God loves the poor and they love God, and it would be just nicer if he did go to Africa instead of getting rich at home."

In2: Girl, age 8

"Yes—he really should. If he promises something, then he must also keep it. Sometimes I promise something, but I always keep it. Promises must be kept."

In3: Boy, age 10

"He really ought to go. Since he promised. Whenever something (major) happens one ought to think of God. God is love, He helps people when they make promises, and if one promises something then one must keep what one has promised." *Why should one keep a promise?* "Probably otherwise one would get punished. God causes one to feel pain inside—a tummy ache or something like it."

• *Question 2: How would you respond to this statement: "It is God's will that Paul goes to the Third World (that is, that he keeps his promise)?"*

▶ *Responses:*

  In1: Girl, age 8

"Yes, it is God's will for Paul to go to Africa; perhaps the people there are very poor, and God loves those who are close to death. And, perhaps, God somehow told Paul to go to Africa in order to help the poor people whom God loves so much. On the other hand, God could provide the poor people directly with the needed medication; God could tell them to go to a certain place where they would be given medication so that they would all get well."

  In2: Girl, age 8

"Yes—one can say that it is God's will." *Why?* "God wants for us to help the poor." *Can God make Paul keep his promise?* "Yes." *Why?* "God is in a person's heart. And God tells a person what he wants or not. He has that kind of power."

  In3: Boy, age 10

"No. God would rather say: 'Don't go, but pray hard for the poor.'" *Are you saying that praying is more important than working for the poor people?* "When he prays, then he goes to Africa and he teaches the people there to pray as well so that they no longer believe in other gods and stuff; rather they ought to believe in the true God. But, God can help much more than people and, therefore, we ought to pray. Since we aren't able to make plants and stuff."

• *Question 3a: In the foregoing story two demands oppose each other: first, Paul's girlfriend and the job offered to him; second, God and Paul's promise to God.*
Which of these two demands do you consider to be more significant, or how do you experience the relation between the two demands?

▶ *Responses:*

  In1: Girl, age 8

"God comes first, God is more important. First of all, one should keep a promise to God. Since God is love and would like for us to do what he says."

  In2: Girl, age 8

"God and the promise. For God is greater than we are. God makes the weather good for us, provides food, clothing, etc. God is worth much more than any person."

  In3:* Girl, age 12

"God and the promise." *Why?* "Because Paul was the only survivor." *Why is that significant?* "Paul has made his promise to go to the Third World—and he must keep it." *But why is God more important?* God always helps us when we promise God something. God protects us . . . and God created us and the animals. He watches us and sees everything."

• *Question 6: Do you believe that the decision not to keep the promise will have any consequences for Paul's future life?*

▶ *Responses:*

In1: Girl, age 8

"Yes, something will happen to him—because God told him, you must go to Africa; God said to him: 'You must not say later that you don't want to go.' God was in the plane with Paul, God told him there: 'You must go to Africa.' Paul said yes and thus nothing happened to him; now he is not going—and the people in Africa are perishing, the children there are unable to do anything, are unable to go to school; God does not like that and thus God is sad."

In2: Girl, age 8

"He should keep the promise. Something might happen to him. For example, God could force him to go to the black people—or Paul can't stand it anymore, then perhaps he will go there."

In3:* Girl, age 12

"Yes—and he did promise. It is possible that something might happen to him. Another time, God won't help him."

• *Question 7a: Does this accident have any connection with the fact that Paul did not keep his promise to God?*

▶ *Responses:*

In1: Girl, age 8

"Perhaps it has to do with the fact that Paul did not go to Africa; God told him to go to Africa, and Paul did not go, thus God just dropped him, God no longer cared what happened to Paul."

In2: Girl, age 8

"Perhaps God punished Paul for not keeping the promise—for God wants that one keeps the promises one makes."

In3: Boy, age 10

"Indeed, the accident is the punishment for not keeping the promise."

• *Question 7b: Do you believe that God punishes Paul for not keeping his promise? Why or why not?*

▶ *Responses:*
  In1: Girl, age 8
    "Yes, because he did not go to Africa; perhaps because he listened to his parents who were against it; thus God punished him."
  In2:* Girl, age 12
    "Yes, I think so; e.g., God makes it so that Paul will have to stay in the hospital longer than usual, that he gets well very slowly."
  In3: Boy, age 10
    "Indeed, God punishes Paul for not going to the poor people in Africa; it is for showing him what he ought to do; perhaps then, Paul will go to Africa after all; yes, that is why God punishes Paul: to make him eventually keep his promise."

• *Question 7c: If this is so, will God intervene in this world without fail? If not, does God manifest Godself in the world at all? In what way?*

▶ *Responses:*
  In1: Girl, age 8
    "Yes, God makes it that houses turn out good, etc. God makes it that people get rich; there are rich people and poor people; but it is supposed to be that the former have a lot and the latter little. God is with us, one cannot see God, but he affects that things turn out well; God is with us always, in our hearts."
  In2: Girl, age 8
    "Yes, e.g., through guiding, punishing, protecting, rewarding, and helping us, etc. God is invisible, but one can feel God. God is everywhere."
  In3: Boy, age 10
    "God affects everything; God created the animals and all; God makes everything work; all things are from God."

Stage 2

• *Question 1a: Should Paul keep his promise to God? Why or why not?*

▶ *Responses:*
  In1: Boy, age 9
    "Yes, he must, God saved him. Perhaps he saved Paul because Paul had always been nice to him. He did not do much evil stuff. If we are good to God, then perhaps in return God will help us some time." *Why does God help us?* "God's aim is our survival. If God helps us, then, at times, we can do something in return for God. First we do something, then perhaps God helps us." *How does God help us?*

"With the powers he possesses. God can do miracles. But he does not always perform them. It all depends on how one behaves toward God."

In2: Boy, age 16

"When he made the promise, Paul was panicky, and while in a panic one generally says a lot without thinking about it. Actually, I am in favor of him keeping the promise; on the other hand, I think, it should be possible for him to marry his girlfriend. No, the promise must be kept, because there is a commandment that says: 'You must not lie'; at least he did make a promise to God. But even if he does not keep the promise, God would forgive him. God would be like a person whom one has promised something, and in this case one simply ought to keep the promise."

In3: Male interviewee, age 20

"He really should keep it; otherwise it is not a promise, by not keeping it, I mean. If one promises something, one ought to keep it, that is obvious. Promising something is a question of honesty; also one ought to keep the promise in order to ease one's conscience."

Should one keep promises made to other people for the same reason?
Yes, if one wants to be fully consistent. God, of course, ranks higher, and one must keep each promise made; actually this is true for promises made to people, too, especially if the promises are important, don't you think?"

Why should one keep all promises made to God?
"Well. God is the one who will judge us later; and I've got a feeling that that is the big problem. With people, on the other hand, consequences are naturally less severe, although one might suffer some. However, if one breaks a promise to God, and then comes before the Final Judgement . . . for that reason one should be good to God and try to live according to the commandments."

• *Question 2: How would you respond to this statement: "It is God's will that Paul goes to the Third World (that is, that he keeps his promise)?"*

▶ *Responses:*

In1: Boy, age 9

"Well, he did promise God and thus one should keep it. One should always keep a promise, otherwise God will no longer help us." *Do people know when God stops helping them?* "Yes, when one faces a problem and one just cannot solve it."

In2: Boy, age 16

"I believe that every person has a task, and if God wants for Paul to go 'down there' (to Africa), then he is likely to go, or he should go. But I really don't know; Paul made the promise in a state of panic, he probably felt bad. If it is God's will for him to go, and if Paul obeys, then I don't believe that God will let Paul starve 'down there.'"

In3: Male interviewee, age 20

"Well, it is God's will, for God made sure that Paul survived after he made the promise. Thus, God wants Paul to keep the promise. God also wants to test Paul. He lets him survive in order to see whether he really does what he promised. If Paul keeps God's promise, that is God's will, and that pleases God."

• *Question 3a: In the foregoing story two demands oppose each other: first, Paul's girlfriend and the job offered to him; second, God and Paul's promise to God.*
Which of these two demands do you consider to be more significant, or how do you experience the relation between the two demands?

▶ *Responses:*

In1: Boy, age 9

"The promise is more important. Perhaps God will help him again. In the beginning it may be difficult for him . . . but he should do it anyway, because he can help the poor people."

In2:* Boy, age 15

"The promise is in any case more important. A promise is like a laborer doing some type of work for which he will be paid afterward; he needs to be told how much he will earn. It wouldn't be right if one told the laborer afterward: The work is done, but you aren't getting any pay."

In3: Male interviewee, age 20

"I already touched on this earlier; one must obey God, because God is more important and a higher authority. Paul must keep his promise. The earlier promise to the girlfriend is thereby practically voided, and God agrees with this course of action."

What if the girlfriend protests?

"That is to be expected and one has to disregard it; one has to try to explain to her that the promise to God is more important, and she will have to accept that."

If one trusts God like that, does that mean that one will no longer suffer?

"Well, people will have to stand certain pains, i.e., earthly pains; but they will be compensated even more after the earthly life."

• *Question 6: Do you believe that Paul's decision not to keep the promise will have any consequences for his future life?*

▶ *Responses:*
  In1: Boy, age 9

> "It is probably not good the way he did things; something could happen to him later, an accident or something else. God does that because he is no longer pleased with him."

  In2:* Girl, age 10.5

> "It might very well be that nothing will happen to him, but the next time Paul gets involved in an accident and prays to God, God would not listen to him and not help him either, because Paul has already done that once and not kept his promise."

  In3: Male interviewee, age 20

> "Yes, I believe that this decision will have consequences in Paul's life; he will blame himself; he will have a guilty conscience; he will not be at peace with himself. Also, he acted against God's will because he did not keep the agreement."

Question 7a: Does the accident have anything to do with Paul not having kept his promise to God?

▶ *Responses:*
  In1: Boy, age 9

> "No, but maybe Paul thinks: Now, I can't do anything. He did not even pray to God. But maybe God did not punish him so harshly, because he continued to pray afterward."

  In2: Boy, age 16

> "Not necessarily. In my mind, God is someone who forgives—but it is possible that God will run out of patience, if one keeps making the same mistake over and over again. But I believe that he is forgiving; and with prayer one can resolve many things. God does not punish."

  In3: Male interviewee, age 20

> "Yes, the accident has to do with the broken promise. It is a sign from God that Paul did something wrong."

• *Question 7b: Do you believe that God punishes Paul for not keeping his promise? Why or why not?*

▶ *Responses:*
  In1:* Girl, age 10

> "I say yes, because God was angry afterward. Paul did promise to help all poor children and not to get married. This is supposed to teach him a lesson so he won't do it again. Perhaps he doesn't quite respond to it at the time, but if it happens to him a second . . . maybe when he has

a little boy who dies, maybe then he will pay attention." *What shall he do?* "He should pray to God and simply and sincerely apologize. One should just pray in the evening."

In2:* Boy, age 14

"Certainly. At least in part. Although not in all cases. Those who believe in God will most certainly be helped by God somehow, and those who do not believe in God will not be helped. God makes some people happy by making others unhappy."

In3: Male interviewee, age 20

"Yes, God punishes and admonishes; but it is always a meaningful punishment; God wants for Paul to change; God punishes for pedagogical reasons, because God wants people to behave in accordance with God's expectations. This is also one of God's ways of providing security for people, i.e., by showing God's presence."

• *Question 7c: If this is so, will God intervene in this world without fail? If not, does God manifest Godself in the world at all? In what way?*

▶ *Responses:*

In1: Boy, age 9

"Yes, on behalf of good people. But not for bad people, because they did foolish things."

In2: Boy, age 16

"Of course, God can intervene in the world. For example: I am studying hard at home and still get a poor grade. It could be that God is using this detail to point something out to me; maybe I am doing something stupid and I am supposed to think about it and apologize. But I don't think that God applies as drastic a punishment as a fractured skull or a concussion, etc. God does not apply such harsh punishment; God punishes so that one begins to think about it."

In3: Male interviewee, age 20

"Yes, by all means, God intervenes in the world—not only does God want to straighten out Paul, God expects everyone to act accordingly. God is almighty, everything comes from God, God 'makes' everything."

STAGE 3

• *Question 1a: Should Paul keep his promise to God? Why or why not?*

▶ *Responses:*
In1: Female interviewee, age 23

"I feel I am stuck in a dilemma, because I do not know whether I would keep this promise. I do not doubt the existence of God, but I do doubt that God has such a great influence on people that Paul's future life would take a turn for the worse it he did not keep his promise. Furthermore, I don't know at all whether I could or would want to relinquish the good position at the clinic. Also, I could not back off from marrying the girlfriend."

In2: Male interviewee, age 17

"I do not see the reason for him making such a promise. I find it absurd. In that situation he begins to pray and begins to make grand promises. In my mind, he only made the promise because of the situation he was in. . . . I believe he did that because it was an emergency situation and he did not think what the consequences might be if he survived, since he was fully convinced that he was going to die. Still, I do not see the reason for making such a promise."

Let us assume that you had made such a promise in a similar situation. How would you feel afterward?

"I can't do that. Either one feels drawn to working in the Third World or one doesn't. Take my father, for example, it was one of his life-goals, he worked there . . . for twenty years . . . that was his goal, yet he did not make a promise to God in an emergency situation. He felt drawn there, because it is a job which appealed to him the most. He also had an offer from the president of a bank who told him that he would be his successor. Then, my dad would have had a lot of money and status; yet he preferred doing something that gave him more than that. Therefore, I cannot imagine that, even in an emergency situation, I would make such a promise without carefully considering what consequences might result."

In3: Female interviewee, age 34

"The mistake lies already in Paul making a deal with God. In such a situation I consider that infantile. The question is what is left of Paul's life once he has to give up everything that brings him pleasure and satisfaction. I would have a guilty conscience for taking the well-paying job, because I, personally, made the decision to use my life on behalf of poor people. I would have to do that because it is an inner need and because I made the decision in an important moment of my life, but not because I promise something to God."

• *Question 2: How would you respond to this statement: "It is God's will that Paul goes to the Third World (that is, that he keep his promise)?"*

▶ *Responses:*
  In1: Female interviewee, age 23
> "In my personal opinion I don't think that it is God's will. I would not keep the promise, because I would not want to forgo all the plans I have made.
>
> If Paul keeps the promise, he will later be dissatisfied with his life anyway, because he had to give up things that meant a lot to him. I would not be willing to put life on the back burner just because of a promise. I am who I am and I want to live my life according to what I consider right. I do not want my life to be sidetracked by a power (God) of whose existence I am not even convinced. Unless keeping the promise would mean a whole lot to me. Maybe then I would keep it. But that would be keeping a promise for its own sake and not because it was made to God. Of course, I do believe that, somehow, such a power exists. But I do not know whether its name is God or something else or whether this power even exists the way I imagine it. I imagine God as an old man with a white beard. I do not know if he exists. But I do believe in predetermination. Is this predetermination done by God or some other power? I do not know. Since everything is predetermined in life, the keeping of a promise cannot alter or influence the predetermined course of one's life."

  In2: Male, age 17
> "I do not believe that. If one wants to speak of God's will . . . I would say, it depends on how Paul gets along with himself, so that he does not have a guilty conscience. In the end, he must know for himself what he wants."

  In3: Female, age 34
> "Paul has to sense a duty to himself about going to the Third World, and in that regard I cannot see God's will at work. People keep promises made to themselves and not to God. People tend to put God up front, but they make promises to themselves."
>
> *But what should Paul do?*
>
> "He does not have to do anything. I see it like this: One says that God is implied in every person. God is simply the conception of morality in us human beings. This conception of morality is called God, the Inexplicable. Normally, we would not bust a person's skull just because we want the $50 he is carrying. It is not the fear of punishment which prevents us from busting his skull, but the inhibitions we have about such actions. Such inhibitions are inexplicable, and I believe that at some point someone just invented a term for this inexplicable phenomenon and called it God."
>
> (3-4 transition)

• *Question 3a: In the foregoing story two demands oppose each other: first, Paul's girlfriend and the job offered to him; second, God and Paul's promise to God.*

Which of these two demands do you consider to be more significant, or how do you experience the relation between the two demands?

▶ *Responses:*

In1: Female, age 23

"I consider the girlfriend and the position more important and more meaningful, because I cannot imagine a personal relationship to God. I can only have a relationship with someone with whom I can engage in personal interaction. For that reason, persons and their free will are more important to me."

In2: Male, age 17

"I would decide in favor of the person." *Why?* "Because I need and love that person—that is why I would decide in favor of the person." *But what does the relationship to God look like?* "To be honest, I do not feel any obligations toward God. Well, obligated in the sense of going to church every Sunday—but I think one can be just as well a good person without going to church. To come back to my relationship with God . . . If one asks: 'Who or what is God? . . .' then there is already a huge 'hook' on which one can get stuck . . . if one cannot go any further. One can only believe in God if one has clarified for oneself who or what God is and what one can receive from God. For, in my view, everybody has to believe in something . . . in oneself, in other people, or in God. Because that is what gives us strength . . . namely faith. Yet, according to my point of view, it does not have to be faith in God."

In3: Female, age 34

"Paul has to be true to himself: He has to go to the Third World. If he does not go, his conscience will bother him until he has totally changed. Paul can only be happy if he remains true to himself.

For me, ideals are more important. The expression 'God' disturbs me because to me God is a daddy with a beard. And the Bible says that one should not have any images of God. God requires that rightfully, and one ought to obey. It is really impossible to make an image of God. As soon as one creates an image it is no longer about God but becomes an idol."

How shall one conceptualize God, if one ought not make any images? "God is something abstract that cannot be imagined. At the very best one can get an intuitive grasp of God."

• *Question 6: Do you believe that the decision not to keep the promise will have any consequences for Paul's future life?*

▶ *Responses:*

In1:* Female, age 14

"Probably not from God's angle, but from within himself—his conscience will bother him for a long time. He won't be able to get away without any complications. . . . I would not be able to stand it. . . . I do not know how I would react."

In2: Male, age 17

"It is most certainly possible. It can result in a guilty conscience for Paul. It is possible that it will keep bothering him until he actually goes to the Third World. The decisive element is, however, that he learns to decide for himself, that he learns to be at peace with himself."

In3: Female, age 34

"Well, yes, as mentioned earlier, Paul will neglect his job because of pangs of remorse, and, most likely, he will also start fighting with his girlfriend. Since he knows that he is in the wrong, he will always be in a bad mood."

• *Question 7a: Does this accident have any connection with the fact that Paul did not keep his promise to God?*

▶ *Responses:*

In1: Female, age 23

"If it was predetermined that Paul was supposed to keep the promise, then the automobile accident had something to do with him breaking the promise. Maybe the accident was just a coincidence."

In2: Male, age 17

"That is so far-fetched. He could have just as well gone to the Third World and been hit by a falling tree. I find it extreme to say 'that has to do with that,' 'I knew that that would happen. . . .' For example, why did he not die on the plane? Because he had made a promise? I don't think so. I think all the other passengers on the plane also made promises, but they did not survive. Maybe they even promised the same. . . . Maybe even more. Why, then, did they not survive?"

In3: Female, age 34

"Yes, somehow Paul did provoke this accident. It is the beginning of a whole series of misfortunes which will befall him. He must attribute them, however, to his own behavior. If one has a guilty conscience, one commits all sorts of mistakes, simply because one is no longer able to do the right thing."

• *Question 7b: Do you believe that God punishes Paul for not keeping his promise? Why or why not?*

▶ *Responses:*
  In1: Female, age 23
     "I have never conceived God as a punishing power. Of course, if a power exists which directs our paths, this power does have other means than punishment for guiding us."
  In2: Male, age 17
     "No, that is really far-fetched. I just don't believe that the one is related to the other." *Related to what?* "To the promise . . . I think he could have died just as well in the Third World. I can fall down the stairs here and die. . . . Life is full of dangers; therefore, I cannot say: If I do this or that, then this thing or another will happen."
  In3: Female, age 34
     "No, Paul is punishing himself by not keeping his promise. His own soul will punish him. God cannot punish." *Why?* "Who or what is God? *Who or what is the soul?* "I am saying that the soul is something undefinable, simply something that is in us. I have spoken with priests and asked them what they think about God. But they were unable to give me any answers. They always said that one just had to believe in God. They could not even give a clue about what it is exactly that one ought to believe in. Does anybody know who or what God is?"

• *Question 7c: If this is so, will God intervene in this world without fail? If not, does God manifest Godself in the world at all? In what way?*

▶ *Responses:*
  In1: Female, age 23
     "God does not become visible, except in my imagination. God can become visible in the predetermination of a particular path—but in such a situation one always reflects on whether this is really guidance from God."
  In2: Male, age 23
     "God certainly intervenes, but not in a way that we consider logical. Of course, we create such connections. . . . In our thought-systems we cannot perceive God's activities. The divine domain and the human domain are somehow separate, although there is some sort of inner connection."
  In3: Female, age 34
     "No, not in this sense. God does not reveal Godself because God cannot reveal Godself. There is no being with the name 'God.' For God to reveal Godself, God would have to be a being."

STAGE 4

• *Question 1a: Should Paul keep his promise to God? Why or why not?*

▶ *Responses:*
   In1: Male, age 44
   "He does not have to keep the promise because he made it in a situation of psychological stress. If, however, he wants to keep the promise and actually does it, then things are different. In any case, he is not obligated to keep it.

   Personally, I would be guilt-stricken; but I believe I would not necessarily keep it—unless there was an additional motivation for me, and I would have to tell myself that applying myself in the Third World would be a thankful task for me. In order to be able to keep a promise one needs to be able to deliberate such things freely and calmly."

   What is the basis on which one has to keep such a promise?
   "I believe it is a certain commitment to a decision freely made. Human beings have no obligation toward God; they are invited, by reason of their humanity and their freedom, to certain actions toward God. They are not coerced to act one way or another. They act because of their own free will, because of an autonomous 'yes' to an offer made by God."

   In2: Male, age 53
   "First, I would like to say that he did not make this promise because of an autonomous conviction but because of fear; thus, it was an unfree decision. I mean, a life totally dedicated to God cannot result as a fully autonomous decision from such an emergency situation. I would say that the freedom to decide a total commitment to God constitutes the basic condition for an authentic religious attitude. The presupposition for such a promise is his faith in God. If he does not believe in God, then he cannot be obligated to do anything. Second, if he does believe in God and desires to live his faith, then his sense of obligation does not arise out of coercion. Rather, the awareness of his creaturely and redeemed nature motivates him to certain actions and attitudes toward God. However, he does not have to do it; he has other options as well, for he is autonomous and free; the point is, however, that free does not mean that he can do as he pleases, for his nature and his redemption tie him to a certain course of action. In that sense, I would answer 'yes' to the question; if he believes, then certain obligations arise logically. Still, they arise out of an inner need and freedom. The same is true here as was in the case of the first point: that what has not been given freely by God has no value."

In3: Male, age 58

"Not necessarily, because he made it under stress. He could not reflect upon the consequences. A promise that interrupts one's life to such a great extent ought to be considered at length. . . . Paul ought to consider the situation carefully and then make a decision. If he concludes that he cannot and does not want to keep the promise, then he ought to act correspondingly. A promise ought to be kept only if it has been carefully considered. . . . Such a promise ought to be honored; unless the circumstances change and create a new situation.

I mean that human beings ought to view their existence as a created one and not—as the existentialists call it—just thrust into existence; God has given us life as an opportunity. People should affirm their situation."

• *Question 2: How would you respond to this statement: "It is God's will that Paul goes to the Third World (that is, that he keeps his promise)?"*

▶ *Responses:*

In1: Male, age 44

"How can one determine God's will? That is nonsense." *Why?* "Well, it is the same nonsense as in the obituaries: 'It is God's will to call him home.' Of course, it is God's will. But, going to the Third World, I mean, he can be helpful just as well at home, if he does it in the right spirit. I mean, money does not have to be primary, people could just as well be primary. It may be that it was an indication of where he is really needed, but it had nothing to do with God's will: now you have to go. It could be a guidepost for an individual."

In2: Male, age 53

"First, I would like to say that it most certainly is God's will that people help each other, in a sense that includes Paul, i.e., by fulfilling the command to love one's neighbor, a command which also corresponds to human nature. But in this concrete case, I don't think God is going to judge Paul, if careful reflection led him to not keeping the promise. I don't think that Paul would fail to meet God's will. I would like to add that each person is called to do good for others. Concretely it all depends on whether, after the emergency was over, he was able to decide freely in favor of service in the Third World; in that case, his going was surely in line with God's will.

In3: Male, age 58

"It certainly is a serious call, but Paul ought to consider it carefully." *Did God provoke this promise?*

"No, hardly, for we determine our attitude toward God. Of course, God is omnipresent, but I don't think it is God's will that Paul goes to the Third World." *Why not?* "I cannot imagine it." *Why not?* "All my actions toward God take earthly routes, whether I bind myself personally to God such as in a monastery or in marriage. There are different ways to God. One reaches God through the world. Ultimately we are dealing with the issue of taking a position. God must be brought to the world again and again, and the world must again and again go to God. There is always a process at work. I can choose to take a position out in the world. It all depends on where I feel at home. However, the circular movement is unavoidable: If I am with God, then I must return to the world and vice versa. . . . It appears to me that God and the world imply each other and that a compartmentalization is inappropriate."

• *Question 3a: In the foregoing story two demands oppose each other: first, Paul's girlfriend and the job offered to him; second, God and Paul's promise to God.*
Which of these two demands do you consider to be more significant, or how do you experience the relation between the two demands?

▶ *Responses:*
In1: Male, age 44
"I consider it horrible if he just went ahead and left his bride or girlfriend. Therefore, it can not be God's will for him to go to the Third World. I really believe he can fulfill God's will at his present place, here, by helping other people. The one ought not exclude the other."
In this context, what is meant by fulfilling 'God's will'?
"It means doing one's duty wherever one is placed, simply by being there and by trying to be there for others. For, after all, God's will is for us to help one another. Of course, it would be wrong if Paul were so egotistical to consider only his fine position and the nice salary that comes with it. If Paul were to decide in favor of the position at the clinic based only on these positive external factors, then it would be the wrong reason. If, however, he were to say: I will accept this position, for I can help my neighbor here just as well, that I would regard as a valid reason."
Why is it more meaningful to be neighborly?
"First, because I view God as creator, as creator also of human nature. And to the extent that God is creator and that neighborliness is part of our nature, we are connected with God whether we want to be or not."

In2: Male, age 53

"I like the second part of the question better. I would not place the two values in frontal opposition. I discern in the love for other people and in working as a physician more than only something worldly; and perhaps it was necessary for Paul to perceive that concretely. He got onto a superficial fast-track, putting his career first, thinking about success, etc., and suddenly he was brought to his senses. I would not place the two issues in contradiction; in absolute terms, of course, only God is relevant. God exists without human beings. But in this world there are people—he wanted it that way—intended for a purpose, part of a plan God has for them. And in that respect, human beings—in contrast to the animal world or the rest of the created order—are of special importance for creation and God's plan for salvation. God doesn't do anything meaningless."

In3:* Female, age 24

"Well. I believe we should live through God. The one is impossible without the other. We were created by God, without God we would not even exist. I have a feeling that God might also live through us."

• *Question 6: Do you believe that the decision not to keep the promise will have any consequences for Paul's future life?*

▶ *Responses:*

In1: Male, age 44

"Yes, there will be very negative consequences for him. He will constantly be under some pressure because of not having kept a promise he was supposed to keep. If the question is phrased like this, I would have to say that Paul has to go to the Third World and provide assistance there."

In2: Male, age 53

"I would say there will be consequences in any case. Whether they will be good, bad, or disastrous for him, whether they will destroy his life or cause him inner turmoil so that he cannot get his life back on track, all depends on the reasons which led to his decision."

In3: Male, age 58

"It all depends on how he can deal with this conflict. If he can't deal with it, he will certainly face consequences, otherwise he won't."

• *Question 7a: Does this accident have any connection with the fact that Paul did not keep his promise to God?*

▶ *Responses:*

In1: Male, age 44

"It is quite possible that the accident is related to Paul's failure to keep the promise. But that has to do with Paul himself. It might be a compulsive act or something similar, but not God's will or a punishment."

In2: Male, age 53

"No, in the sense that God caused the accident in order to show Paul that he did something wrong. God does not move the clouds about and does not create obstacles, that is not the issue. I could imagine, however, that Paul realizes that he made the wrong decision. Further, I could imagine that he is experiencing internal unrest and thus causes an accident. Hence, the accident is the consequence of an internal unrest."

In3: Male, age 58

"Not directly. Indirectly, I would see a purely psychological connection, e.g., his inner state is one of uncertainty which makes him unequilibrated and unfree. . . . I don't think that God causes such an automobile accident. . . . God does not intervene if such an intervention would disrupt the normal course of events."

• *Question 7b: Do you believe that God punishes Paul for not keeping his promise? Why or why not?*

▶ *Responses:*

In1: Male, age 44

"I would put it like this: God does not punish people but people punish themselves, because they disobey God's will. For everyone who breaks a law, the transgressing of the law already implies, somehow, a punishment internal to the person. But not in the sense that God administers punishment or says: Because you do not obey, you are getting a serious illness.

Put differently: God is beyond human beings; they can decide freely whether to accept or reject God's offer. Yet, God is not unconcerned. . . . I would like to show this with an example. If a teacher has to give a poor grade to a student who has not done any work, the teacher is not unconcerned. Not because of the poor grade but because the student does not study and thereby hurts him- or herself. I want to say with this example: God is beyond such things. Yet God is not indifferent when people get themselves into trouble."

In2: Male, age 53

"No, it all depends on the motivations; if he truly recognizes that he ought to do something and fails to do it, then he punishes himself. People cannot act against their nature without hurting themselves."

In3: Male, age 58

"I cannot imagine God intervening in the world. I view the entire situation more like a call, and the consequences might be that Paul commits his life to a service which gives his life a meaningful direction."

• *Question 7c: If this is so, will God intervene in this world without fail? If not, does God manifest Godself in the world at all? In what way?*

▶ *Responses:*
In1: Male, age 44
"If we view historical time as a circle, then God stands simply in the center at the same distance from everywhere. Yet, viewed from the plan of creation, I would say that all the events, all of evolution, and everything has been instituted in nature; God is equally near to all people at all times, God is always present even without intervening at different points."

In2: Male, age 53
"First in creation, that is a revelation; people who don't have much use for religion are often enthusiastic worshipers of nature, which, for them, can become a real experience of God. I believe God is revealed as described in the book of nature. God is also revealed to human beings in their nature, in their inclination to do good, to be there for others—that is surely God as well. More concretely, as far as I am concerned, I would like to say that God is revealed in the person of Jesus Christ; that, for me, is the second revelation. Not only that Christ came into this world to redeem us; that alone is powerful. There is something else, i.e., what Christ taught and did is actually nothing else than nurturing human nature. He retrieved the good parts of people, he showed them how to become liberated and happy, not necessarily liberated from misery, disease, and what have you, but liberated on the inside so that they can really grow. And related to this is that people living out of this revelation radiate some of that quality that one could call divine."

In3: Male, age 58
"Everything has to do with God and God has to do with everything. All events are related to God. God is present even in everyday occurrences. Depending on how I take something, I can see the God-connection more or less clearly. Of course, I can resist, but that is then finally a question of my disposition toward God.

STAGE 5

Preliminary Remarks
In our samples we discovered hardly any respondents at stage 5. Since

we were dealing essentially with random samples, the possibility of finding stage 5 was extremely slim. One would have to be selective and choose unique individuals, e.g., activist groundbreakers on the edges and margins of society, in the underground, in solitude, persons of wisdom or holiness, great thinkers or courageous theologians. The possibility of such persons being in a random sample is obviously very small.

J. Vasudev, a woman from India, who is very familiar with our theory conducted a sample test in India. She had intended to conduct the interview with Mother Teresa who had agreed to it. However, the fact that Mother Teresa has to face real (and not artificial) dilemmas daily and that in resolving them Mother Teresa "reveals God through a human being," as Vasudev put it, dumbfounded Vasudev. And instead of doing the interview she worked for several months with Mother Teresa. According to her own statements, Vasudev is not a believer.

Perhaps one criterion of stage 5 is that instead of speaking, communication happens in such a way that the Ultimate becomes unambiguously immanent and that, vice versa, in this encounter human beings appear completely transcendent. (Or in the language of the Bible, that people live for proclaiming liberty to the captives, giving sight to the blind, and setting free those who are oppressed, Lk 4:18b.) Put differently, in this instance the sacred and the profane, the transcendent and the immanent, hope and absurdity, freedom and dependence, trust and anxiety, eternity and ephemerality, functional transparency and opaqueness (magic) are arranged in an optimal equilibrium.

Our attempt to present here, nonetheless, an example of stage 5 needs to be viewed with great caution. For the interviewee, a theologian and philosopher, is in a position where he or she would like to move often away from the dilemma to general, meta-cognitive reflections. Perhaps that too is a possible indicator for the necessary decentration-power of stage 5.

• *Question 1a:*   *Should Paul keep his promise to God?*
                    Why or why not?

▶ *Response:*   *Male, age 40*
                "The question is always: What is the meaning of God, what is the meaning of someone making a promise to God in a moment of terror and fear. The man tries to find some way out of this situation and, because no human being can help him, turns to the one final power which can still help him in this situation. That is the ultimate Other; all this-worldly possibilities are useless. There are no more technological possibilities, and he is unable to do anything. It is normal that he uses the term 'God.' From the perspective of having a

responsible relationship to this God, that promise, however, is an irresponsible act; there is no choice left, it is a situation of blackmail. According to my perspective and according to a Christian relationship with God, such a way of relating to God is irresponsible. My faith would lead me to say: Of course, he ought to take the position. I would not accept this situation, because the love of God, when turned into coercion, destroys love."

• *Question 2:*   *How would you respond to this statement: "It is God's will that Paul goes to the Third World (that is, that he keeps his promise)?"*

▶ *Response:*   "Mostly, the expression 'the will of God' has historically stood for the claim to power by groups which have been able to interpret the will of God, e.g., the Crusades. The will of God must be mediated by and interpreted in the spirit of the gospel, the great theologies, and the situation of the individual: For me, the decisive criterion would be the needs of others. The will of God is what others need from me, where they lay claim to my freedom; the formulation of God's will according to the Law is absolutely insufficient."

• *Question 3a:* *What is really important for this world: human beings or God?*

▶ *Response:*   "The either-or is an impossible alternative. It presents a choice that actually does not exist, for according to the New Testament and the prophets (he who loves God but hates his brother has not understood anything; he is a liar and a hypocrite) there is not to be any separation; otherwise it is impossible to know the meaning of God. That means: It is impossible for me to realize a relationship to God and to do justice to God if I cannot do justice to my girlfriend. Of course, by entering into this love-relationship Paul realized freedom which must not be separated from the relationship to God but rather must be understood as an interpretation of God's will, an interpretation of the situation, i.e., the love for his girlfriend and the love for his job. The fact that he is the best applicant for this surgical clinic constitutes, in my opinion, a direct call from God, a manifestation of God's will. I have always practiced that in my own life. That is, when I would wonder what I should become I would always

ask others; and when they said you are capable of doing
this or that, then it was something I ought to do or at least
an important criterion for what must be realized in the relationship to God: How am I going to spend my life, if I want
to live it in light of the inbreaking kingdom of God. To
what can I give my life? This question brings to the surface the needs, the criteria, and judgements of others whereby—and this is important—the needs of the oppressed carry
more weight than the needs of those in power. The alternatives as posed by Paul are wrong. I cannot conceive my
relationship to God independent of my communicative relationships and my relationship to my work. That would
empty my God-relationship of its content and would constitute an escape. A relationship to God can only be realized
within historical relationships—although it is not exhausted therein."

• *Question 3b:*   *Does God reveal Godself in this world at all and in what*
        way?

▶ *Response:*   "I would not say that in Paul's life as described there is no
        evidence of the meaning of God—but not without an aware-
        ness of his responsibility and without his interpretation of his
        own life. Here God is depicted in the context of natural
        causes and not in the context of freedom—that is impossi-
        ble, for as far as I am concerned the revelation and mani-
        festation of God can only be placed within the context of
        freedom. First, I would reject that God reveals Godself only
        in the context of miracles or in punishment and reward.
        Second, I would begin with the event in which God reveals
        Godself, i.e., in the Crucified and Resurrected One.
        Correspondingly, in history God is revealed where people are
        beaten, where the narrative of liberation and freedom is
        realized under extreme conditions; for me, that is an impor-
        tant locus of God's manifestation.
        Another important locus is love, and hatred, where it
        becomes evident what humans are, what they are not, and
        what they can do; God is revealed in communication as
        well as in the breakdown of communication. All of life can
        be interpreted as a manifestation of God—and natural his-
        tory must be viewed from this perspective. I cannot speak
        about evil without speaking of God. It is possible to say
        that evil is good; that the will to power must finally suc-

ceed. This raises the following question: Why is that not possible? The distinction between good and evil is only possible when people have been liberated for it. Something like the unconditional claim about realizing the good, about not interfering with the other's freedom can only be taken up when one is redeemed by another freedom and set free as a self."

In reading the example of this forty-year-old theologian and philosopher we get, on the one hand, the impression that we are dealing less with a deep-structure but more with epistemic, learned knowledge. On the other hand, it is refreshing and liberating to encounter this kind of theology applied to a concrete dilemma. We sense in it what implications a theological model of stage 5 would have in regard to the direction of further development. We sense what the world would be like if persons at stage 5 would shape the real world in accordance with their judgement. The cognitive structure discovered here embodies the matrix and correlation of immanence and transcendence, dependency and freedom, absurdity and hope. We find polarities in complete interrelation, they almost completely depend on each other.

Horizontal Differences: the Modes of the Concept of Transcendence[5]

Once again, we would like to take up the issue of structure versus content. This time, however, we will not proceed from the perspective of developmental psychology. We are asking whether statements and confession about the divine that differ in regard to content have the same meaning when viewed structurally? Are they able to satisfy the claim to universality?

In an attempt to clarify this question, we suggest the hypothesis that two principled forms should be distinguished in the way of human transcending: a personal form and a nonpersonal one. This distinction makes it possible to grasp the structural-universalistic core of the various approaches to and expressions of the divine without having to harmonize these in their respective individual forms.

As we come to the end of this chapter, we would like to examine once more the issue of structure versus content, but this time from the angle of the

---

5. We are adding this section because it presents important additions for the coding process. A coder must recognize clearly the difference between mere horizontal and actual vertical transformations.

claim to universality. We are asking if statements about existence, the last things, the Ultimate (God, the divine, a godhead), statements which differ in regard to content, can mean the same thing structurally. Especially if coping with darkness and uncertainty in a religious way constitutes a mother-structure for all people, although articulated in various ways, it ought to be possible to distinguish the modes of transcending as well as to juxtapose them functionally.

The different modes must not only be examined from a historical perspective but also understood from the point of view of developmental psychology. The phylogenetic losses mourned by Ernst Bloch have an ontogenetic parallel in the loss of each person's childhood, although it continues to live on in some way:

> Fullness has often come about by the creation of emptiness behind it. And light has often been dearly bought by the over-hasty diminution and darkening of what came before. So it was when nature, which was at least implicit in the astral myth, suddenly disappeared altogether from the milieu of man. Superstitious, pagan magic of mountain and valley, of storm and blue sky is now passé: it has drifted away in the face of the Bible's spiritual breeze (1972, p. 224).

From this point, over the emanation-doctrines, to the image of the omnipresence of a personal and, eventually, loving God, the disequilibrium of the seven polar dimensions obtains highly different and often conflicting faces. Cosmos and logos, fate and being, an all-encompassing reality and salvation-history executed by God—all these are metaphors, which represent, for theologically untrained interviewees, the external pole in contrast to their interiority, their soul, even when the exterior entities manifest themselves in one's interiority. We are not concerned with the normativity of these images, and our research does not address the study of God-images. Put more generally: We are not guided by a "conceptual" knowledge interest. Since our research spells out how persons establish relationships in concrete situations it is unavoidable that various forms of God-images automatically and in very complex fashion enter into the religious judgements. This is to enable radical transcendence-thinkers, pantheists, those who only conceive of a personal God-human relationship, and atheists to reveal their deep-structures. For example, believers may be able to conceive of "God's reign, and with it of God, in no other way than as present *as well as* in-breaking" (Schoonenberg, 1977, p. 199). However, the corresponding content—such as: "God's word and logos lives in Jesus and thus God's spirit comes through him" (p. 199)—may occasionally, yet generally surprisingly seldom, find entry into one of the judgements elicited and investigated by us.[6]

If one desires to categorize the diversity of images, it proves helpful to distinguish two forms of the mode of transcendence: the first one, tacitly, conceptualizes the divine as a person; the second one, generally defensively and argumentatively, images the divine as being, i.e., some entity that exists outside of us, as "world-spirit," as animated fate, as the sacred in nature, etc. Those who perceive transcendence as being in the second sense, combine theological with ontological elements, up to the point where the different revelation-based religions are rejected. We maintain the hypothesis, as yet unverified, that philosophical consciousness about the reality of transcendence is possible only beginning with stage 3. We derived this hypothesis intuitively from our research data. Obviously, this question must be taken up again and investigated empirically.

Reducing the diversity of all sorts of creeds to only two types has advantages as well as disadvantages. Spaemann (1973, pp. 43f) raised the objection, later adopted by Lübbe (1980, pp. 82f), that functional definitions of religion leave open the truth of a religious orientation. That is correct, but a functional perspective can be fruitful nonetheless. We consider as more decisive an aspect which Rendtorff formulated as follows:

> Structurally, persons' religiosity, religious behavior, and religious consciousness constitute a relation to something other than their own existence, their own actions, and selfhood. Only in this relation, and mediated through it, do religiosity, religious behavior, and religious consciousness constitute an essential form of self-perception or self-determination. Religion is not an immediate form of self-actualization, but that process with which persons enter into a relationship with an Ultimate Reality which transcends all empirical certainties.

> Explications of the general content of religion or of its general function frequently have the tendency to correlate religion and religious processes with successful living, perfection, and promotion to eternity, etc. Generally, this happens under conditions of empirical situations of conflict of all sorts. Thereby, these explications determine the discovery of an ultimate identity as the essential achievement of religion. However, this can never be an internal or empirical possession of a religious individual. In that case, religion could appear only as an imperfect version of what constitutes its substance. Rather, the essential significance of independent forms of religious expression must be seen in the fact that they facilitate and concretize the establishment and execution of human behavior in the matrix of a rela-

---

6. Nonbelievers often express themselves negatively by rejecting fixed religious formulations and rely on the terminology of fate and an all-encompassing reality.

tionship between persons and a reality which supports them. This does not mean that the general substantive claims of religion become ineffective. On the contrary, they become concretely applicable and can play an active role in the lives of persons in world and society (1980, p. 199).

However, a relation to an Ultimate, to the reality which transcends all empirical certainties, can be realized even if the mode of transcendence is not personal. Both conditions are admissible; the second one, the nonpersonal, can be ascribed to a stage much more easily than the first one which is a melange of generalities and specifics and also strongly shaped by content factors. We have gathered that the interview raters tend to ascribe higher stages to those persons of faith who appear to have an intense personal relationship with their God, in comparison to those who refer to fate, to the unknown, which they also frequently reject. For that reason it is important that raters acknowledge and treat, i.e., code, both modes in the same manner.

These explications by no means exhaust the issue. Two things need to be investigated empirically: (a) what role the concepts of the Ultimate play in religious judgement, and (b) which conceptions of the Ultimate can be accepted as religious. Both issues were addressed partially in the context of research on images of the world [*Weltbildforschung*] (for initial reasults, see Fetz and Oser, 1986).

In this chapter we have introduced the method for ascertaining and measuring religious judgement. We have employed this method in a variety of research projects and validation studies. They are described in detail in chapter seven. Readers with a strong interest in the empirical foundations of the theory are encouraged to consult that section. Readers interested primarily in the philosophical and theological implications of this theory are encouraged to continue with the next chapter. Those who are looking for the practical application of the theory will find chapter six most helpful.

Chapter Five

On the Range of Structures of Religious Cognition

In this chapter we elaborate in cursory and preliminary fashion the limits, opportunities, and implications of the present proposal.[1]

It is important to us to portray the possibilities for religious education if it is concerned with leading people to a higher stage of religious judgement. Persons at higher stages exhibit greater freedom, greater capacities for transcendence, a more foundational sense of hope, a more reflected form of trust, a better equilibrium between the profane and the sacred, and a more balanced perspective of time.

We also inquire into the relationship between the structure of cognitive judgement and the transmission of knowledge; we discuss the didactic and pedagogical implications and we raise the question about the motivational aspect of religious judgements. Finally, we draw out some theological implications.

The Basis for Goals of Education in the Domain of Knowledge Transmission

Every cognitive reception of (religious) content and knowledge occurs under certain presuppositions. The most fundamental presupposition and basis for any (religious) knowing is represented by the structures of religious cognition. They form the basic con-

---

1. For a detailed discussion of the pedagogical implications see Oser, 1988. Special attention is paid to a research project with high-school students conducted in the framework of the present work.

ditions of religious learning and religious meaning-making. Each stage constitutes the shaping context within which knowledge and content are assimilated and processed. Each of the different structural stages assimilates the same content and knowledge from a different perspective and processes them according to different criteria.

If, as is customary in all cultures, religious education and religious socialization transmit a certain content, then the basis for comprehending this knowledge as well as for applying it in religious actions is the cognitive-religious structure in its various forms. The reading of the Koran, the study of the Torah, and the explanation of the concept "kingdom of God" in religious education have commonalties in that the basis of the images used is constituted by a certain type of structure, i.e., either a particular structure or a transition. This structure forms the a priori foundational condition for religious learning and religious meaning-making. This fact is probably best illustrated in regard to preaching: A preacher speaking of the love of God and using a socially based illustration can expect various interpretations in his or her audience. For some, the expression (love of God) relates to the fulfillment of some type of preventive action (stage 2); for others it refers to the preconditions of possible social engagement, i.e., freely given without any requirements, tied however, to the execution of human potential (stage 4). The language used in the two cases reveals different preconscious, stage-specific, fundamental meanings which are not articulated but form the foundation for the religious reconstruction of reality. Regardless of the specific meaning of a religious concept for an individual, regardless of the way a certain segment of the religious-ontological domain of reality is construed, the regulating systems of the stage characteristics are the blueprints according to which cognitive religious assimilation and accommodation take place. Each developmental stage provides a different frame for comprehension, interpretation, and change. And therein consists the relation between development and learning.

There are certain texts, such as parables or fables, which are presumably fashioned in such a way that they are immediately accessible to persons at every developmental level. Their transparency is given by the fact that they cannot be assimilated *tale quale* as texts but must be interpreted in order to yield meaning. Since this reconstructive process is a necessity it becomes clearer than in other instances that such an interpretation is executed within the framework of a particular stage.

The basis of all religious knowledge, regardless of the different ways of structuring and grounding it, is the structural interpretation of the relation between persons and the Ultimate. This holds true even in concept research. The images of God, in regard to their abstractness, presumably do not correlate linearly with the stage sequence, i.e., relatively child-like images of God (e.g., a person drifting in space) may surface even at stage 3. Of course, cultural context plays an important role.

It would undoubtedly be intriguing if we could report on data which illuminate the relation between ontogenetics and phylogenetics. That, however, must be postponed until a future project. But we can point to two interesting writings investigating that relation. The first one, by G. Murray, is entitled, *Five Stages of Greek Religion*. The author describes the stage development of Greek religion across long spans of time. The first three stages are "natural": (a) the Age of Ignorance; (b) the age of the great Olympian gods who created order in the world, and (c) the Hellenistic period reaching from Plato to St. Paul and to the early Gnostics, wherein a certain skepticism took over the function of introducing further development. From there it was possible to perceive a fourth stage which, in the face of progressive loss of hope and in the disintegration of empires, postulated a religious individualism vis-à-vis an eschatologically charged future, i.e., the striving for personal holiness.

The second writing is entitled "Evolution of Medieval Mentalities: A Cognitive-Structural Approach" (Ch. M. Radding, 1978). It compares medieval rules and behaviors with the arguments of children about moral situations according to Piaget, and later according to Kohlberg. For example, an Anglo-Saxon code is correlated with stage 2 of the child's judgement, something that is quite obvious when one reads: "One Anglo-Saxon code allowed thirty shillings for an ear, sixty shillings for an eye, the tongue, a hand, or a foot, eight shillings for a front tooth, and so forth" (p. 586). This very meticulous and by no means uncritical study reveals that, for example, in the eleventh and twelfth centuries a transition of moral-religious consciousness occurred from a more individualistic orientation to one more oriented toward obligation to one's "neighbors" and to society, i.e., in effect, a phylogenetic stage change.

Such comparisons must be taken up anew on the basis of our stage descriptions. They address objectified knowledge of persons engaged in reasoning processes behind which can be discerned a fundamental structure in a particular historical context. The explanation of historical facts by means of a system of historical rules obtains thereby a third dimension: the blueprint of religious or ontological development which, by extension, measures the up and down of human development in wave-like fashion. We speak of "up and down" because higher development also implies greater liability for ruptures and new beginnings. Unlike the cognitive development of an individual, historical development is probably not linear. Rather, generations appear to develop toward a breaking point where the fragmentation of other generations is frequently recognized only with difficulty. However, this assumption would have to be tested hermeneutically by means of intensive

literary analysis. In the future, even classroom transcripts featuring sufficient student comments and religious questions about a nonreligious reality
must be investigated in regard to the general level of religious development.

The Development of Religious Judgement: Educational and Didactic Implications

The educational and didactic implications will be outlined in
five points: 1) The stages of religious judgement serve as an
instrument to understand better the religious reasoning of persons
at all ages. 2) They make clear that a stage change necessarily
manifests itself as a transitional crisis. 3) They illuminate why a
particular, concrete (knowledge-) content is being viewed in an
entirely different way at each of the stages. 4) The stages of religious judgement represent an instrument for the teachers themselves to reflect critically on their own positions and their methods of argumentation. 5) They serve to facilitate the reconstruction
of one's own historical constitution of religious identity.

The actual discussion of the possibility of stimulating development to a
higher stage of religious judgement appears in another writing.[2] Nonetheless,
in anticipation we would like to make a few comments on the educational and
didactic consequences of our knowledge of the stages of religious judgement. A sketch of the following issues must suffice at this point:

1) The stages of religious development constitute an instrument for comprehending the reasoning of children, adolescents, and adults all around us.
It becomes possible in many decisive moments to follow other persons' line
of reasoning by properly employing this instrument.

It is one of the a priori demands in the pedagogical literature that students need to be engaged at their actual level of knowledge and comprehension. A segment of the anthropological presuppositions of the learning process consists in connecting new learning experiences with existing structures
or, more precisely, in engaging new situations in the process of assimilation or accommodation with existing structures. In day-to-day education of
the school this process is realized spontaneously. But disciplines like history, literature, political, social, ethical, and religious education frequently
face the danger of rupture in the learning process, since the degree of complexity, the level of abstractness, and the subjective ranges of students are not
considered. Thus, a stage concept like the present one can assist in creating that sort of communication basis which allows for a learning-relevant
interaction between the teacher and the student.

---

2. Oser, 1988.

2) A transition from one stage to the next is characterized by a crisis-attitude which frequently can be understood and accepted only with knowledge of the stage descriptions and their transformations. In the process of identity formation, the transitional phase, for example from stage 2 to stage 3, is a necessary ingredient. In young people, this process evokes the rejection of their "old" structures as they perceive them in others. (For instance, they reject the influence of a God in this world, and they assert that persons have to assume their own communicative responsibility. The consequence of this can be the rejection of all things ecclesial, of the sacred, of theological language in general, of religious dilemmas, etc.) Knowing about the necessity of transitions from one stage to the next, the shape of the transitional crisis can be identified and supportively guided (*désintégration positive*).

3) The lack of closure of religious development requires that all knowledge of traditional (e.g., biblical), cultic, and currently interpreted actions must be processed, integrated, and externalized again at each developmental stage. For the stages describe a depth-dimension of human being in the sense of Tillich (1958, pp. 76f). Only from the perspective of this depth-dimension is it possible to understand concrete religions, their symbols and their institutions. If religion, in the Tillichian sense, is "the state of being concerned about one's own being and being universally" (1958, p. 76), then a certain content must be reconstrued afresh at each stage of this interpretation of meaning. This concerns everything that is "tangibly" religious, the cultic expression, prayer, revelation, etc. Now, Bruner's "blind" concept of a curriculum-helix (1960) is confronted with a structurally filled stage concept, a hierarchy of levels which assigns to the curriculum-helix clear shape and form and which reflects on the content-elements at each stage in a new way. Thus at the different stages, the same content is viewed entirely differently. This fact necessitates a pedagogical concept which articulates the essential contents at each stage from the new perspective of relevance.

4) The stages of religious judgement are also an instrument for "measuring" a teacher's course of argument. In a study on the stimulation of religious judgement we discovered that meta-cognition, i.e., reflecting on one's own ways of reasoning can be a means for motivating and improving religious dialogue itself. I myself reflect on how I might accept religiously a teacher's desperate act of suicide religiously. I provide reasons, I create an equilibrium among the seven polar dimensions described above. But I must expose this equilibrium again to my own critical meta-reflection in the light of the knowledge of the stage characteristics. This is a truth-finding process that occurs on two levels. One level concerns the various elements of the argument at any particular stage; the second concerns the connecting of these elements with the theoretical stage concept. This is a reflexive level which Peukert (1982, pp. 99f) has introduced under the perspective of a "new" concept of praxis.

In that case, praxis would mean: In light of systematic contradictions which one has experienced, from which one has suffered, which have deformed one's life-world, and therewith in light of alienation, actions of change are initiated toward a nonalienated form of life, i.e., a form of life in which identities can be formed jointly so that changing conditions can lead to changing subjects and vice versa. At its core, this sort of praxis would itself be a transformatory learning process.

5) Finally, the ontogenesis of religious consciousness presented here serves for the reconstruction of each person's individual history of identity formation. Our process of becoming subjects always reflects, at any one time or another, our relationship to the Ultimate as well as our communicative moorings. The task is to see oneself, via the reconstruction of successful and unsuccessful situations of meaning-making in the various phases of the life cycle, in a process of growth and transformation, in particular with respect to a highest stage which, due to a religious dimension without a primarily religiously colored content, makes possible a personally responsible faith stance coupled with high tolerance and true solidarity. To educate ourselves religiously would thus primarily mean fathoming the depth-dimension of the Ultimate in all life situations. This would happen existentially with a new, liberating introduction of religion and religiosity into all phenomena of life.

Religious Judgement and the Motivational Aspect

Claims that religious judgement concerns only the cognitive realm of the person are incorrect. For when we speak of identity and thus also of judgement, we refer to the personality and that which is absolutely valid for it. Persons processing crises (e.g., the death of a friend) in a religious manner do so not merely in a rational, cognitive fashion. They stand by what they say, they live it out. Thus, religious judgement refers also to the deep-structure and therewith also to a comprehensive part of the person. Even if this judgement is expressed with different forms of "character," it still concerns in essence the whole person.

The present theory of the development of religious judgement may be criticized for lacking the motivational, the psychodynamic aspect. What does this mean? Presumably it implies that religious judgement consists only of discursive processes, of cognitive connections of logically correct reasoning-patterns without the engagement of the person. To this critique we must now respond.

First, limits in the range of the present theoretical concept are not only real but even desirable. The stage concept says nothing, for instance, about the processing of religious dreams, or about the formation of relationships to religious ideals or mentors, or about the processing of cultic experiences in the domain of religious education, or about the formation of epistemic structures, etc.[3]

These domains are touched on indirectly by the various patterns of religious reasoning. It would be wrong to dismiss our theory as a pure logicism [*Logizismus*].

Second, we must also inquire into the range of their applicability and how they touch on the psychodynamic elements. At the beginning of this book we mentioned that we are addressing what we have designated as "the religious" from the perspective of the subject. Now we add an existential framework to it, because the subject speaks about "the religious" in concrete situations, mostly in situations in which there is no other way to cope with contingency. "The religious" is grounded in a concept of experience, i.e., in experiences where persons engage subjectively in a practical issue which does not concern preformed contents but rather the demand, in a concrete situation, to articulate the Ultimate-human relationship and, thereby, to cope with it in the mode of self-determination. This relationship, then, is in no way abstract but a process which challenges the whole person.

In other words, we are talking about the analysis of truth from the perspective of subjective obligation. Chisholm remarks on this: "A *belief* or *assertion is true* provided, first, that it is a belief or assertion with respect to a certain state of affairs; that that state of affairs exists, and provided, secondly, that that state of affairs does exist; and a *belief* or *assertion is false* provided that it is a belief or assertion with respect to a certain state of affairs; that that state of affairs does not exist" (Chisholm, 1966, p. 103). Applied to our work this means that truth shifted to the subject surfaces existentially by means of the open-ended definition of the situation (the dilemma). Therefore, the motivational aspect ought not be viewed so much as the degree of an external tension. Rather, we interpret this aspect in the holistic nature of the situation and in the grounding of the subjective religious judgement in persons' existential experiences.

Third, another aspect needs to be considered. We said that structures of religious cognition are condensed assimilations and accommodations which have been developed over years of religious socialization and which constitute the individual's disposition. Thus what is really produced in a situation of coping with contingency is that segment of the person which, via its theoretical competence, yields the true deep-structures, i.e., the true possibilities of intellectual [*geistig*] knowing. We know from other studies, e.g., on the resolution of religious problems in groups, that this competence can be increased (cf. Oser, 1981). Nonetheless, what is produced is a "faith-statement," i.e.,

---

3. It also omits from consideration phenomena like withholding of love, overprotection, power, group dynamics, religious pathologies, etc.

a belief or assertion and not just a cognitive skeleton. The task of the researcher, however, goes into an entirely different direction: He or she filters from this material structural elements which are interindividually compatible, i.e., condensed material, which makes possible a theory of development and which reconstructs the possibility of growth.

Fourth, the classical approach of genetic epistemology generally describes the motivational aspect with reference to the disequilibrium and the reequilibration of the structures. This is certainly an important aspect, for the coordination between religious reference-systems (religious content, religious community, etc.) and possible acquired structures results from the disruption of the equilibrium in the dilemma.

Dilemmas require us to reconstruct the relations between what we externalized and what exists socially. Perhaps the process of "widening equilibration" [*ausweitende Äquilibration*] (cf. Furth, 1982, p. 212) occurs nowhere nearly as much as in the raising of questions about the ultimate meaning of life, about hope, about freedom, about transcendence as relationship and as condition for the possibility of social life. At the same time, "widening equilibration" is the driving element in the momentary actualization of possible reasoning patterns concerning the Ultimate and thereby the driving element in religious development in general.

Implications for Theology: Theological Statements in a Developmental Mode

The most important implication for theology consists in fundamentally adopting into its theorizing and research the structural developmental concept of development. This means, for example, that different developmental stages are taken into account in the case of texts and their analyses. Also, in many cases it would be possible to reconstruct the development of individual persons (ontogenetics) in the history of religions (phylogenetics). Many inconsistencies in the history of religion are perhaps often related to the stage of religious development of the persons responsible for shaping that history. The relevance of the developmental concept, as set forth in the stage model, is illustrated with individual theological disciplines.

We want to sketch briefly certain implications which arise for theological thought from the developmental theory presented in this book. We are doing this because we dare to hope that the deliberations presented here may lead to fruitful discussions not only in the domain of social science but also in that field of scholarship which traditionally and rightfully has been charged with investigating religious reality, i.e., theology. This is the case because theology, as a "science of faith"* has to "produce *knowledge in faith, knowledge derived from faith* and finally *knowledge about faith*" (Seckler, 1977, p. 168).

In the face of macro- and micro-structural experiences of crisis which profoundly shape our present age, the question arises with great urgency: "What exactly are human actions? More specifically: What are actions which truly encourage human life and community, and what are the guidelines for action?" (Peukert, 1981, p. 280). Not only are the social sciences but also, and especially, theology is challenged by this fundamental contemporary issue. It is the result of its historically long-standing and repeated claim that religion, religious praxis, is capable—even by taking into account its basic ambivalence—of opening up the true situation and the fundamental constitutiveness of the person and the world. We already emphasized in the first chapter that in the interest of human self-becoming the religious dimension is necessary for the formation of identity and that it, therefore, must co-determine the socialization process for the achievement of true humanity (cf. Mette, 1979, p. 136).

Nevertheless, we must admit that wide gaps still exist in the domain of theory formulation as well as in the area of practical reflection.

a) We do not possess much substantive empirical knowledge in the field of religious socialization.

b) When we do have knowledge of rules and procedures, such as in the structural developmental approach, it is rarely taken into account.

Systematic theology, for instance, has taken little notice of the structural developmental point of view. This neglect may be due to several reasons. However, certain obstacles are, on the one hand, the partially critical attitude of the social sciences toward religion and, on the other hand, the attempted insulation of theology from empirical research. As far as interdisciplinary dialogue is concerned, for example with the social sciences, it appears as if theology has managed to steer itself into irrelevance. The result is that theology can no longer benefit from the opportunities and possibilities which arise from the practice of interdisciplinary research. It might be possible for theology, for instance, to "become the advocate of questions not addressed by the different social scientific disciplines, the ongoing questions about the whence and whither, about the ground, the meaning, and the goal" of existence (Fries, 1981, p. 64). The social sciences could, in turn, remind theology that truth is always concrete.

That truth is concrete is also reiterated by the deliberations about the ontogenesis of religious consciousness presented in this work. This means that—faced with increasingly precarious conditions for the maintenance

---

*Translator's note: The background for the European designation of theology as a science, as in *Glaubenswissenschaft*, is outlined in E. Farley's *Theologia*.

and expansion of Christianity (cf. Kaufmann, 1979)—theology should no longer be interested only in what "ought" to be. But it should develop an atmosphere, a body of knowledge, and strategies for reaching the "ought." In other words, theology must address the way things *are*, the way things *ought to be*, and how to get *from is* to *ought*. The central challenge to theology concerns its attitude toward empirical research (cf. H. Schroer quoted in Mette, 1978, p. 297). One possible response might be

> that theology, as a science, has to begin with concrete situations and their challenges, i.e., with empirical issues in the widest sense. Therefore, it has to rely on the methods of empirical research, although these methods and the theories connected with them are not sufficient for knowing a reality that is structured on multiple levels (Mette, 1978, p. 302).

When we connect this response with our own project, we arrive at a particular insight that bears implications for theological conceptualizing: Since theology must be understood profoundly as a practical science—and since, according to the current status of the discussion in the philosophy of science, a practical science can also be conceived as a theory of communicative action—the developmental theory of communicative competence and identity applied in our work receives a key position.

Our starting point is that knowing [*Erkenntnis*] in the most original way is tied to action and that it must be conceived as a construction of the subject. In the words of Fetz: "The prior structure of our knowing—regardless of its actual existential shape—is always the result of a *developmental process* and thus points to its own genesis" (1979a, p. 183). This implies that for an adequate understanding of persons one must understand their genesis. The implication for theological thought is, first, that it begins with a theory of religion that contains a developmental theory of religious consciousness, thus enabling the analysis of historical manifestations of religious consciousness according to their respective structure and level. A second implication is the formation of a concept of the subject, via reliance on statements in the Old and New Testaments, which conceives of the believer as experiencing crisis-like transformations. Since faith is conceptualized as a fundamental process of transformation, reliance on a theory of the ontogenesis of religious consciousness allows theology to reconstruct historical models as well as the various personal histories of (religious) identity-formation.

These insights of the structural-developmental approach into the domain of religious development should be carried into the individual theological disciplines and be applied there fruitfully. How this could occur will be outlined for practical theology, moral theology, systematic theology, and biblical exegesis. Generally, these disciplines deal predominantly with content and barely discuss the structural-developmental, comprehensively universalistic point of view. Therefore, we want to integrate this point of view into the approach and central issues of each discipline.

The relevance of our approach for practical theology, which, as an action theory, concerns itself with the explicit and concrete manifestations of Christian actions, is obvious. What is valid for theology in general, applies especially to this discipline: It is not primarily concerned with learnable and applicable knowledge, for

> the issues with which theology is concerned cannot be transmitted as factual information. Rather, it is a question of communicating a reality, which is the stimulus for changed communicative behavior; i.e, the knowing and acting subjects are immediately involved via their own identities" (Mette, 1978, p. 352).

Therefore, attention must be paid to the presuppositions of cognitive knowing, coupled with the qualitatively religious equilibrium-characteristics in the practical-theological field of action. For the proclamation of certain revelation contents, the personal counseling session, the shaping and interpretation of religious rites, etc., addresses persons with different sensibilities for religious content, with different intellectual capacities, and also at different stages of religious development. Whatever is said can no longer be treated without taking into account the presupposition of the structural developmental approach. Even in the simplest situations, where, for example, people view biblical scenes in the stained glass windows of a cathedral, listen to a devotional or sermon on TV, observe or participate in a baptism, listen to the interpretation of a text, discuss the question of theodicy in religious education—the same particular content is always assimilated differently, according to the various stages. To take into consideration the structural developmental presuppositions means, for example, to distinguish between statements made at different stages, to simplify, to begin at those stages at which persons are presumed to be, and to deliberate about possible transformations.

Moral theology, as our second example, must also transform its own normative and telelogical systems in order to bring them in line with the structural developmental approach. In this sense, it must include in its reflections the *becoming* of the autonomous person. If moral-theological hermeneutics is concerned with shedding insight on ethical autonomy, the final ground of human action and obligation, this cannot happen without concrete references to the forms of moral and religious knowing as they are manifest in the concrete accomplishments of contemporary persons. The stage theory of religious judgement contributes in an explanatory and illuminating fashion to the mediation between asymmetric relations, between competing claims in religion and morality. "We are dealing with the question whether belief in God transcends the ethical autonomy of the person, whether persons suddenly become puppets again, connected to the strings of the will of God, which move them, who are without a will of their own, about at liberty" (Hoffmann, 1979, p. 215). This means that moral theology must learn to interpret the stages of religious judgement from the perspective of morality and, vice versa, the stages of moral judgement according to Kohlberg from the standpoint of their theological claim.

Through the themes it addresses (the doctrine of revelation, God and creation, Christology, soteriology, eschatology, ecclesiology), systematic theology provides information about the historical as well as contemporary structure, meaning, and function of faith statements. The character of theology as a system comes to expression in the fact that theological reason makes explicit the structure of its knowing, thereby demonstrating the connections in its structures. And if we assume that the most general foundations of systematic theology are to be found in anthropology (cf., for example, Pannenberg, 1976), then its special task can be summarized as trying to "work out the religious implications of the empirically determined state of affairs. It will be concerned with investigating the theological relevance of the psychological, sociological, and anthropological insights" (Greive, 1975, p. 68).

The extension of systematic theology in the sense of the structural developmental approach must be conceived fundamentally in such a manner that the becoming of theological systems can also be considered as a comparison of ontogentical and phylogentical approaches. On the concrete level, this would mean, on the one hand, the correlation of the various systematic-theological concepts, such as the doctrine of God or Christology, with the stages of religious judgement. On the other hand, it would be necessary to include the structural-developmental approach into the systematic conceptualization efforts in such a constitutive fashion that fundamental theological statements such as "God is love" are always structurally plausible and reproducible. Furthermore, events in the personal life history of great theologians must be included from the ontogenetic perspective whenever attempts are made to understand and interpret the development of a certain approach. In the field of systematic theology, the ontogenetic point of view could contribute to the illumination of the connection between historical and contemporary faith statements in regard to their subjective and existential relevance. Thus it could also contribute to an improved understanding of the requirements necessary to comprehend theological systems and concepts.

Finally, the historic-phylogenetic trajectories as preconditions for the ontogenetic approach must be considered in particular in biblical exegesis. In addition to etiological, text-critical, historical-critical, etc., analysis, statements of the Old and the New Testaments must also be examined as to whether the phylogenetic development of religious thought corresponds in any particular way to the development of the religious judgement of individual persons. It would be equally important for biblical exegesis to examine individual text-formations as to their inherent structure of judgement, since it may be assumed that the levels of the structure of the religious judgement in the biblical texts may vary substantially due to the differences in context, audience, and social forms.

The above thoughts are only intended to be suggestions and examples. They are equally applicable to the history of religion, psychology of religion, and the philosophy of religion. Especially in philosophy it has happened repeatedly that speculations about development have been undertaken without direct empirical substantiations. Designs about developmental stages can be found, for example, in Hegel, Kierkegaard, Nietzsche, and Fichte. Take, for example, Fichte's developmental model which, in its differentiation, deserves attention still today. In his 1806 teachings on religion, Fichte—in the essay, "The Way Toward the Blessed Life"—distinguishes in this model five possible practical life-stances or worldviews:

> The first and lowest being that of the prevalent Philosophy, in which reality is attributed to the World of Sense, or Nature. The Second, in which reality is placed in a Law of Order in the Existing World addressed to Freedom;—the stand-point of Objective Legality, or of the Categorical Imperative. The third, which places reality in a new Creative Law addressed to Freedom, producing a New World within the Existing World;—the stand-point of the Higher Morality. The fourth, which places reality in God alone and in His Existence; the stand-point of Religion. The fifth, which clearly discerns the Manifold in its outgoings from the One Reality—the stand-point of Science (1977, p. 292).
>
> Science goes beyond the insight into the *fact* that the Manifold is assuredly founded on the One and is to be referred to it, which is given to us by Religion—to the insight into the *manner* of this fact; and to it that becomes a genetic principle which to Religion is but an Absolute fact. Religion without Science is mere Faith although an immovable Faith;—Science supersedes all Faith and changes it into sight (1977, p. 377).

As a second example of a speculative developmental logic we would like to mention Jaspers. He states:

> The liberation of man proceeds from dark, savage forces to personal gods, from gods beyond good and evil to moral gods, from the gods to the one God, and on to the ultimate freedom of recognizing the one personal God as a cipher. We may call this last liberation the ascent from God to the Godhead, from the ciphers to what makes them speak. It is our liberation from the hobbles with which our own conceptions and thoughts prevent us from reaching the truth that halts all thinking (1967, p. 284).

Such statements and systemizations constitute a possible starting point for a comparison of philosophical "stages" of coping with reality with the empirically substantive descriptions of a stage development of religious judgement.

For theology there emerges at least one important implication: Its efforts of knowing must no longer be directed abstractly toward the possibility of religious experience, faith, etc. It has to go further and engage in a constructive process of studying and analyzing theologically normative statements in regard to their development. As indicated above, this could happen in each sub-discipline. In the historical-theological debate between emancipation and revelation it can be shown, for example, that the development of cognitive stages of religious judgement becomes objectified in the historical process of religious systems of interpretations and that this objectification, in turn, shapes the development of the individual (cf. Singe, 1982, pp. 72f). Eicher (cf. 1975, esp. pp. 15-49) indicates, for example, that the problem of revelation versus emancipation was not an issue until the Council of Trent, since faith and reason had never before diverged as separate principles of knowing. This level of judgement according to stages 1 and 2 changes into a stage 3 and 4 judgement under the impact of the cultural trends of the Renaissance, the Reformation, and Deism. Armed with the humanistic thought of the Renaissance, the Reformation opened the fight against natural reason and Catholic ecclesial authority. With the criteria of reason based on the experiences of the natural sciences and history, Deism questioned the principle of revelation itself. In the Enlightenment, this breach between revelation and reason became more radical. At the same time, however, the breach is overcome. An example in this respect is the work of G. E. Lessing, who conceived of the inner truth of revelation as twofold: (a) as a rejection of revelation-faith determined by authority and (b) as the emancipation of persons for reason.

Surely, in this rough schematization of a development toward the stage 5 level, it might be possible to discover regressive tendencies. Also, the development described can never grasp all of the sub-systems. Thus, the Catholic reaction to the Enlightenment, for example, was an insistence on a supranatural revelation-authority versus emancipated reason.

This particularly clear debate about the relationship between revelation and emancipation, raging since the Enlightenment, is a symbol for the dependency of the evolution of a stages 5 and 6 level on societal conditions of socialization. Depending on their structures, different economic, political, or ideological systems can sponsor either productive or regressive developments. The historical evidence reveals that the various systems of rules were used repeatedly to play revelation out against emancipation or to reject revelation in light of emancipation. The principle of emancipation by means of revelation (Eicher, 1975, pp. 34f), suggested by Eicher as the biblical action principle, becomes possible only at the higher competency levels of religious judgement.

What, then, are the implications of these results? On the one hand, there is the biblical action-principle of "emancipation by means of revelation," which can only be achieved at stages 5 and 6. On the other hand, we find the majority of the population still at stages 1-4. This discrepancy between "is" and "ought" can be addressed theologically in various ways. Generally, one attempts to provide analytic "insight" into the precarious situation with the aid of more or less plausible causal explanations. This usually produces rather hapless and ineffective appeals. Thus it becomes necessary that theology's still predominant speculative mode of scholarship be supplemented with empirical research. Constitutive theological categories and assumptions of the development of the personality must not only be principally open to empirical validation but, furthermore, empirically grounded.

A theory of the ontogenesis of religious consciousness can provide insight into and reasons for the fact that, for example, appeals at stage 5 elicit in persons at stage 2 either no response at all or confusion. Since a developmental logic of religious consciousness reveals the development of religious judgement, it becomes possible, on the one hand, to ascertain the discrepancy between what is (e.g., stage 2) and what, ideally, ought to be (e.g., stage 5). On the other hand, it becomes possible also to provide mediating steps in the sense of structural transformations of consciousness. That this is of great importance for the domain of faith education does not need to be stressed separately.

Let us summarize. If theology wants to unearth the possibilities for future faith education, it cannot limit itself to advancing abstract speculative arguments as an indispensable contribution for the formation of the subject. Rather, it becomes necessary to do theology decisively from the perspective of structural development, even if the distinction between phylogentics and ontogenetics—as illuminated above with the example of the relation between emancipation and revelation—must be clarified further with new and progressive research.

Chapter Six

Educational Implications and
Applications of the Theory
of Religious Judgement
(with Anton Bucher)

In recent years, the aesthetics of textual criticism have increasingly gained prominence in literary studies. They emphasize the active roll of the reader in the act of reading. But in order to become more useful for the teaching of texts, especially the teaching of moral and religious texts, they must be complemented with structural developmental theories of moral and religious cognition. A parable from the New Testament, the workers in the vineyard (Mt 20:1f), serves as an example to show how readers at different stages of religious cognition actively reconstruct the parable. We introduce data from a pilot study which make it plausible to assume that persons at different levels of religious cognition interpret religious texts according to their respective stage of religious cognition. This leads to the claim that religious education needs to pay more attention to the different levels of children's interpretive capacities as well as to the structural-developmental orientation in general.

Borrowing from Thomas Aquinas

"Quidquid recipitur, secundum modum recipientis recipitur" (That which is received, is received according to the recipient). This statement made by Thomas Aquinas (1224-1274) can be translated today without any major problem into the language of contemporary literature aesthetics as well as into that of structural developmental theory. The statement says that persons per-

154

ceive texts with those cognitive structures held by them at the time of encountering the text. Put differently and more precisely, persons *actively* impact the text in the process of reading and perform processes of adaptation.

This activity by the reader has been pointed out in recent years particularly by the field of literature aesthetics—although only in a very general fashion (cf. Warning, 1975; Iser, 1984). In contrast to that view which ascribes to literary texts in particular and to pieces of art in general something like an absolute metaphysical status and consequently views the reader as a mere "receiver" of precast meaning, the theory of literature aesthetics stresses the central role of the reading-act and, therewith, the central role of the recipient. Only when he or she reads the text does it, and its meaning-potential, become "activated." The reader "actualizes" one or more of the possible interpretations when the text becomes congruent with the reader's preunderstanding and limits of meaning-making. Thus understanding is achieved. Correspondingly, Iser (1984, pp. 37f) suggests that inquiries about *the* meaning of the text ought to be replaced by questions about the "actualization" or "realization" of texts by the reader. Thus, reading becomes a creative activity of the individual and is no longer the passive receiving of given contents and meanings (cf. Iser, 1975; Ingarden, 1975).

Unfortunately, the contributions of literature aesthetics remain rather general. Above all, what is missing is an inquiry into shared dispositions among readers as well as an awareness that readers' cognition develop along general lines while their moral, social, religious, and even aesthetic consciousness develops more specifically. The operations described by literature aesthetics exhibit certain particular features. They correspond to those structures which individuals have "evolved" or, put differently, they correspond to their intellectual development up to the present. For that reason it seems obvious—and for the didactics of textual criticism even indispensable—to unfold the developmental dimension of literature aesthetics. That would mean the application of Thomas Aquinas' aforementioned statement to the conceptual language of structural developmentalism or of "developmental semiotics" the task of which, according to R. Fetz (1981), is the reconstruction of the origin and development of *all* higher symbol-systems like science, morality, the arts, or religion. In this sense, then, we can suggest that readers at different stages of development will interpret the same texts differently. We can further assume that interpretations which correspond to higher stages will hardly be understood by readers who have not yet developed to those stages. This fact needs to find recognition in the pedagogy of literature aesthetics (F. Kreft, 1982) as well as in text-based religious and moral education. At the same time, further empirical research and explanation is needed.

A first such attempt has been made by J. Kreft (1986). Building on Kohlberg's stages of moral development and on literature aesthetics (Warning,

1975; Mukarovsky, 1974) he made the assumption that morally relevant texts, such as fables, will be interpreted differently at different stages of development. This hypothesis was proven with transcripts of classroom lessons in German literature in which children and youth discussed a fable entitled "The Bear at the Forresters' Dance." Only adolescents were capable of recognizing the social-critical relevance of this fictitious text, while elementary school students appropriated the story in the category of physical facticity—that means, not *yet* as a fable. In their interpretations of the various characters' actions they also made preconventional moral judgements; young adults, however, made postconventional judgements suggesting, for example, that the fable critiques popular role-stereotypes.

On the whole, Kreft concludes that morally meaningful texts provide interpretations which correspond to the various developmental stages of morality as well as literature aesthetics. This leads not infrequently to a situation where an advanced teacher-interpretation demands too much of students.

Nipkow reaches the same conclusion (*Z.f.Päd.*, 33, 1987, No. 2). He analyzed students' interpretations of the Old Testament narrative of Elijah and the priests of Baal who are killed by Yahweh (1 Kgs 18). Nipkow stresses that for a somewhat adequate comprehension of the texts the development of students' social and moral cognition needs to have reached the stage of conventional judgements. Otherwise, the interpretations will be distorted by moving the aspects of physical violence into the center which obfuscates the actual social-critical and prophetic statement of the narrative.

The Theological-Normative Claims of Matthew 20:1f

Matthew 20:1f is one of the parables about the kingdom of God. Its opening verse states: "For the kingdom of heaven is like a landowner who went out early in the morning to hire laborers for his vineyard" (NRSV). The narrative continues by portraying the wage negotiations between the landowner and the laborers. They agree on the one-day wage of one denarius, the customary wage during Jesus' time (Jeremias, 1966). At different times during the course of the day—even close to nightfall—the landowner goes back to the marketplace to hire more laborers. At dusk the workers receive their pay. *Every one* of them gets one denarius, which greatly upsets those who had been hired early in the morning. Their complaints about being treated unjustly are countered by the landowner's reply that he kept the agreement made with them and that he is free to act *generously* any time he chooses.

It is precisely in the breaking with the economic performance-reward scheme that significant interpreters locate the center of this parable which, in the history of theology, has received manifold and contrary interpretations (Kissinger, 1979). According to Harnisch (1985, pp. 177f) "It is an expression of love." When the parable, which must be understood metaphorically in the sense of Ricoeur (1974, 1977), reverses the everyday world and breaks one of its main principles, the possibility of a new world and the summons to a new way of life, which is identified with the kingdom of God, breaks into the consciousness of the listener.

Weder (1984, pp. 218f) takes a similar position: According to his interpretation the parables liberates the listeners from their performance/reward thinking and offers to them the kingdom of God in a liberating fashion. Aurelio (1977, pp. 166f) identifies the owner of the vineyard, who is constantly on the way to the market-square for the purpose of hiring and providing an income for the unemployed, with God who is always reaching out to humanity and who is concerned about the salvation of all of them—regardless of their achievements. In Israel, the owner of the vineyard was a popular metaphor for God. According to Jeremias (1966), the unearned merciful actions of Jesus for the people, in particular on behalf of tax-collectors, sinners, and the poor, is illustrated by the parable and justified before the self-righteous, especially the Pharisees. The parable is also ascribed certain pedagogical intentions: On the one hand, it describes and teaches about the kingdom of God, and, on the other hand, it calls people to a corresponding way of life, i.e., to engage in human and social relations motivated by the goodness of God.

These are, in brief, the currently significant interpretations of Matthew 20:1f. They have in common an emphasis on God's goodness which always precedes all human accomplishments. Does this not seem like a reflection of the religious judgement at the fourth stage? This assumption seems plausible, since in an empirical study (cf. the following section; Bucher, 1987a) exactly those persons whose responses were coded as stage 4 spontaneously reconstructed structurally isomorphous interpretations.

How, then, does the parable relate to the lower stages of religious judgement? According to our hypothesis, interpretations at the lower stages should be characterized by less complex structures. A quick glance at the *Formgeschichte*, i.e., the exegetical discipline investigating the *Sitz im Leben* of the biblical texts and how they were received by the gospel writers (Dibelius, 1971; Bultmann, 1963), indicates that numerous places in the parable lend themselves to various interpretations. Already the author of the gospel of Matthew (approx. 90 AD) radically altered Jesus' original intention of the parable in the redaction-process by relating it back to verse 19:30, i.e., the exhortation about wanting to be among the first, "for the first will be the last." This appears to be a reference to self-righteous and over-eager members of Matthew's Christian congregation (Weder, 1984, pp. 229f) whom the parable identifies with the laborers hired at the first hour and who are reprimanded for being self-righteous and envious. Thus, the owner of the vineyard, and—since represented by him—God as well, is conceived as a "judge" who will reward those who try to rush ahead of others less than those who are humble and unpretentious. Without much difficulty one can perceive herein the polar reciprocity, i.e., the punishment/reward concept of stage 2. This scheme was construed, for example, by Weiss (1927) who ascribed to the workers hired at the tenth hour that they had worked ten times harder than those hired at the first hour. Such a concretization of the vagueness in our literary text—it reveals nothing about the accomplishments of the individual workers—surfaces also in our empirical study, particularly in the interviews with persons at stage 2. Their subjective interpretations literally reverse the normative-theological one.

Empirical Evidence on the Reception of Matthew 20:1f

In the context of an exploratory structural-developmental research study, twenty-eight persons, equally distributed according to age and gender, were asked during lengthy semi-structured interviews what lessons could be learned from Matthew 25:14f (the parable of the talents), Luke 16:19f (the parable of the rich man and Lazarus) and, finally, Matthew 20:1f (the parable of the laborers in the vineyard). The subjects were also invited to evaluate whether the main character in the parables is a convincing representation of God, why Jesus might have told the parables in the first place, and what each parable's overall point might be, etc. In the following we will concentrate on the interpretation-types of Matthew 20:1f. Unfortunately, we cannot report extensively on the development of "text-type-perception" [*Gatttungsverständnis*] and the aspect of literary-aesthetical cognition. However, it is important to note that elementary school pupils perceive parables as "mere stories," while students on the verge of Piaget's formal-operational stage of cognition exhibited the ability to interpret the texts properly according to their literary type, i.e., as parables (cf. Cometa/Eason, 1978; Küppers, 1980; Kreft, 1986; Hoppe-Graff/Schell, 1987; Bucher, 1987b).

Q: Why do you think Jesus told this story?
A: So that one will give more money to those who work more.
Q: And why might that be?
A: Those who work more also get more.

These statements are excerpted from an interview with a seven-year-old girl. The cognitive structure of the religious judgement corresponds to stage 1. In contrast to the exegetes cited above, the girl was not yet able to accept the actions of the landowner and to project them onto God, who, in her opinion, would not act like the owner of the vineyard.

Q: Would God act like the owner of the vineyard?
A: No.
Q: Why not?
A: Because it is not right.
Q: What would be right?
A: When he would give more to those who worked more.
Q: Can we learn something from this story?
A: Yes.
Q: And what do you think that is?
A: Not to be unjust.
Q: And why not?
A: Because that does not make God happy.

The following excerpt shows that, on the one hand, the child was not yet able to draw the analogy, landowner = God, which was required by the text-type. On the other hand, the child consistently rejected the actions of the landowner when asked to relate them to God:

Q: Again: could the owner of the vineyard be like God?
A: No.
Q: And why not?
A: Because he is not like God, he does not look like God. And the man gave the same amount of money to all the laborers, while God gives more money to those who work more.
Q: And why does God give more money to those?
A: Because they worked more.

This interpretation of Matthew 20:1f, which was for the child both plausible and existentially meaningful, collides with that of the theologians and the religious textbooks. However, the interpretation does match the child's cognitive structure of religious judgement which obviously determines the interpretation of the parable as well as the child's relation to God.

An eleven-year-old girl at stage 2 construed an interpretation that was largely isomorphous in regard to structure and very similar in regard to content:

Q: What kind of things can God do?
A: God can help us, but we also have to muster our own will, and occasionally we ought to put some money in the offering-plate, so that we too are helping a little bit.
Q: And if we do not do that for God?
A: Then God won't help us much either.

The child articulated the possibility of influencing God with good works. In response to the question, why Jesus told the parable of the workers in the vineyard, she explained:

A: Maybe he wants to show something else; that we can do better. And he uses an example like in the other stories.
Q: And what does he want to show us?
A: Maybe when we are in a position to hire an apprentice that we ought to give him or her an hourly wage. That we must not give very little to some and a lot more to the others.

It is hardly surprising that the girl rejects the transposition of the landowner's qualities onto God with emotional vehemence:

Q: And if I tell you now that the owner of the vineyard is an image for God, that God would act similarly—what would you say?
A: That is certainly wrong. God would have paid the same hourly wage to all workers.
Q: And why?
A: God would have wanted that all receive the same wage for the hours they worked.
Q: Does God in fact act that way or not?
A: God makes sure that everything is just, that everyone gets what he or she deserves.

"Thus God acts like the landowner . . ." wrote Joachim Jeremias (1966, p. 111). The girl, however, was in no way willing to alter *her* interpretation, not even after unambiguous interventions of the interviewer:

Q: Listen to me: actually, this story wants to show how caring God is, that God gives more than God has to. The owner of the vineyard did not have to give that much. He could have given the last ones only five dollars, but he did give them more simply out of love. And God acts the same way. What do you think?
A: It simply isn't right. He could have already stated in the morning that there would be an hourly wage. I don't think he likes those hired in the morning. He would have to give them more, too. It just isn't right.
Q: And if we regard the story as an image, as a comparison, attempting to illustrate God's goodness to us?
A: That is not true; the story simply wants to show that there are better ways of settling matters than the landowner's way. It is an example of how things should not be done.

Here, too, exists an obvious structural isomorphism between the religious judgement and the pupil's interpretation which, to her, was fully binding and plausible. In both domains she employs structural elements like bipolar reciprocity, punishment-reward, etc.

A structurally isomorphous interpretation of this parable was also provided by one respondent, age twenty-five, who was assessed as stage 1-2 transitional. At best, she managed to interpret the biblical text as a moral admonition against being envious like the early laborers.

Q: What did Jesus want to achieve with this story?
A: He probably wanted to see what people are like, he wanted to test them.
Q: Which people?
A: Those people. Or, he just wanted to test how they get along with each other, whether they would quarrel, become envious, or be satisfied.

Both the owner of the vineyard as well as God are perceived by this respondent through "the window" of her stage of religious judgement; both were accepted as authoritarian entities who more or less determine human fate. People must be obedient to them and engage in preventive, sanction-avoiding behavior. The structural elements which determine this respondent's relation to the Ultimate (bipolar reciprocity, external expectation-pressure, the punishment/reward pattern) consistently characterized her interpretation of the parable.

Quite different are the interpretations of respondents at stage 3. Most of them spontaneously performed allegorical transformations in order to "equilibrate" the parable with their religious self-understanding. For example, one respondent, age twenty-five, who understands God as a contrafactual entity conceding to humans their own domain for decision making without interfering in it, brought into focus stage 3's typical structural element of solipsistic human autonomy:

Q: And what did Jesus intend to convey with this parable?
A: Exactly what I mentioned before: that there is always a possibility to join the church or a religious community, regardless when one receives a call; one can join whenever one wants to.
Q: What do you perceive as the most important element in the text?
A: Exactly that—and I clearly see it in this parable—that one can change one's life at any time . . . at three o'clock, five o'clock, that is transposed to one's life.

The different hours of the day, thus, are interpreted as different stages in the life cycle, and the core of the parable is seen to consist in the theme of always being in charge of one's religious dispositions. Thus, this interpretation exhibits the autonomy which persons achieve at stage 3 and which is not yet present in the interview excerpts of the respondents quoted above. In contrast to those, this twenty-five-year-old respondent no longer perceives the parable as an exhortation. When confronted with the typical interpretations of persons at earlier stages, he reacted negatively.

A twenty-three-year-old respondent made a similar statement. She remembered quite well how, in religious education, she had found the story unjust and had not been willing to connect it with God. At the time of the interview, however, she affirmed the parable and mined it for the structural elements typical of stage 3, i.e., responsibility for oneself and the engagement by the individual. These she ascribed to the day laborers:

Q: In your view, what might be the deeper meaning (of the parable)?
A: In my opinion, the deeper meaning concerns the fact that the laborers are freely engaging in a service and by their own decision want to do something, want to apply themselves. It's not a question of being evaluated by the owner but rather of the quality of the engagement, that one fully applies oneself, works hard without regard for the owner's assessment.

When asked if the parable has anything to do with the kingdom of God, she responded:

A: Yes, somehow, for if such a realm indeed exists, then surely it will not have any evaluations. But I am not a person to just wait until God decides to establish such a realm—that's not what I believe anyway. It really depends all on us humans, how the world is ordered and managed, whether it is just or unjust.

This response, too, is dominated by the responsibility for oneself and the autonomy typical for stage 3. God can no longer directly intervene in the affairs of the world—such as "to establish his realm," as assumed by those children who identify the kingdom of God with a concrete sphere of authority ruled by God.

At stage 4, finally, all respondents, even those who had not listened to a sermon for years, presented interpretations which were compatible, even identical, with those of prominent exegetes:

Q: Do you find the image of God provided by the parable still acceptable?
A: Yes, I do. It does not contradict my image of God, the Creator. The God in the parable does not act according to human standards, but rather is

truly generous. And that is how I view God, the Creator, that he is quite different from those gods which are floating around in our culture.

This interpretation comes from a man, age forty-two, who has long been alienated from the church. In all the interviews, he massively rejected the "merchant-image" of God which portrays God as rewarding persons according to their achievements and punishing them according to their offenses. Rather, he was able to understand and accept the goodness of the vineyard's owner as a metaphor for God being the one who always makes human action possible and who is concerned with free people who themselves act in goodness toward their neighbors.

Interestingly, a woman, age fifty, reconstrued the parable entirely according to the line of thought of the theologian, Aurelio (1977, pp. 174f.), without ever having heard of him.

Q: And does God act like the owner of the vineyard?
A: Yes, I would think so. God comes to us humans again and again just like the man who went to the market square again and again. He does not want to disappoint those who trust in him, he approaches them, wants to provide them with work and wages.

The respondent remembered how she had understood this parable as a child, i.e., as unjust and unbelievable. Only in later years and only after she had grown into a new relationship with God did the current interpretation begin to make sense to her.

Figure 11 shows the aforementioned types of interpretation in relation to the stages of religious judgement.

A: The parable demands that no one is to be envious like the early workers.
B: The parable summons everyone not to imitate the unjust actions of the master.
C: The parable is an offer for one's self-actualization and for one's engagement which can take different allegorical forms.
D: The parable portrays the goodness of God, the kingdom of God.

Moralizing interpretations of the parable, which are characterized by bipolar reciprocity and an "authoritarian" image of God, were encountered most frequently at the earlier stages of the religious judgement. Those of type C, which are based on the structural elements of solipsistic autonomy and individual responsibility even toward God, center around the third stage. The interpretations of type D, which correspond to the normative-theological interpretations—for instance, in Bible commentaries or religious textbooks—

Figure 11: Types of Interpretations of Matthew 20:1f and the Stages of Religious Judgement

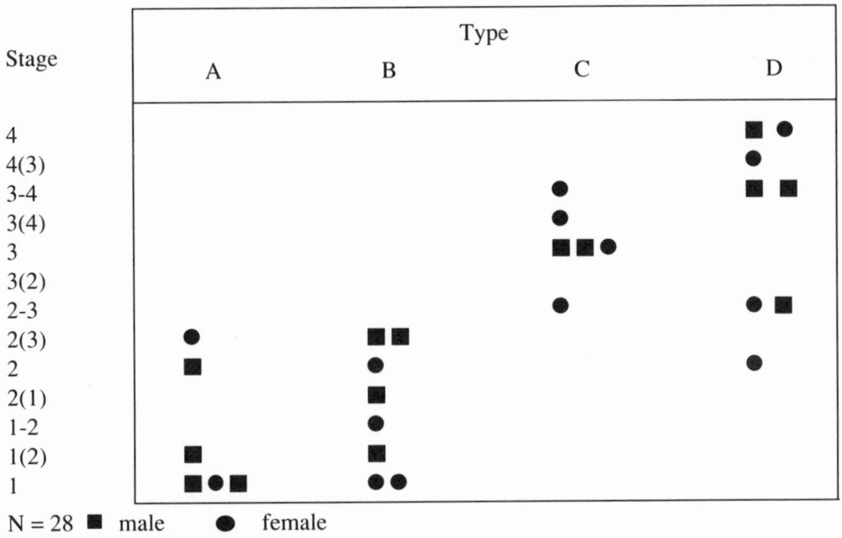

Stage	Type A	Type B	Type C	Type D
4				■ ●
4(3)				●
3-4			●	■ ■
3(4)			●	
3			■ ■ ●	
3(2)				
2-3			●	● ■
2(3)	●	■ ■		
2	■	●		●
2(1)		■		
1-2		●		
1(2)	■	■		
1	■ ● ■	● ●		

N = 28   ■ male   ● female

exhibit a broader spread, although with a clear concentration at stage 4.

The results were similar in regard to the parable of the talents (Mt 25:14f; cf. Figure 12). That parable tells about a businessman about to embark on a long journey calling his three servants together and entrusting them with some money. The first two doubled their amount through smart and courageous business deals; the third one, however, was scared and buried his money. After his return, the businessman held the servants accountable. He rewarded the first two very generously; the third one was reprimanded and fired.

In their interpretations, the theologians (Weder, 1984; Jeremias, 1966, et al.) emphasize that the text does not represent a threat regarding God's judgement or Christ's return (both of whom may be represented by the businessman). Rather it shows that God has given us his "kingdom" and our talents which we are to apply in freedom in order to create space for the kingdom of God which, like the money in the parable, wants to grow dynamically (Weiser, 1971, pp. 262f).

The data indicate that respondents at earlier stages of the development of religious cognition actually do construe the parable as a threat concerning God's judgement. Only respondents at stage 4 reconstructed and spontaneously submitted theologically adequate interpretations. Quite a few respondents, however, rejected such interpretations as too "naive" and an inappropriate description for God (for they viewed the parable as reflecting a stage 2 image of God).

A: The parable summons one to engagement on behalf of God, like the first two servants; otherwise one gets punished.

B: The story suggests not to treat other people too harshly, not like the master treated his servants; otherwise one will be treated by God just as harshly.

C: The parable calls us to actualize ourselves in freedom and to develop our talents.

D: I reject this parable as too primitive and too naive; God does not reward and punish like the employer in the story.

E: The narrative is an appeal to share, in freedom, the gifts which God has first given me so that the kingdom of God may be advanced.

Figure 12: Types of Interpretations of Matthew 25:14f and Stages of Religious Judgement

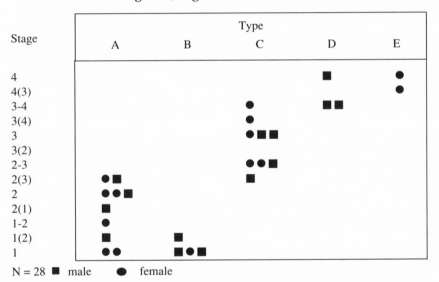

N = 28 ■ male   ● female

Pedagogical and Didactic Implications

We can draw three educational implications:

1) The work students perform with texts is intended to lead to a higher stage of religious development or, put differently, to increased religious autonomy.[1] Religiosity becomes the process of coping with contingency situations revealing—with increasing freedom and critique—the relation between individuals and the Ultimate. This cannot happen directly, but only

---

1. A more detailed explanation of this goal and concept of religious education can be found in Oser's book, *Wieviel Religion braucht der Mensch?*

when teachers encourage students to develop new arguments for themselves and to question or transform familiar ones. For this end the developmental model can provide an interpretive frame which is otherwise unavailable.

Applied concretely to the parables this means: students whose interpretations of Matthew 25:14f (the parable of the talents) feature the punishment-reward scheme—i.e., believers must be industrious servants in order to be rewarded by God—should be engaged in role-play and transactive discussion of so-called n+1 arguments (Blatt/Kohlberg, 1975) in order to develop to the point where they themselves recognize the responsibility of people for that which has been entrusted to them. In role-play and transactive discussion they can also emancipate themselves from the image of the punishing and rewarding God. The new interpretation of the parable is more autonomous in the sense that it is no longer understood as exhortation (*paranesis*) nor as threat.

2) The adaptive activity in working with texts must be underscored. Children perform processes of religious interpretations without any initial change in the fundamental structure of religious reasoning and without the beginnings of a stage transition. But while in use, this structure undergoes an extension or widening which leads to the achievement of religious identity. This horizontal aspect is frequently neglected. In their application, cognitive structures must be stimulated with an intent toward greater flexibility; otherwise they deteriorate.

In regard to the biblical parables and metaphors it becomes therefore necessary to create a sensibility for image and metaphorical language. This may, for instance, be achieved by initially remaining for a long time with the image of a text and only later attempting to deduce or abstract issues from it. Consider, for example, Mark 4:30-32: "The kingdom of God . . . is like a mustard seed, which, when sown upon the ground, is the smallest of all the seeds on the earth; yet when it is sown it grows up and becomes the greatest of all shrubs" (NRSV). Before any conclusions are drawn about the kingdom of God, students should be afforded the opportunity to plant seeds (e.g., wheat seeds) and to observe their growth. This is just as applicable to the action sequences in the parables: Students should role-play and experience them before they interpret them in their theological intentions. However, this would mean for religious education that much less content and fewer biblical texts would be treated thematically, although those that are addressed would be dealt with much more intensively.

3) We must consider, however, that the interpretations of the biblical texts in general and of the parables in particular must be accomplished by the students. We must maintain with Halbfas (1968, p. 265) that "a textbook must never just give answers to students. Rather they must be forced to reach the answers themselves in a process of wrestling with the texts step-by-step." To that end, however, the students' structures of religious judgement

must be taken into account. Although the textbook interpretations are generally theologically adequate, they frequently presuppose capacities of knowing which are not yet available to the students. This means that teachers cannot simply start with biblical commentaries and they ought not try to transfer these onto the students in a one-way fashion. Rather, teachers must accept as valuable the students' interpretations as such and as the best possible ones. Because they correspond to the students' respective stages of religious development, they are appropriate interpretations. Only in a secondary approach can teachers attempt to introduce new interpretation elements. Even then, they must take into consideration the reconstructive reaction of the students. This means, for instance, that children often perceive the contrary intention of the text, as was demonstrated repeatedly with the parable of the workers in the vineyard (Mt 20:1f): "God would never act like the owner of the vineyard. God would pay just wages." This interpretation, too, although contrary to the normative theological one, must be recognized as someone's best religious judgement. If the teacher immediately questions it or brushes it aside as false, he or she can discourage a child from reading and interpreting the Bible independently. Furthermore, he or she may thus be practicing—although in a weakened form—religious indoctrination which disregards the child as a subject and views him or her instead as an immature object to be taught. This is an attitude which, rightfully and frequently, has led to criticism of religious education.

The intention of all these normative statements is to indicate that the final goal, particularly of Bible didactics, is the formation of autonomous readers of the Bible; that is, receivers who no longer *tale quale* accept interpretations from others but become hermeneutically active themselves, unlock texts for themselves, and acquire for themselves the instruments for interpretation (Oser, 1987).

Does this mean that theologically adequate interpretations have completely lost their normative claims and need no longer be consulted? Does this open the door to a limitless subjectivism, as is occasionally critiqued in regard to literature aesthetics (Iser, 1984, pp. 43f)? Certainly not. The convergence between the theological interpretations and those that are plausible and comprehensible for individuals remains a long-distance goal of religious education and Bible didactics. That goal cannot be achieved by jumping to it via simple information transmission or indoctrination. Rather, it will take a long time and will, in any case, appear in the transformation of religious deep-structures. This holds true for children, adolescents, and adults—in short, none other than the recipients who, metaphorically speaking, again and again "breathe life" into texts of all sorts, including biblical ones. For: *Quidquid recipitur, secundum modum recipientis recipitur.*

Religious Pedagogy in a Structural Developmental Mode?

To what degree has religious education taken seriously the aforementioned statement by Thomas Aquinas? If one takes a look at the history of this discipline, which for a long time was conceived only as the application of dogmatics and exegetics, one soon discovers that children and their religious development have frequently been neglected, just as the fact that children interpret religious contents differently from adults (cf. Loch, 1964). Rather, children were regarded as *objects* to be tamed and taught. Religious education was based on the catechism. Lecture and memorization were the common methods.

Since Wegenast's (1968) call for the "empirical turn" in religious education, the field has opened itself to the social sciences and adapted theories of developmental psychology. Now there are theories of religious education that are especially indebted to Erikson (1966; Fraas, 1973, 1983), oriented toward socialization research (Morgenthaler, 1976), and grounded in Piaget (Goldman, 1964, 1971).

However, even a cursory look at the current trends in religious education, especially those favored by the (German) churches, indicates that several deficiencies made apparent by the structural developmental approach have not yet been addressed. On the contrary, there are signs of a return to a content-oriented kerygmatic concept in which proclamation and dogma are dominant (Englert, 1986).* After lengthy and nonproductive debates on method, Kasper (1987, pp. 67f) demands that the center of religious education should consist of the core contents and dogmas of the church. Developmental theories (such as Kohlberg's) are accused of "marginalizing" the seriousness of the Christian message, such as the experience of guilt (Schmidt, 1986, pp. 158f). From the perspective of a structural developmental approach such a trend raises concerns. It runs the risk of labeling children once again as mere recipients of orthodoxy and of those dogmas to which is ascribed a metaphysical status-in-itself (cf. Werbick's critique, 1985). However, this overlooks the fundamental insight of literature aesthetics (and therewith of Thomas Aquinas) as well as of structural developmental theory. It overlooks that contents, including religious contents, are not only actively affected by their recipients but actually first activated in that process.

Similar problems are mentioned in commentaries on textbooks. They are still mostly concerned with theological reflections about correct interpreta-

---

*. Translator's note: While this diagnosis reflects the situation in Central Europe, it might serve as an encouragement to North American readers to examine the current trends in their context, particularly in light of the churches' reactions to recent revelations (e.g., Gallup, SEARCH Institute) concerning widespread theological and biblical illiteracy among the laity.

tions of biblical texts and with methods best suited to convey those interpretations in class. A contemporary example are the teachers' commentaries
by Halbfas (1983, 1984, 1985). They are chock-full of religious studies and
theological analyses of symbols and metaphorical texts, whose essence must
be imparted to the children without employing any insights from educational or developmental psychology. Rather, children are assumed to possess
a so-called "third eye" (Halbfas, 1982), i.e., the capacity to understand symbols already on a first-grade level. This is a serious relapse into an obsolete
Christian anthropology which assumes that an inborn "religious organ"
enables children to comprehend religious things, even catechetical statements, one way or another.

It appears as if the "Copernican turn" has not yet taken place in religious
education, i.e., the shift which moved children and their religious actions
and interpretations into the center and which assumed that they can be
"exegetically" active and interpreting on their own.

Chapter Seven

Validation of the Stage-Concept of Religious Judgement

The stages of religious development postulated by us can be validated empirically. This chapter introduces a cross-sectional research project which we conducted with 112 persons of different ages in the clock and watch manufacturing town, Grenchen, Switzerland. The clearest result of this study is an unambiguous age-related trend until age twenty-five. This means that the stage-progression of religious judgement corresponds to an increase in the participants' age. Other interesting results are: (a) across almost all dilemmas employed by us, persons' responses were stable as far as the stages of their religious judgement were concerned; (b) no denominational differences were discovered; (c) persons in old age seem to judge again at lower stages; and (d) socially speaking, members of the middle and upper classes seem more likely to develop higher stages of religious judgement than members of the lower class. All of these results contribute to the strengthening of the validity of the stage-concept, "religious judgement."[1]

In order to generalize the stage-concept of religious development a series of studies is necessary to fulfill various theoretical requirements. We are introducing several such studies toward the end of this chapter after we have made a few statements about the issues related to measuring religious judgement.

---

1. We would like to thank the pastors of the participating congregations, and especially the principals of the schools and the city officials of the city of Grenchen for their support in gathering the data.

170

Introduction, Research Sample, Controlled Independent Variables

It might be interesting to the reader to obtain more detailed information about our research study. We included in the research project ten age groups representing three different denominations. The major issues and questions concerned (a) developmental-psychological tendencies; (b) general differences among the distinct groups (e.g., denominational differences); and (c) differences in regard to various contents and the different dilemmas.

Our first study was conducted in a town far removed from the influence of a university, i.e., Grenchen, in Solothurn County, Switzerland. Grenchen is home to the clock and watch manufacturing industry. The 20,000 residents divide almost evenly among Roman Catholics (44 percent) and the Reformed (46 percent). Eight percent are Old Catholics. Two issues were of importance when we selected the research sample:

1. The sample should come from a typical Swiss town with a mixed economic structure, e.g., industry, business and trade, and agriculture.

2. The residents ought to divide evenly among the main denominations.*

Various questions and issues were under consideration. The major points were:

1. Does a developmental-psychological trend, confirming the stage theory, actually exist or is it impossible to characterize the stage-differences as age-specific?

2. Does the stage-sequence show differences in regard to denomination, gender, socio-economic class, and education?

3. Are there stage differences that could be attributed to differences in the content of the situations described in various dilemmas rather than to structural development? If these differences are significant, they would have to be designated as *décalages* or they would be in contradiction to the theory.

These three issues will lead into the hypotheses elaborated below.

The sample comprised 112 persons of the following age groups: 8-9, 11-12, 14-15, 17-18, 20-25, 26-35, 36-45, 46-55, 56-65, and 66-75. Each age group had an equal number of male and female members. Religious membership was another controlled variable. Approximately, half of the partic-

---

*Translator's note: In terms of religious pluralism, Switzerland, like most European countries, is different from the United States of America. There are fewer denominations, but they are much larger in size. The predominant ones in Central Europe are the Roman Catholic, the Reformed, and the Lutheran Church, as well as a combination of the latter two, the Evangelical Church of the Union. There are, however, various smaller groups.

ipants were Roman Catholic (N=49) and Reformed (N=47). In the age groups 8-9 and 11-12 we also distinguished the Old Catholic tradition (N=16). The educational level and the socio-economic status (SES) of the adult participants (age 20 and up) varied according to chance. The adult participants of the study represent a random selection from the city statistics of Grenchen. The children and youth were chosen at random from Grenchen schools.

In addition, two self-assessments and the socio-economic status (SES) of the adult participants ascertained:
1. their interest in religious issues and questions;
2. their basic religious attitude: believer or nonbeliever (not presented here);
3. the socio-economic status of the adult participants.

Research-Design, Data-Gathering, and Presentation of the Dilemmas

The research-design contains statements about the order in which the various dilemmas were presented for we had realized that it was impossible to give all eight dilemmas to every participant because of a tiring effect.

Each participant was presented four of the eight dilemmas described below. The selection and the sequence of the dilemma presentations for each participant occurred in a balanced distribution of all possible cyclical variations of the numerical columns listed below. The numbers represent the eight dilemmas.

For example, participant 1:   1 2 3 4
                            2:    2 3 4 5
                            3:    3 4 5 6
                            4:    4 5 6 7
                            5:    5 6 7 8
                            6:    6 7 8 1
                            7:    7 8 1 2
                            8:    8 1 2 3 etc.

This procedure assured that the various types of dilemmas were presented equally often, though in eight different sequences, in order to control certain seriation-effects. The number of participants in each age group varied between four and eight persons.

For the gathering of the data we intensively trained twelve students of the Pedagogical Institute of the University of Zurich in the procedure of the "semi-clinical" interview. If a dilemma-discussion is to yield good results, it is necessary to assure an in-depth and personal discussion of the dilemma at hand as well as an intensive give-and-take communication between the discussion partners. The goals of the training were to convey the significance of the following for the interview process:

1. The creation of a pleasant climate; making the issues and questions at hand optimally transparent for each participant; openness for any type of communication.

2. Obtaining certainty that the dilemma has been understood and that the research-subject is able to develop an experiential grasp of the situation.

3. Asking follow-up questions, because the cognitive structure is relevant and because the response-competence of the participant must be unearthed.

4. Answers are informative for their religious reasoning rather than their compiling of action-alternatives.

First, we developed a series of dilemmas. They originated by asking a variety of persons about their religious experiences. From the numerous experiences of the respondents we selected those which, on the one hand, created in the listener a certain disequilibrim, and which, on the other hand, brought to expression certain pairs of religious dimensions. In a pilot-study we attempted to measure the degree of the various disequilibria.

The dilemmas were presented in such a way that, in some dilemmas, the word "God" appeared in the dilemma description. In other cases, especially in the case of the dilemmas pertaining to issues of guilt (numbers 4 and 5), the reference to the Transcendent appears explicitly only in the catalogue of standardized questions. In the following we are presenting a survey of the individual dilemmas.

1: Paul-dilemma

In this dilemma, the promise (made to God in a critical situation) to renounce a successful career is opposed to a strong need for security in career and personal life.

Before his wedding, a young physician takes a plane trip. The plane has technical difficulties and is heading for a crash. In his great distress the young man makes a significant promise to God which he will fulfill if he survives. He is the sole survivor, and back home he is offered a very good position. Should he keep his promise?

2: Job-dilemma

This dilemma deals with the question of theodicy. It asks about the being and nature of God in the face of suffering in the world.

In a small town lives a well-respected, devout judge. He is very thankful to God for his happy life and he engages himself personally on behalf of the poor. Without any fault of his own he loses his good reputation and has to resign from office. Unfortunately, his daughter falls very ill. All his savings become used up for medical expenses. Yet, the daughter does not get better. How shall he act toward God in this situation?

Dilemma 3: Unjust Suffering

This dilemma deals with the issue of theodicy in a different way. In this case, the one who proclaims God's message is struck with suffering.

A pastor who engages himself for the well-being of his congregation is attacked by an insidious and incurable eye disease. Despite earnest prayers he becomes completely blind. He is plagued by great doubts about his faith. He begins to question the righteousness of God. A friend suggests to renounce his faith in God, because it is nonsense. How shall he respond to his friend?

Dilemma 4: Eternal Salvation

In the face of death, a persons rejects any sort of comfort, mercy, any relationship with God.

A criminal accused of murdering a father and his three children is sentenced to life in prison. He demands to be put to death. The judge accommodates him. The criminal refuses to see the prison chaplain. Some people think that perhaps the widow and mother of the murdered victims could make him change his mind. What shall the widow do?

Dilemma 5: Guilt-dilemma

In the face of death, forgiveness is to be given for having caused unbelievable suffering. Faith in forgiveness is opposed to hatred.

A German baker lives as a respected citizen. Yet, a rumor is going around that he was an SS-commander at a concentration camp and responsible for the death of thousands of Jews. He himself knows that the rumor is true. One day, he is seriously injured in an automobile accident. A passer-by happens to be a Jewish physician who escaped from the camp headed by the baker. They recognize each other. The dying baker begs the physician for forgiveness. Shall the physician grant it?

Dilemma 6: Love-dilemma

Love as a supportive power is opposed to the doubt about its power in the face of a deadly disease.

A young woman suffers from a terminal blood disease. She falls in love with a successful politician and faces the problem of whether to inform him of her illness. She fears he might leave her and that she might be in his way. He protests and stresses that he would like to marry her in any case. However, she still entertains the thought of leaving him without telling him. What should she do? How shall we judge her thoughts?

Dilemma 7: Suicide-dilemma

The value of human life is opposed to the meaning-making power of a career.

For thirty years, a chemist has been participating in the research and development of a fuel which is supposed to be cheaper, more effective, and less damaging to the environment than gasoline currently used. One day he discovers the decisive chemical formula. His life-goal has been reached.

At night the laboratory catches on fire. As the chemist tries to enter the burning building, he is held back by a fire-fighter. Yet, the researcher wants to enter the house by all means; without his documentation, life would lose all its meaning. What shall the fire-fighter do?

Dilemma 8: Marriage-dilemma

An obligation to a church community is opposed to personal needs.

In a South American country, a young Roman Catholic woman and a Protestant pastor from Switzerland, who is fully loyal to his church, get involved. The young woman gets pregnant. Both would like to move to Switzerland and get married. When applying for a marriage license, the young woman is faced with having to leave the Roman Catholic Church which is very meaningful to her. If she does not renounce her church, her home country will not issue the papers needed for the marriage. She is plagued by heavy scruples. Yet, she would like to marry the young man. What shall she do?

The questions pertaining to these eight dilemmas correspond to those of the Paul-dilemma. They are conceived in close resemblance. They consist of approximately sixteen questions divided into different clusters. Each of the questions elicits certain elements of the interviewee's structure of religious judgement. However, their primary function is to encourage the respondent to produce an equilibrium between the seven of the bi-polar dimensions listed in chapter one.

Again, we designate the interview as semi-standardized, because the same questions are given to each person but each person is pushed for the reasoning for his or her decision until he or she can no longer go beyond his or her own competency. The stimulation takes the form of questions like, "Please, explain further" or "Why do you think this or that is the case?" One purpose of leading persons to the limits of their respective competence is to obtain as much material as possible in order to abstract the structure with as much validity as possible. The standardized questions guarantee further that the interviewees do not drift onto a meta-level or articulate general confessional statements but rather stay attuned to the dilemma as closely as possible. Only material which illuminates the relationship between an individual and the Ultimate (God) in a concrete situation can be used for analysis. All other materials could, at best, be used for the study of conceptual types.

Data Analysis, Hypotheses and their Rationale

The hypotheses constitute a core element of the theory of religious development. With their aid we will attempt to examine whether the most important elements of the whole concept can be falsified. As long as falsification is possible, we can at least maintain that the theory cannot be easily dismissed. Important hypotheses refer to the age-related trend, the special case of old age, differences in denominational membership, gender, educational level, socio-economic status, and finally the assumption that all dilemmas provoke the same structure of religious reasoning (trans-situationality).

All of the 448 interview transcripts were coded by two raters. Rater A determined the global score, rater B coded the interviews according to the partial scores as well as according to the global score. The agreement between the partial scores and the global score was 85.0 percent; the agreement among the raters for all dilemmas was 70.13 percent. The coding process took place against the background of the stage descriptions and a provisional coding manual. The consistency (test-retest-reliability) across three weeks was .85 (Kendall's *tau*).

We have assigned the hypotheses to three groups:

1. Group: Age Trend and Old-Age Hypothesis
(1a) Age Trend

Until age twenty-five, the stage level of the religious judgement increases with increasing age. That means that the older a person grows the greater the probability that he or she will grow correspondingly in his or her stage of religious judgement. (If this hypothesis can be confirmed it would mean that all of the subsequent analyses would only be meaningful within the same age-group, since otherwise the stage-results would be confounded with the age-variable.)

If the age hypothesis can be confirmed, we can assume, at least partially, a sequence of religious stages. Complete sequentiality can only be proven, however, with longitudinal data.

We must also stress that we are postulating the age-trend when it is measured across all dilemmas and persons but also when it is measured only with the main-dilemma, the story about Paul.

The reasoning for this hypothesis about the influence of age on the development of religious judgement is based on the fact that "sample tests of individuals (S1-Sn) from different age groups (A1-An) are studied once (O1) with the same or a comparable measuring instrument at a certain point in time (T1)" (Trautner, 1978, p. 21). Thereby, the issue is not the constitution of an age-trend, since age is not a psychological value. Rather, it is merely possible to assume correlational connections with probable, surmised factors of influence.

Although in our trial-design we did not determine population-groups in advance according to intelligence, emotional stability, social background, etc., the age-variable is nonetheless important for supporting the progression-hypothesis and for legitimizing the stage-inclusion model (cf. Flavell, 1983).

1b) Adult Age and Maturity

The stage level remains relatively stable during the adult years. No regression can be detected in old age.

The stability- and nonregression-hypothesis has been discussed in many essays and articles. Schaie (1979, pp. 185f), for example, pointed out that this hypothesis is still meaningful. It assumes that the organism at the point of maturity has assimilated from the environment all the information of significance for the variables of the measuring process so that no structural growth in knowledge is necessary. The regression-hypothesis, however, is mainly being discussed in the field of intelligence-research (cf. Wechsler, 1972). There it is assumed that the "construct" intelligence begins to regress at about age twenty-five and that regression can be calculated by means of the so-called regression-coefficient. In contrast, we assume that the pattern of cognitive religious judgement is not dissembled and does not regress with increasing age, since we are dealing with structures. What regresses or is dissembled in the construct intelligence are: knowledge, general understanding, mathematical thought, discovery of comparisons, etc., i.e., predominantly contents. Structures, however, which underlie those contents, as well as the content-related capabilities, can only remain stable or progress.

2. Group: Denomination, Education, Status, Gender
2a) Denominational Affiliation

This factor has no general influence on the stage development of persons' religious judgement. Denominational affiliation is clearly a content-aspect and not a structural aspect of the religious judgement. Furthermore, we cannot assume that one denomination offers more opportunities for dealing with religious issues than another. If impulses for change are the possible disequilibria in the explanatory matrix of the seven fundamental dimensions, then a difference-hypothesis would mean that reasons must be supplied for the fact that such opportunities are more frequent in one denomination than in another.

2b) Education

A person's level of formal education does exert an influence on the stage development of the religious judgement. The higher a person's educational level, the greater the probability that this person's religious judgement is more developed than that of a person with less education. (This can be explained with reference to the higher, generally cognitive prerequisites for higher stages.)

2c) *Socio-economic Status (SES)*

The higher a person's SES, the greater the probability that his or her stage of religious judgement is higher too. The differences in education and social status are derived from the study of Candee (1978) which we deem important. It shows that upper-level professional positions correlate with a higher stage of religious judgement at an above-random frequency. The probability that persons in leading positions "need" stage 4 in order to create a transparent, interactive climate of justice is higher than the probability of persons in lower-level positions reaching stage 4.

2d) *Gender Differences*

Generally, there exist no gender differences. However, we suspect that among adolescents between the ages of fourteen and eighteen, girls, on average, develop higher stages of religious judgement than boys. This hypothesis relates to studies with gender-specific questions (cf., for example, Oser, 1981, pp. 397f; Kürthy, 1978; Weitz, 1977).[2]

3. Group: Trans-situationality
3a) *Trans-situational Consistency*

A person employs the same structural pattern of religious reasoning across various dilemmas which differ in regard to content.

3b) *Horizontal Décalage "Guilt"*

In the case of dilemmas 4 and 5, which deal with the issue of guilt, persons at stage 3 display a tendency toward stage 2 when compared with the other dilemmas. (This hypothesis is not sharply distinguished from the first one, since we do not expect significant differences but only trends and tendencies.) No other regression-effects are expected across the different dilemmas. The differences between the median score are not singularly concentrated but distributed normally.

3c) *Horizontal Décalage "Church"*

We assume further that persons exhibit tendencies toward stage 3 when church-related values and content are addressed. (We say this, however, without expecting differences of any significance.)

---

2. In this context we must note our critical stance toward the work of Gilligan (1977, 1982) who attempts to demonstrate that women deal with reality in a different cognitive fashion than men and that the development of moral judgement in women follows a different stage-design than that of men. We believe Gilligan is pointing to differences in regard to content rather than lifting up structural differences. Independent of that discussion, however, we must follow the deliberations of theories of maturation and assume that during certain age-spans girls generally are developed further than boys.

The verification of the hypotheses concerning trans-situational consistency is an important piece for validating the stage-hierarchy. Trans-situationality means that persons employ the same structure of religious judgement in *different* dilemma situations. Little empirical evidence is available documenting that persons apply different stage patterns in different situations (cf. the discussion about domain-specificity, Seiler, 1973; Nisan, 1981). Thus it must be correct that the structural patterns and their hierarchical ordering in stages represent trans-situational, consistent entities. As such they are a function of the complexity of a certain environment and of age (cf. Levine, 1979, p. 228). The structural forms become more differentiated when the environment increasingly stimulates the discussion of religious problems, the religious interpretation of interactionist problems, the employment of new forms of religious meaning-making of reality, and the correlation of religious dimensions of interpretation with other forms of coping with reality. Neither the content of the dilemmas nor the various situations stimulate stage-development. Rather, development is stimulated through the employment of progressive-developmental methods which present religion as that particular perspective of human reality which facilitates the possibility for renewal and transcendence of human existence (cf. Rössler, 1976, pp. 123f).

According to our theory, it must be possible to obtain one particular stage pattern from all of the aforementioned dilemmas. If cases were discovered where different dilemmas would yield significantly different stages (e.g., stages 5 and 2), we would have to conclude that the trans-situational hypothesis is incorrect, and the "structural" element in the system would be on shaky ground. Minor stage-differences, however, can be attributed to (a) errors or mistakes in the measuring process, and/or (b) horizontal *décalage* (timelag) as Piaget describes it, and/or (c) certain situational influences.

In extreme cases one might suggest that stage-differences are a result of "segmentation," i.e., the phenomenon of persons disclaiming or changing or conforming their own judgement under social pressure (cf. Döbert/Nunner-Winkler, 1975, p. 107). One could also speak of "partial regression."

We assume that neither any significant differences between the dilemmas nor a demonstratable regression-effect will be detected.

We base this assumption on the presupposition that the progression of the stages can be proven to be valid, i.e., that our first hypothesis is clearly verifiable with cross-sectional data.

Results

Most of the results presented here confirm the hypotheses. The general age-trend until age twenty-five deserves probably the most attention, for in the case of blind ratings a different distribution of the stages is easily possible. Further important results are the absence of denominational or confessional differences. This result points to the fact that structures — at least to a great extent — go beyond different contents, i.e., structures must not be explained with reference to denominational practices. The independence of the structures from content is also explained by the fact that, in most cases, different dilemmas lead indeed to the same stage results.

However, we must also refer to empirical facts which falsify one of our hypotheses. We initially assumed that no structural "regression" occurs in old age. But our data showed the opposite, and although we only have a few interviews, that fact initiated much speculation and debate.

1. Group: Age Trend and Nonregression

We stated that up to age twenty-five, the development of religious judgement dovetails with chronological age. The results are presented in Figure 13. This table clearly shows that stage 1 occurs most frequently at age 8-9, that it almost completely disappears at age 14-15, and that at age 17-18 it is no longer present at all. Stage 2 shows a transposed trend: It is most frequent at age 11-12 but vanishes completely with age 20-25. Stage 3 surfaces first at age 11-12; it is most frequent in the age-group 20-25. Finally, we also see an

Figure 13: Percentages of Stage 1, Stage 2, Stage 3, Stage 4 responses in various age-groups (comprising all dilemmas)

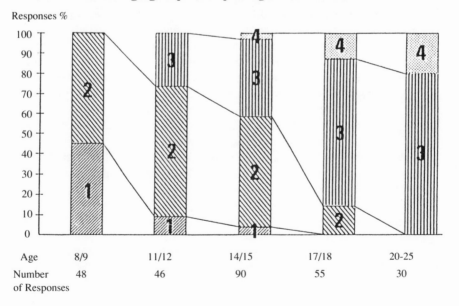

Responses %

Age	8/9	11/12	14/15	17/18	20-25
Number of Responses	48	46	90	55	30

increasing age-trend for stage 4 beginning at age 14-15.

The entire picture reveals a correlation between aging and the development of religious judgement. (Let us emphasize again that this does not mean that age is a psychological value. It is nearly impossible to identify all the socialization effects that influence the age-trend. Nonetheless, a clear age-trend confirms the developmental hypothesis.)

When we advanced the hypothesis that a stage-level remains stable during the adult years and does not regress in old age, we took a position against the regression-hypothesis. Figure 14 shows the results in regards to middle-adult ages and old age.

In Figure 14 it is immediately evident that no significant changes occur

Figure 14: Percentages of Stage 1, Stage 2, Stage 3, Stage 4 responses comprising all eight dilemmas for adult age

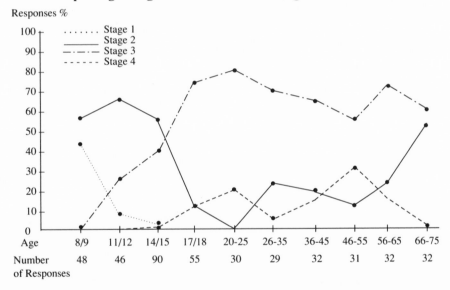

between the age-groups 20-25 and 56-65; one could only say that to the extent that stage 3 decreases, stage 4 shows an increasing development. This means a silent, almost undetectable increase until age 56-65. There is, however, a surprising sudden rupture at old age: The age-group 66-75 contains barely any persons at stage 4, and the number of those at stage 3 actually decreases. On the other hand, there is a tremendous increase in stage-2 judgements. How can this regression in old age be explained? Why must our hypothesis be rejected?

Let us look at Figure 15 where the same data are presented with median-values comprising all ages and dilemmas. The figure shows significant differences among the adult groups.

This is important concerning the stage regression in old age, because there the degree of regression is extreme. In the other adult age-groups the differences could be ascribed to sample-related effects, since the increases and decreases are similar. In other words, the extreme variations of the values would be related to the small number of persons forming one group. We must also consider that we hardly can make any statements in regard to the issue of randomness in small samples.

Figure 15: Average age-trend (age-trend hypothesis) of the religious judgement comprising all eight dilemmas

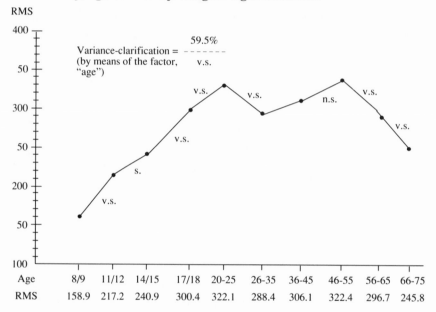

Age	8/9	11/12	14/15	17/18	20-25	26-35	36-45	46-55	56-65	66-75
RMS	158.9	217.2	240.9	300.4	322.1	288.4	306.1	322.4	296.7	245.8

n.s. = not significant
s.   = significant at the 0.05-level
v.s. = significant at the 0.01-level (very significant)
      (difference test with the Duncan-test)

Figure 16 clarifies again that regression in old age is of such a significance that it cannot be ascribed to the randomness of the sample. If we accept this age-trend as given, three explanations are possible:

a) We are dealing with an age-cohort effect. An argument against this position suggests that other age-cohorts, e.g., those persons now age 46-55 who grew up during WWII, should also show trends in one direction or another. Furthermore, it is doubtful that age-cohort effects can be detected with the rough measures of developmental psychology.

An argument in favor of the age-cohort effect is the fact that those generations growing up during and after WWII experienced enormous secular-

Figure 16: Influence of age on the stages of religious judgement without considering childhood and youth (comprising all dilemmas)

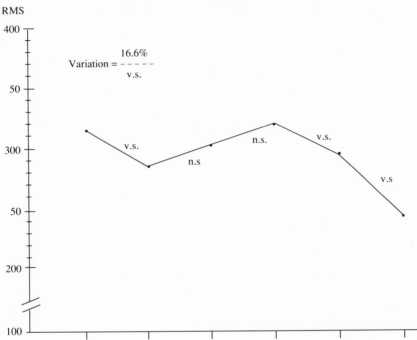

izization processes in their development from adolescence to adulthood. The older generation appears to have marshaled great resistance against those secularization processes.

b) We are dealing with a classical age-related regression-effect. Arguments against this position are those advanced in our explanation of the age-related regression-hypothesis. An argument in favor of this hypothesis suggests that the organism, during the process of general deterioration, can also slowly dissolve the deep-structures.

c) We are dealing with a so-called "age-related socialization process." This concept refers to the condition of disequilibrium into which persons of our times frequently slide after their retirement due to the loss of their function and meaning in society. In earlier societies, aging persons were entrusted with great tasks of providing counsel and decision making which drew on their experience and wisdom. Today, in contrast, persons are condemned to accepting their "learned helplessness," to find meaning in activities which are frequently socially irrelevant, etc. Thus, it could be stated that the particular socialization of aging and no-longer-employed persons would explain a stage-regression. An argument against this assumption is the lack of unambiguous evidence for such a social-ization effect. An argument in favor of this position suggests that, pre-sumably due to the changes in meaning, aging persons begin to draw more from and on the past — more so than younger generations. Thus, individual dilemmas will be answered more likely at stage 2 because its content reminds persons of certain experiences in their adolescence. This form of "compartmentalizing" is confirmed by the enormous breadth of intrapersonal spread across the various types of dilemmas among per-sons of old age.

The age-trend and regression hypotheses were tested with the same sam-ple by employing only our standard Paul-dilemma. The measures of only this one dilemma, i.e., not including the values of the other dilemmas, are shown in Figures 17-19 and in Table 1.

Figure 17: Absolute frequency of the stage-scores for all age-groups in the Paul-dilemma

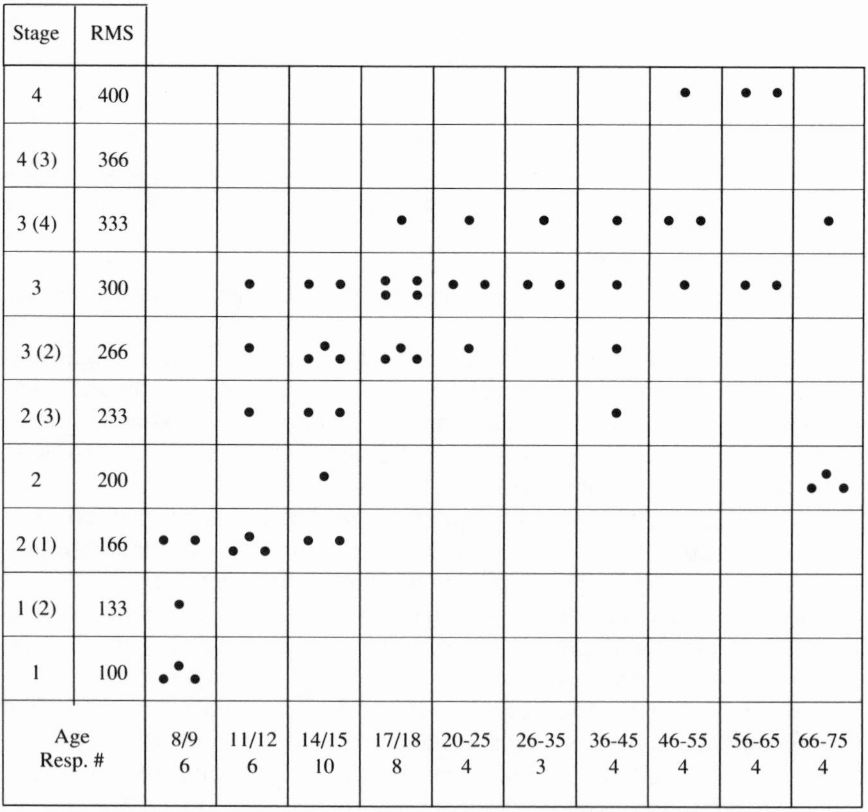

Stage	RMS	8/9	11/12	14/15	17/18	20-25	26-35	36-45	46-55	56-65	66-75
4	400								•	• •	
4 (3)	366										
3 (4)	333				•	•	•	•	• •		•
3	300		•	• •	: :	• •	• •	•	•	• •	
3 (2)	266		•	•°•	•°•	•		•			
2 (3)	233		•	• •				•			
2	200			•							•°•
2 (1)	166	• •	•°•	• •							
1 (2)	133	•									
1	100	•°•									
Age / **Resp. #**		8/9 / 6	11/12 / 6	14/15 / 10	17/18 / 8	20-25 / 4	26-35 / 3	36-45 / 4	46-55 / 4	56-65 / 4	66-75 / 4

Figure 18: Percentages of the stage-scores for the Paul-dilemma comprising all age-groups

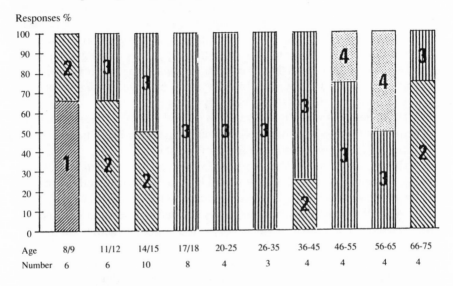

Figure 19: Absolute frequency of the full stages for the Paul-dilemma responses

Stage										
4								•	• •	
3		• •	• • • • • •	• • • • • • • •	• • • •	• • •	• • •	• • •	• •	•
2	• •	• • • •	• • • • •				•			• • •
1	• • • •									
Age N	8/9 6	11/12 6	14/15 10	17/18 8	20-25 4	26-35 3	36-45 4	46-55 4	56-65 4	66-75 4

Table 1: Median RMS for the Paul-dilemma sample comprising all age-groups

Age	8/9	11/12	14/15	17/18	20-25	26-35	36-45	46-55	56-56	66-75
RMS	128	216	240	291	300	311	283	342	350	233
N	6	6	8	8	4	3	4	4	4	4

Summing up our remarks concerning the age hypothesis, we can say that the share of higher stages clearly can be seen to increase with advancing age. This increase does not occur linearly. Stage 3 increases to a greater degree than stage 4. Furthermore, it appears as if the majority of persons are at stage 3. Finally, let us make the following concluding remarks:

• Significant interruptions of the cognitive patterns of religious judgement are rarer in adulthood than in childhood. Therewith, changes in persons' overall personality are rarer too. In our system, however, a stage transition always means a change of the personality structure.

• The structures formed by adults are in general relatively fragile. They are structures of knowing, mediated via school or mass media, which affect no qualitative transformations in the sense of our stages.

• The age-related regression (ages 66-75), though highly interesting, is not easily explained. At this point, we would have to examine whether it might not be possible that at this age different patterns of reasoning can be employed at the same time. In other words, the five stage patterns begin to separate out from each other and the respondents begin to reconstrue them anew in their respective situations according to an unconscious recollection of those situations in which the structures had been formed at earlier times. Thus the organic dissolution of the structures is insufficent explanation for the regression in old age.

• The fact that we have falsified our hypothesis in this section means at the very least that even structures (schemata) can dissolve in old age. It appears to us that until today this has barely been documented in the literature.

• A different interpretation of this circumstances might say that the stage regression in the age group 66-75 could have been caused by effects related to age cohorts or historical epochs. We tend to prefer the explanation of a so-called age-related socialization effect. Further studies must be aimed at clarifying the issues surrounding this question.

2. Group: Denomination, Education, Status, Gender

The hypothesis that no differences in the stages of religious judgement exist among Roman Catholics, Old Catholics, and Reformed Protestants was tested initially with a variance analysis [*Varianzanalyse*] comprising all age groups and all dilemmas. No statistically significant group differences were discovered.

The assumption that denominational affiliation does not influence religious judgement can thus be confirmed with our data. We must point out, however, that this result is valid only for our sample. It must not be generalized to the population as a whole. In short, since the denominational affiliation of our sample population did not exhibit any structural differences, it can be maintained that the same structural religious patterns can, even viewed sociologically, be construed with different contents (denominations).

For testing the educational influences on the stage development of the religious judgement we divided the adult respondents into two groups: high educational level (college and beyond), or low educational level (unskilled laborers, high school, apprenticeships, on-the-job training, service-job-oriented or vocational colleges). Low educational level corresponds significantly to lower stages (t=2.33, p=0.03).

The differences become even more pronounced in the case of socio-economic status (SES). The results are presented in Figure 20. Persons with high SES have, on average, higher scores; those with low SES have lower ones. The difference between median and lower SES is very significant.

Figure 20: Influence of the variable "status" (SES) on religious judgement

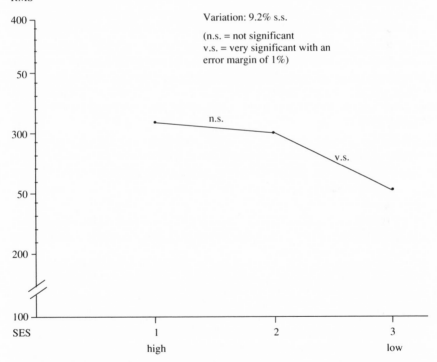

RMS

If one considers the interactional effects between social class and age, then its variance numbers 15.4 percent (v.s.). But a clear trend cannot be proven. Why the age-groups 46-55 and 56-65 of the middle-class respondents show higher values than those of the upper class cannot be determined with clarity (cf. Figure 21).

Now we would like to address the issue of gender-influence: On the whole, this influence on the development of the religious judgement is

Figure 21: Interactional effects between age and social status (median values)

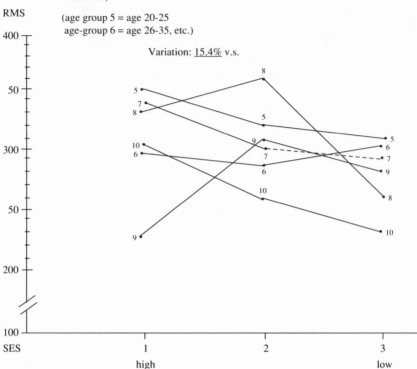

insignificant (variation 0.05 percent n.s.). It is a different matter as far as the interactional effects between age and gender are concerned (cf. Figure 22).

The interactional effects indicate that girls achieve higher scores than boys, especially at age 14-15 but also at 17-18 and already at 11-12. In contrast, men show higher values in childhood (age 8-9) and in adulthood. This is particularly clear for the age-groups 8-9 and 66-75. For the ages 20-65 the "no-distinction-hypothesis" ought to be maintained, although male respondents always receive higher scores, except for the ages 56-65.

In summary, we can make the following statements about the interactional effects between age and gender: In childhood, boys display a higher level of religious judgement; in adolescence, the girls are clearly more developed; in adulthood, there are no actual differences — those that exist in the data are probably accidental; in old age, the male respondents again show higher scores.

We would like to point out again that these results must be treated with great caution due to the small size of the sample.

Figure 22: Interactional effects between age and gender concerning religious judgement

(age-group   1 = age 8/9; age-group 2 = age 11/12; . . .
(age-group 10 = age 66-75)

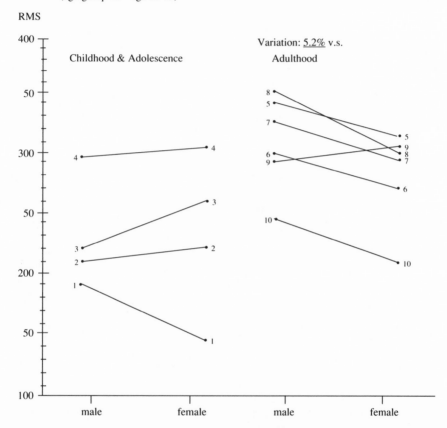

3. Group: Trans-situationality

The hypothesis suggested here states that persons are reasoning with the same religious structure in response to dilemmas with different contents. We attempted to test this assumption in three ways: (a) by examining the general distribution of the scores in regard to the individual dilemmas; (b) by comparing the individual dilemmas in pairs; (c) by presenting the scores of individual persons for all dilemmas. Let us begin with a look at the general distribution across all dilemmas (cf. Table 2 and Figures 23 and 24).

At first glance, one sees few differences in the distribution. Based on that distribution, one could assume that no significant domain-specificities appear. However, if one discerns more discriminatingly it becomes apparent that — just as predicted by our hypotheses — all dilemmas with church-related

Table 2: Absolute and percentage distribution of stage-assignments for eight dilemmas

RMS		PAUL 1		JOB 2		UNJU 3		LOVE6		SUIC 7		ETSL 4		GILT 5		MARR 8	
		N	%	N	%	N	%	N	%	N	%	N	%	N	%	N	%
100-133	stage 1	4	7.5	2	3.9	2	3.7	3	5.7	3	9.3	3	5.7	4	7.8	4	7.5
165-233	stage 2	15	28.3	22	42.3	22	40.7	19	35.8	16	29.6	27	50.9	25	49.0	10	18.9
266-335	stage 3	31	58.5	23	44.2	25	46.3	24	45.3	30	55.5	14	26.4	18	35.4	37	69.8
366-433	stage 4	3	5.7	5	9.6	5	9.3	7	13.2	3	5.6	9	17.0	4	7.8	2	3.8
		53		52		54		55		54		53		51		53	

content show a tendency to cluster at stage 3. This is especially the case with the marriage-dilemma #8. The responses to it show an upward tendency of the lower stage-scores and a downward tendency of the stage 4 scores. It becomes apparent that in the case of church-related themes, more persons are inclined to stage 3 judgements, i.e., toward the free and solipsistic separation of the sacred and the profane. This means a *décalage*, a timelag, in the sense that in the case of church-related topics persons are more likely to include individual secularization-processes in the making of a religious judgement than they would be in the case of general topics describing human existence in the face of contingent realities.

An obverse trend must be noted for those dilemmas which deal with the question of guilt, i.e., the dilemmas 4 and 5, "eternal salvation" and "guilt" (cf. hypothesis 3b). For dilemma 5, we diagnosed a trend from stage 3 to 2; for dilemma 4, a trend toward stage 4. In one case, we find claims of retribution and images of restitution for things done; in the other, the objectifications of guilt typical of stage 4. In other words: In the case of guilt issues, persons are much more willing to favor preventive measures and jurisdiction over individual responsibility (stage 3).

Thus, we can speak of domain-specificity. In the case of certain topics, persons exhibit a tendency toward a certain pattern, i.e., toward an adjacent, i.e., higher or lower, stage. Of course, at this point, we must assume that these types of *décalage* or timelag are culture-specific. Yet, they are quite clear in their consistency: In the case of church-related themes, the letting-go of a relatively closed and authoritarian (ecclesial) system in favor of an open, public church which offers reference-points for everyday actions in the individual as well as social sense is still in process. More likely is a rejection of church in the old sense, but without the occurrence of transformations of the old images into new ones. Such a state of affairs mirrors the character of the stage 3 pattern. In contrast to persons at stage 2, persons

**Figure 23: Percentage shares of stage 1, stage 2, stage 3, stage 4 judge-
ments in the eight dilemmas: PAUL 1, JOB 2, UNJU 3,
LOVE 6, SUIC 7, ETSL 4, GILT 5, and MARR 8 (N = 425
stage assessments)**

Stage 1 = RMS 100-133;   Stage 2 = RMS 166-233
Stage 3 = RMS 266-333;   Stage 4 = RMS 366-433

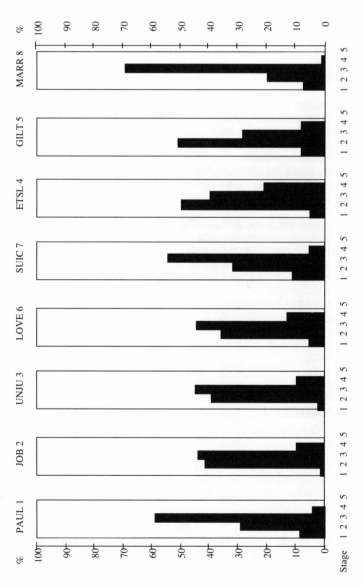

**Figure 24: Percentage shares of stage 1, stage 2, stage 3, stage 4
judgements in the eight dilemmas**

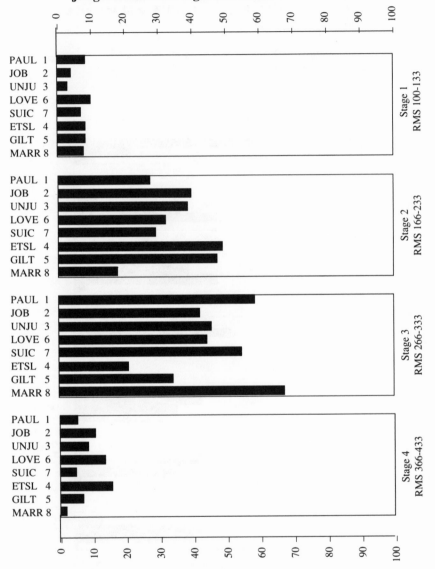

at stage 3 possess the courage to transform their patterns with regard to
church.

The same holds true for the domain of "guilt." In its case the societal
image of *do ut des* lags far behind the autonomy typical of stage 3. At stage
3, guilt would have to be interpreted from the perspective of human freedom

and responsibility, whereby the transcendent dimension receives little attention. These differences, then, stand out as highly significant in the results of
the Chi^2-test (Chi^2 = 45.05; df = 21).

It is interesting that on the whole the stability-hypothesis must be viewed
as confirmed. This is the result of an additional co-variance-analysis: if we
treat "age," "status," and "gender" as co-variants, no significant effect can
be detected for the various dilemma-types (F=1.04, P=0.402). All of the
variance is related to the variables "age" and "status," at a measure of 12.6
percent. This means that we can maintain the trans-situationality hypothesis as valid: Persons' judgements about different contents (dilemmas) are
formed at the same stage. Discrepancies and tendencies toward any one
certain stage can be designated as *décalages* or timelags in the classical
Piagetian sense.

Let us return now to the effect of age in regard to the various dilemmas.
We stated that (b) we conducted comparisons in pairs in regard to the medi-

Table 3: Median age-scores for the different dilemma-types

Dilemma	Stage 1	Stage 2	Stage 3	Stage 4
PAUL 1	8.7y. (0.5)	25.2y. (22.6)	29.2y. (17.5)	55.6y. (4.1)
JOB 2	9.0y. (0.0)	22.8y. (19.9)	31.3y. (18.5)	46.0y. (17.0)
UNJU 3	9.0y. (0.0)	23.0y. (19.5)	30.4y. (19.2)	36.0y. 14.7)
ESTL 4	9.3y. (1.5)	22.4y. (17.7)	33.7y. (21.7)	40.3y. (13.7)
GILT 5	11.0y. (3.1)	22.9y. (19.3)	38.0y. (20.4)	31.0y. (12.4)
LOVE 6	9.3y. (2.3)	21.8y. (19.7)	30.8y. (17.9)	41.2y. (20.8)
SUIC 7	10.2y. (2.6)	26.5y. (22.3)	32.5y. (19.5)	21.0y. (2.6)
MARR 8	8.7y. (0.5)	36.5y. (29.4)	29.5y. (17.8)	17.5y. (0.7)
TOTAL x=	9.4y.	25.1y.	31.9y.	36.1y

an age-scores of the individual stages. Table 3 is the basis for that comparison.

The individual comparisons reveal that the Paul-dilemma (#1), the Job-
dilemma (#2), the dilemma about "unjust suffering" (#3), the "eternal-sal-

vation-dilemma" (#4), and the love-dilemma (#6) show the clearest age-trend.[3] Surprising are the trends for the dilemmas "guilt" (#5), "suicide" (#7), and "marriage" (#8). Take the marriage-dilemma: Persons with an average age of 36.5 were coded (with great spread) at stage 2, persons with the average age of 29.5 were coded (with medium spread) at stage 3, and those with an average age of 17.5 were scored (with little spread) at stage 4. What does this mean? It appears as if we are dealing with a typical age-cohort effect which caused the reversal of the age-trend (cf. Figure 25). In contrast to the older and the oldest generation, the younger generation is free from absolute ties to the church. Thus, the younger generation can realize the

Figure 25: Trans-situationality study: age- X - dilemma-trends for three different dilemmas

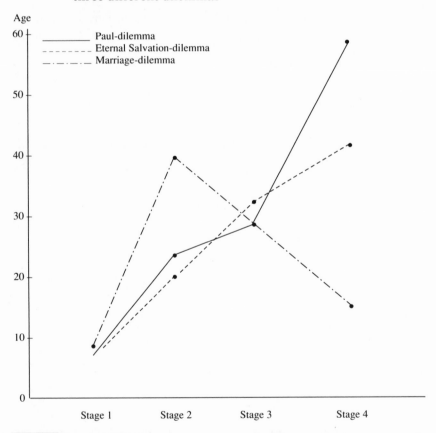

---

3. In regard to the age-validation, future studies must be conducted especially with these dilemmas. The Paul-dilemma appears to be the most immune from age-cohort effects and influences of SES, since it probably contains the most generalizable and history-independent religious elements.

connection between their own relation to God and the demands of the church more easily, more clearly, and more "correlationally," while the older generation seems more likely to reproduce the patterns of church-obligations without reference to the Ultimate. Figure 25 also indicates that the dilemma about eternal salvation represents the most harmonious age/stage-trend.

Looking at Figure 26, we discover that the median scores of the Job-dilemma represent a normal age-trend, while the other two dilemmas display an increasing age-effect which breaks off rapidly at stage 4. In both cases the spread is relatively narrow. Again, an age-cohort difference becomes visible. Stage 4 respondents were generally younger people, with an average age of 21 for the suicide-dilemma and 31 for the guilt-dilemma. It appears that, in the domain of these two topics, older generations reason less frequently at stage 4; i.e., for them guilt seems to be more a matter for the individuals and their privileged relations and less a universal obligation. And for them suicide has little to do with the Ultimate as such.

Figure 26: Trans-situationality study: age - X - dilemma-trends for three different dilemmas, including two with age-cohort effects

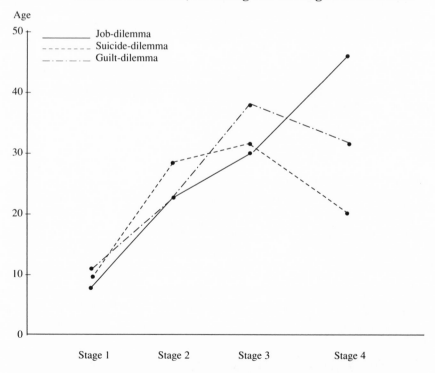

Let us summarize: It is important that trans-situationality always make apparent the age-cohort effects in regard to the *décalages* or timelags.

Presumably, older persons were educated differently from younger ones in certain religious domains. Also, the church leaders of older generations often prevented persons from having their own thoughts concerning religious problems. Suicide, for example, is still understood as a turning away from God. And guilt is still viewed from the perspective of personal efforts concerning forgiveness (confession) and restoration (contrition). These knowledge-elements also flow into the religious judgement. If the assimilation of content occurs neutrally in regard to the different historical trends of the church's teaching, different content-domains yield an ideal, increasing stage-score curve in all age groups. For example, this generally appears to be the case with the theodicy-questions.

Despite these differences, we do want to maintain the trans-situationality-hypothesis. Additional assumptions, such as certain age-cohort effects and *décalages* related to specific contents, explain the deviations of the trends too clearly.

We would like to add that the relation between membership in a certain socio-economic class and the frequency of certain stages does not reveal a clear-cut trend. Table 4 shows — probably due to an accidental sample error — that persons at stage 4 are more likely to belong to the middle and lower classes (median score 1.73), persons at stage 3 generally belong to the middle class (median score 1.98), and persons at stage 2 belong to the middle and upper classes (median score 2.33).

Table 4: Frequency and socio-economic status in the individual dilemma for stage 1 - 4 (left figure = absolute frequency; right figure =average socio-economic status)

Dilemma	Stage 1	Stage 2	Stage 3	Stage 4
PAUL 1	0	4/2.5	16/1.8	3/2.3
JOB 2	0	5/2.4	14/1.9	4/2.0
UNJU 3	0	6/2.0	13/1.8	4/1.5
ETSL 4	0	7/1.7	9/2.3	8/1.6
GILT 5	0	7/2.1	12/2.0	3/1.6
LOVE 6	0	4/2.5	13/2.0	6/1.6
SUIC 7	0	5/2.8	13/2.0	6/1.6
MARR 8	0	4/2.7	20/2.0	0

c) Furthermore, we said that trans-situationality is best presented by juxtaposing the data of individual persons for all dilemmas. Since we cannot present the whole body of data, we would like to introduce three examples (cf. Table 5). The first example represents an ideal group, the second one conveys differences of median value, the third shows a value of extreme discrepancy. The calculation of the frequency of those responses with a variance not

Table 5: Three groups with widely discrepant correlational values (200 = stage 2; 333 = stage 3 (4); etc.)

	Person No.	PAUL	JOB	UNJU	ESTL	GILT	LOVE	SUIC	MARR
(1. group w/ 1/3 stage permitted)	20				200	200	200	200	
	22	333					333	333	333
	29					300	300	300	300
	41	300	300	333	333				
	49	266	300	300	300				
(2. group w/ one stage variance)	3			200	200	200	300		
	13					200	200	233	166
	21					266	233	300	333
	30	266					300	266	333
	34		233	233	300	200			
(3. group: variance betw. dilemmas too great and un-explainable)	2		166	300	300	300			
	35			300	233	200	400		
	12				233	266	400	300	
	55	333	200					233	300
	64	266	400	366					300

exceeding one stage yields a result of 97.21 percent. Table 6 presents the results for all persons, comprising five dilemmas.

88.35 percent do not vary by more than two-thirds of a stage. Only in 2.79 percent of the cases does the trans-situationality hypothesis not correspond

Table 6: Stage-score variances for all persons, comprising the dilemmas 1, 2, 3, 6, 7: frequency of differences
The differences are given in RMS-variances; an RMS variance of 1-33 points corresponds to the difference of 1/3 stage. This means that the stage assessment in one dilemma was higher by 1/3 stage compared to the other.

RMS-variance	Frequency		Cumulative Frequency		Max. Variance
	N	%	N	%	
0	75	41.90	75	41.90	0
1 - 33	62	34.64	137	76.54	1/3 stage
34 - 66	21	11.73	158	88.27	2/3 stage
67 - 100	16	8.94	174	97.21	1 stage
100-133	5	2.79	179	100.00	1 1/3 stage

to the additional assumptions made earlier. We assume that *décalage*, domain-specificity, and sequentiality can still be explained within the range of a one-stage variance. When we examine the interview transcripts we see that the 2.79 percent with a variance of more than one stage could not be clearly rated due to missing information, poor interviews, the lack of follow-up questions, etc. The rationality of coding requires that sufficient objective information is elicited by the questions structuring the interview so that a higher correlation is achieved. That this is not so for 2.79 percent of the cases can be considered a "measuring error."

It is important to realize that the percentage of 97.21 percent was achieved without any attempts by the raters to erase the differences via discourse and consensus. Normally that would be desirable for such a procedure. Nevertheless, the variance of one stage across the individual dilemmas in the case of individual respondents can still be explained by as yet to be determined horizontal *décalage*.

If one applies the same calculation to all eight dilemmas, i.e., if one includes even those content-domains which diverge from the normal distribution (guilt 4, 5, and marriage 8), the result is still 92.46 percent and not exceeding a variance of one full stage.

Instead of comparing the variance for all persons, a comparison for only one person, still yields 79.12 percent of the coded scores falling into the category of two-thirds-stage variance. Table 7 indicates the differences in the stage-score for the dilemmas 1, 2, 3, 6, and 7 for one respondent.

Table 7: Variance in stage-assessments for one respondent

RMS-variance	Frequency		Cumulative Frequency		# of Codings	
	N	%	N	%	2	3
0	31	34.07	31	34.07	22	9
1 - 33	31	34.07	62	68.13	11	20
34 - 66	10	10.99	72	79.12	3	7
67 - 100	15	16.48	87	95.60	11	4
100-133	4	4.39	91	100.00	0	4
Total	91		91		47	44

The principle of *décalage* was described earlier. At this point, we would like to provide an example with concrete and exact figures: In the case of the dilemma, "eternal salvation," 32.46 of stage 3 respondents displayed a tendency toward a lower stage of religious judgement; for the "guilt-dilemma" the percentage is 26.09 percent. For both dilemmas taken together, the total percentage of respondents exhibiting a tendency toward a lower stage is 32.65 percent. Put differently, for approximately two-thirds of the persons at stage 3, the *décalage* hypothesis does not apply. This can be gathered from Table 8.

Table 8: Frequency with which persons at stage 3 (cf. above) were assigned to stages 1, 2, 3, 4 for the dilemmas "ETSL 4" and "GILT 5"

	ETSL 4		GILT 5		both dilemmas	
STAGE	N	%	N	%	N	%
1	0	0.0	0	0.0	0	0.0
2	10	38.46	6	26.09	16	32.65
3	10	38.46	15	65.22	25	51.02
4	6	23.08	2	8.69	8	16.33

Finally, we would like to provide a survey over all the agreements (cf. Table 9).

According to the third set of hypotheses, we would expect agreement (+) only among the dilemmas 1, 2, 3, 6, 7. The overall number of comparisons (i.e., including all respondents) is 179; out of these 138 were agreements (+) and 41 non-agreements (-). This translates into an agreement percentage of 77.09 percent and non-agreement percentage of 22.91 percent. The least agreement can be discovered between dilemma #3, "UNJU" and dilemma #6, "LOVE," at 50 percent. The greatest agreement exists between dilemma #1, "PAUL" and dilemma #2 "JOB": 84.85 percent. For these two dilemmas, the respondents were assigned almost completely to the same stage.

Summary of the Initial Empirical Findings

> This summary of the results shall provide the reader with a survey of the most important results. We will add the letter of a natural scientist discussing the question of an age-related regression. Despite all the positive attitudes in regard to the results, the limited size of the sample must lead us to caution. Further empirical studies are necessary to aid in the differentiation of the stage concept.

The clear age-related trend in the group of persons age 8-25 leads to the assumption that the construct "development of religious judgement" is reasonably well validated. Problems do exist, however, in regard to the age-related regression. The following is an excerpt from the letter of a colleague, an older university professor:

> When I saw your first page, I immediately wondered whether one could expect a return to stage 1 or 2 in old age. I did expect that, but for entirely dif-

Table 9: Agreements of stage assessments for all eight dilemmas:
(+) agreement, i.e., the respondent was assigned to the same stage in both dilemmas;
(-) no agreement, i.e., the respondent was assigned to a different stage for each of the two dilemmas.

Stage 1 = RMS 100-133; stage 3 = RMS 266-333; stage 4 = 366-433. The figures below the diagonal line indicate the absolute frequency; the figures above it reflect the percentage distribution.

	PAUL 1		JOB 2		UNJU 3		ETSL 4		GILT 5		LOVE 6		SUIC 7		MARR 8	
	+	-	+	-	+	-	+	-	+	-	+	-	+	-	+	-
PAUL			84.85	15.15	78.26	21.74	50.00	50.00	—	—	75.00	25.00	81.82	18.18	70.59	29.41
JOB 2	28	5			79.41	20.59	60.87	39.13	72.73	27.27	—	—	55.56	44.44	57.14	42.86
UNJU 3	18	5	27	7			65.71	34.29	60.87	39.13	50.00	50.00	—	—	63.64	36.36
ETSL 4	6	6	14	9	23	12			71.88	28.12	70.00	30.00	80.00	20.00	—	—
GILT 5	—	3	8	3	14	9	23	9			60.61	39.39	80.95	19.05	100.0	0.0
LOVE 6	9	3	—	—	6	6	14	6	20	13			79.71	20.59	80.95	19.05
SUIC 7	18	4	5	4	—	—	8	2	17	4	27	7			75.76	24.24
MARR 8	24	10	12	9	7	4	—	—	9	0	17	4	25	8		

ferent reasons than given by you in light of the actual results. My reasons are as follows: An older person feels more strongly than the younger, still vital person that he or she has become guilty in this world and thus also guilty before God. He or she declines to justify himself or herself according to stage 3 and surrenders instead. This is obviously reinforced by a resignation over against the world: "We create order and things fall apart, we reorder them and we fall apart ourselves," says the poet, Rilke. Therefore, I maintain that the religious person — viewed statistically — becomes more humble.

Put negatively, one could speak of a fatalistic obedience or submission to God. I prefer to view it positively as an unconditional surrender to God's unfathomable wisdom. Basically, now position (i.e., stage) 2 (and 1) merges with position (i.e., stage) 5. In the face of death, the surrender to the mystery of God (without regard for the desirability of one's own self-actualization) becomes a uni-polar reciprocity: God is everything, I am nothing. This means simultaneously that one waits for God's love, that God is the active one, that I only have to be empty for God.

Thus I surmise that from stage 3 on, a number of trajectories are possible, some of which appear to be discontinuous and even regressive. But this is not a regression in the sense of decline but in the sense of a total "simplification" of the relation to the Transcendent. In that case, the scheme would be as follows:

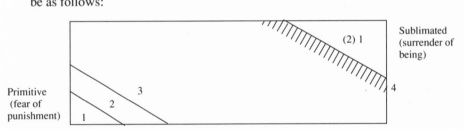

In the scheme, I placed the "2" in brackets, since older persons probably no longer count upon the efficacy of *do ut des* but rather surrender as portrayed by the example of the Saints.

This interesting quote from the letter states that the developmental lines are valid up to stage 3 and even up to stage 4 but that the structural description does not apply beyond that. This would mean that instead of relying for an explanation on the age-related socialization-effect described above the relevance of the stage descriptions themselves is questioned.

However, we would like to insist, at least for now, on our analysis of the age-related socialization-effect. In his letter, our colleague describes in a fine way a certain modus of the stage 4 and stage 5 conception. It becomes clear that we always already possess the conditions of the possibility for stage 4 and 5 but that these are interpreted in a basic attitude of ascetic humility. But in principle nothing new is being suggested in structural terms. However, one must say that the above quotation is very interesting because it represents an attempt to provide an existential explanation-pattern for the age-related timelag.

Other results, like the differences in education, class, gender, and denominational affiliation correspond largely to our presuppositions. In the case of the trans-situationality, however, new studies are necessary, particularly in order to qualify more precisely certain domains, domains which prevent acquired structures from fully executing their functions. It appears as if the guilt-themes in particular exert an influence on persons at stage 3 to judge at stage 2. This would be true horizontal *décalage* in the sense of Piaget. One could speak of domain-specificity in the case of specific church-related topics, for there we discovered a preferential tendency towards stage 3. It is important that these findings are replicated with larger samples. In our case the data can only be viewed as indicating the direction of new questions and investigations.

The Instrument for Measuring Religious Judgement

> We suggest that the following three dilemmas be used in any future research program designed to investigate the development of the religious judgement: (a) the Paul-dilemma; (b) the chance-dilemma; (c) the theodicy-dilemma.

Concerning (a): The Paul-dilemma elicits the relationship between persons and the Ultimate (God), using a situation in which a person commits himself to God. The "promise" made is an old religious action pattern: A person makes an oath which obligates him for the future in a particular direction. This obligatory act lays open the relationship to the Ultimate. It will have to be assessed and explained by the interviewee. In a way, this "oath" throws the interviewees back to their own relationship to an Ultimate. The interviewees' reactions, i.e., consenting or dissenting in regard to keeping the oath, their elaborations of the imagined consequences, and their various rationales, all take the form of (personal) "justifications."

Concerning (b): Things are entirely different in the case of the "chance-dilemma" which had not been used in the first research program:

> Just for the fun of it, a poor woman spends a little money and buys a lottery ticket. She does not expect to win at all. The odds are one in a million. However, she wins, and the grand prize at that. She receives an inordinate amount of money. To her there is only one explanation: It was not chance or good fortune but "God's hand" which made this happen. Her children, however, explain this event by reference to chance. They talk with their mother about it. She, however, sticks with her opinion and cannot be convinced otherwise.

Questions:

1a) Who is right? Why?

1b) Is this pure chance or do other important dimensions play a role? Why? Why not?

1c) What is stronger, chance or God (or a divinity)? Why the one and not the other?

1d) If there is no such thing as chance, what then caused this miracle? Is it something divine, something hidden, an invisible force, a law? Why, why not (or vice versa)?

2) Whenever such miraculous things happen in the world, is that always pure chance? Or are there moments of divine intervention? Why or why not?

3) Some people believe in the existence of something other than pure chance. Such a belief gives them strength and hope. Do you think along similar lines? Why or why not?

4) Some people believe that an Ultimate (God) somehow intervenes in the world, especially on behalf of those persons who believe in the Ultimate (God). Is this view correct? Why or why not?

5) Human beings are capable of doing all sorts of things, e.g., building houses, inventing computers, walking on the moon, etc. But there are also things they will never be able to do, e.g., resurrecting the dead, constructing a living organism, eliciting love by force. Might one say that God or the divine can be found in those things, acts, events where human beings are powerless? Why, why not?

6) The woman won the lottery only once. Might one say that one-time events like that happen by pure chance? Or, if events are clearly evident and continue for a long time must that be attributed to the workings of the divine? Why, why not?

7) Is it God's will if someone wins the lottery? Why or why not?

This second dilemma elicits an entirely different relational structure than the first one. Here, the person is confronted with having obtained a gift without any prior effort. The contingency differences are readily apparent. We are dealing here with the old problem of chance, which can be transferred into many domains within human limits.

Concerning (c): For illustrative purposes we had printed the theodicy-dilemma in the first chapter. Here we are presenting it in conjunction with the original questions:

In a small town there lived a rich man. He was happily married, had four children, and owned a large house. He was very successful in his job as Superior Judge of the city. He prayed regularly and never forgot to thank

God for his good life. Also, he gave generously to charitable causes and intervened personally on behalf of poor people. However, although he was a just man, many persons in the city feared the judge because of his strictness. Certain circles in the city spoke ill of him and spread rumors. Thus, without any wrongdoing, he lost his good reputation. After a certain period of time he was forced to resign from his position as Superior Judge. That, however, was not all. Later on, his daughter developed a type of paralysis which worsened by the day. The former judge could no longer afford the medical expense for his daughter's treatment. He had to sell his beautiful house and use all the money to pay the doctor bills. His daughter's condition still did not improve.

Questions:

1a) The former judge reflects upon his misfortune and wonders about God's role therein. What is he supposed to think of God?
1b) Were the events willed by God? Why or why not?
2) The former judge did not feel personally responsible for his dismissal from the court nor for his daughter's illness. Do you believe that God wanted to punish him for past injustices? Why or why not?
3) Does God punish people? Under what conditions? How?
4) Is it unfair of God to allow such suffering? Did God act unfairly or immorally in this situation? If you believe that God was unjust, please explain why you think so.
5) Why does God permit the suffering of innocent people, e.g., in sickness, natural disasters, and war? If God is almighty, can God not prevent suffering and instead help people?
    Earlier in his life, the judge had thanked God for his good life. In his unhappy situation he now wonders whether he should continue to pray to God.
6) Should the former judge continue to pray to God and believe in God, despite his misfortune? Why or why not?

After a certain period of time the situation of the judge takes an unexpected turn for the better. His daughter recovers and the rumors are discredited as malicious and slanderous. The former judge's reputation is restored and he is reinstated in his old position.

7) Should the judge thank God again and pray? Why or why not?
8) What are the origins of good and evil in the world?

This dilemma resembles a certain version of Job's story. The dilemma raises questions similar to those in the ancient text, without, however, giving any answers. The answer must be provided reconstructively by the inter-viewees themselves. Essential elements of the dilemma are the reference to "evil" in the world and the image of God's "distance" from persons who are experiencing evil and God's "presence" with those who are spared. In this case, the equilibrium in the various dimensions is to be achieved not via the issue of chance but via the genesis of suffering, illness, death, and above all, evil itself.

We are now of the opinion that a good stage assessment must refer to all three dilemmas, because they describe different situations and because each has a different way of launching the polar dimensions into a reconstructive motion. The first dilemma addresses personal initiative and activity vis-à-vis an Ultimate. In the second dilemma, the interviewees are faced with having to balance chance and divine intervention. In the third one, they are con-fronted with striking a balance between God's absence and presence via "evil." According to the discontinuity-paradigm, the differences in the three domains should not exceed one stage.

Additional Research Studies (with Anton Bucher)[4]

This section introduces additional research studies some of which have been completed and published and some of which have been presented in the context of smaller projects or pilot studies. Each individual segment of the research program pre-sented here covers one particular theoretical aspect.

a) One unresolved question concerns the universality of the develop-mental sequence of religious judgement. We continue to assert this univer-sality, although we are able to prove it only partially. To this end, Dick (1982) presented Paul-dilemmas to Hindus and followers of Jainism in Rajasthan (India), to members of Mahayana-Buddhism near the Tibetan border, to Bantu ancestor-worshipers in Rwanda, and to members of a Christian missionary contingent also in Rwanda. These dilemmas were adapted to the socio-cultural and religious context of each group. Each of the samples revealed a significant age-related trend. However, the limited nature of these samples did not allow for cross-cultural comparisons, which led Dick to designate his study as "intracultural." Thus, except for the age-relat-ed trend, the universality claim of our theory cannot yet be considered empir-ically validated.

b) Based on the assumption that even those persons who contest the exis-

---

4. This section is taken essentially from the essay, "Die Entwicklung des religiösen Urteils. Ein Forschungsprogramm" by Oser and Bucher published in *Unterrichtswissenschaft* 15, 2, 1987, pp. 132 -156.

tence of God must cope with the contingencies of their lives, Achermann (1981) presented religious dilemmas to self-declared atheists. The data made possible a description of stages or types comparable to that of the religious judgement stages insofar as the stages move from "being determined from the outside" and "fatalism" to "self-determination via social engagement." Despite these isomorphisms, we consider it appropriate in this case not to speak of specifically religious development. Nonetheless, the numerous structural correspondences should give rise to further reflection.

c) In another sub-project, Von Brachel and Oser (1984) asked fifty respondents — equally distributed according to age, denominational affiliation, and gender — how they saw their own religious development. Contrary to the initial hypothesis that religious structures are broken open and become transformed by certain critical, one-time life-experiences (Filipp, 1981), it became evident that structural changes resulted from ongoing, new experiences such as leaving home or vocational training. It was possible to show that those respondents who, at the time of the interview, had internalized stage 3 were clearly able to recall that, at an earlier time, they had thought differently about religious questions and interacted differently with God.

d) In addition, attempts were made to validate the theory of religious development by means of psycho-historical studies of significant persons considered to be at a higher stage of religious development. This was done following similar psycho-historical studies concerning the development of identity presented by Erikson (1963, 1968, 1980). Presently, only three such studies are available: Hager (1987) traces the development from stage 2 to stage 4 in the biography of Johann Heinrich Pestalozzi. Bucher (1985) reconstructs the religious development of the poet Rainer Maria Rilke from his early childhood to his death. By relying on autobiographical testimonies, letters, and lyrical texts, Bucher is able to identify all stages in sequential order. Brumlik (1985) describes the religious development of Martin Buber by coupling our stage-scale with Erikson's epigenetic ego-identity model.

More of such studies are necessary because they facilitate statements about the possible endpoint or the *terminus ad quem*. To this end, in addition to consulting contemporary theological concepts, it might be helpful to interview older and wiser persons with much life-experience; one such study is presented in Oser, Althof, and Bucher, 1986.

e) In Oser and Gmünder (1984, p. 261) it is hypothesized that variable religious contents, especially in text-form, are assimilated isomorphously to the structure of cognitive religious judgement. Although the small sample of an exploratory structural-developmental research study on the reception of three NT parables by respondents at different stages of religious judgement could not verify this hypothesis, it nonetheless was able to strengthen it (Bucher, 1987a; Bucher and Oser, 1987b). It was possible to extract from the extensive volume of raw data different types of interpretation which could be assigned to particular stages (interrater-reliability coefficients between 0.78 and 0.96). In addition, Bucher (1987a, 1987b) postulated a model with four stages which claims to describe and explain the development of the comprehension of biblical and literary parables and similes.

On the whole, these results appear to be significant and laden with implications, especially for the field of Bible-didactics and for the use of texts in religious education, for these results constitute important evidence for the fact that young students assimilate religious texts to different structures from adults. Therefore, the instructional method of uni-directional transmission of theological explanations is insufficient insofar as their students either do not comprehend them, which may result in disagreeing, or they reinterpret the explanations according to their own religious judgement. This has been demonstrated repeatedly with the parable of the workers in the vineyard (Mt 20:1f), which was presented in chapter six.

f) An intervention study (Oser, 1988) documented that after 2.5 months the average stage of students in an academic high school could be raised by about two-thirds of a stage. The intervention treatment consisted of discussions of religious dilemmas from the life-world of the students, from the Bible, and from other religious writings.

This sensational success was made possible by systematically stimulating the argument and reasoning patterns of the next stage. Frequently this stimulation made the students insecure, but it also provoked them to debate. Finally it "cracked open" their structures of religious judgement and transformed them toward more complexity.

g) In this context the study by Schildknecht (1984) should be mentioned. Examining the development of competence for discussing moral and religious dilemmas and questions, the author was able to show that the number of transactions, i.e., those statements in which the speaker includes the arguments of the dialogue partner (e.g., you are saying that . . .), increases with age. Her age-group 1 (age 5.7 - 8.6) contains no such transactions. They do account, however, for 25 percent of the shared statements in her age-group 4 (age 14 - 17). In reference to these data, Oser, Althof, and Berkowitz (1986) developed the new stage hierarchy of argument-integration and discursive behavior.

h) The connection between religious and moral judgement according to Kohlberg (1981a, 1984) was of special interest. Initially, Gut (1984, pp. 230f)[5] seemed to supply an additional clue for the generally acknowledged thesis that the development of moral judgement structure precedes that of religious judgement (cf. Kohlberg and Power, 1981). Her study measured twenty-four respondents with moral judgement stages higher than their religious

---

5. A more extensive and critical presentation of this study can be found in Oser and Reich, 1990.

judgement stages. In addition, sixteen of her respondents had parallel assessments. However, in the case of ten respondents — contrary to the hypothesis that a particular stage of moral judgement constitutes a necessary though not sufficient condition for the parallel stage of religious cognition — the religious judgement was higher than the moral. This means that the assumptions of Kohlberg and Power (1981) must be examined further. Oser and Reich (1990) were able to show that the stimulation of religious cognition does lead to a higher stage of religious judgement but not to a higher stage of moral judgement. This confirms the hypothesis that domain-specific development (morality, religion, social cognition) depends heavily on the socialization in the respective symbol-system.

i) Another project assessed the stages of religious judgement of fifty-six respondents ages 5 - 20, with equal distribution according to gender and denominational affiliation. In addition, two specifically designed questionnaires were employed to ascertain respondents' worldviews, their "ontology" and "cosmology," in order to clarify which content-related presuppositions enter into the religious judgement (Fetz and Oser 1985). It was established that young children have an "archaic" image of the world, the hallmarks of which are the polarity of "up there" and "down here" (heaven and earth) and finitude. The corresponding cosmogony is characterized by an "artificialistic" pattern of interpretation, i.e., like an artisan, God is presumed to have "made" the world and even artifacts such as big houses, etc. (cf. Piaget, 1965). The literal understanding of the biblical creation account, which is related to this, corresponded consistently to the lower stages of religious judgement. In the course of development, then, both the artificialism as well as the archaic image of the world dissolve — first, into a so-called hybrid transitional stage in which mythological and religious explanations coexist, initially without any problem, with those of a scientific character. Eventually, the scientific and biblical belief-systems become differentiated at a third level which does not seem to be achieved before age twelve. From there on, "heaven" and "sky" can be understood both in their scientific and in their symbolic religious connotation.

k) These data pose the general question concerning the development of the capacity for "complementary" thinking, i.e., the capacity to coordinate two different explanations of one particular state of affairs, e.g., the beginning of the world and the theory of evolution vs. creationism. During a pilot-study, Oser and Reich (1987) presented twenty-five respondents — who were equally distributed according to age and gender — nine different problems with two different explanations to each. Then they asked which one was the correct one, whether both were necessary, etc. Based upon the data, they fashioned a developmental model for "thinking in complementarity" featuring five levels.

l) Important are also those research studies which deal with the relationship between religious judgement and something called "religious climate" (Klaghofer and Oser, 1987, Niggli, 1987a, b). Klaghofer and Oser were able to show that the religious climate consists of two components: 1) "coping with contingency in a religious way" and religious activities in the family and 2) "religious discourse in the family." In conformity with the theory they could confirm that, especially in the case of girls at stage 3, the religious climate is worse than in the case of girls at stage 2. Boys exhibited significantly lower climate-scores only at the transition from stage 2 - 3.

Niggli's work is more pertinent to styles of religious education. He was able to document clearly that religious nurturing (in contrast to compulsion) generally yields a significantly higher stage of religious development. This result is of greatest importance for further educational studies, but also for the praxis of religious education.

We have omitted methodological studies regarding the measuring of the dilemma-effects, treatment-validity (Oser and Patry, 1985), and others.

We must add that the research program presented here is open-ended. It conceives of itself as a contribution to the empirical orientation in practical theology (Schröer, 1974; Van der Ven, 1984). Furthermore, it corresponds to Kaufmann's call for the introduction of empirical data into the theological and pedagogical formation of theories. This last point was the concern of the chapter on the range of cognitive religious structures.[6]

---

6. An additional survey of research projects can be found in F. Oser: "Towards a Logic of Religious Development: A Reply to my Critics," in *Stages of Faith and Religious Development*, eds. J. W. Fowler, K. E. Nipkow, and F. Schweitzer.

Bibliography

Achermann M. (1981), *Kognitive Argumentationsfiguren des religiösen Urteils bei Atheisten.* Unpublished thesis. University of Fribourg, Switzerland.

Aebli, H. (1969), "Die geistige Entwicklung als Funktion von Anlage, Reifung, Umwelt- und Erziehungsbedingungen." In H. Roth (ed.), *Begabung und Lernen (Deutscher Bildungsrat: Gutachten und Studien).* Stuttgart: Klett, 151-191.

Apel, K.O. (1980), *Towards the Transformation of Philosophy.* London: Routledge & Kegan Paul.

Aurelio, T. (1977), *Disclosures in den Gleichnissen Jesu.* Frankfurt.

Baltes, P.B./Goulet, C.R. (1979), "Ortsbestimmung und Systematisierung einer Entwicklungspsychologie der Lebensspanne." In P.B. Baltes/L.H. Eckensberger (eds.), *Entwicklungspsychologie der Lebensspanne.* Stuttgart: Klett, 35-54.

Berger, P.L./Luckmann, T. (1966), *The Social Construction of Reality.* New York: Doubleday.

Berkowitz, M.W./Oser. F./Althof, W. (1987), "The Development of Socio-Moral Discourse." In W.M. Kurtines/J.L. Gewirtz (eds.), *Moral Development Through Social Interaction.* New York: Wiley, 222-253.

Billig, M. (1988), "Social Representation, Objectification and Anchoring: A Rhetorical Analysis." In *Social Behavior, Vol. 3 (1),* 1-16.

Bitter, G. (1981), "Was ist Korrelation? Versuch einer Bestimmung." In *Katechetische Blätter, 106,* 343-345.

Blatt, H./Kohlberg, L. (1975), "The Effects of Classroom Moral Discussion upon Children's Level of Moral Judgement. *Journal of Moral Education* 4, 129-161.

Bloch, E. (1972), *Atheism in Christianity.* New York: Herder and Herder.

Böckle, F. (1980), *Fundamental Moral Theology.* New York: Pueblo.

Broughton, J.M. (1978), "Development of Concepts of Self, Mind, Reality, and Knowledge." In *New Directions for Child Development, No. 1: Social Cognition,* 75-100.

210

_____ (1980a), *The Development of Philosophical Thinking in Adolescence*. A Progress Report on a Longitudinal Study. Harvard: Working paper.

_____ (1980b), "Genetic Metaphysics: The Developmental Psychology of Mind/Body Concepts." In R. W. Rieber (ed.), *Body and Mind—Past, Present and Future*. New York, Academic Press, 177-221.

Brumlik, M. (1985), *Die religiöse Entwicklung von Martin Buber*. Unpublished manuscript. Pedagogical Institute, University of Fribourg, Switzerland.

Bruner, J. (1960), *The Process of Education*. New York: Vintage.

Bucher, A. (1985), *Die religiöse Entwicklung des Dichters Rainer Maria Rilke*. Berichte zur Erziehungswissenschaft, Pedagogical Institute, University of Fribourg, Switzerland.

_____ (1986), "Entstehung religiöser Identität. Religiöses Urteil, seine Stufen und seine Genese. Eine Darstellung sechsjähriger Forschungsarbeit zur Frage nach der religiösen Entwicklung von F. Oser und Mitarbeitern. In *Christliches ABC, 4*, 161-210.

_____ (1987a), *Wenn zwei das gleiche Gleichnis hören, so ist es nicht das gleiche. Strukturgenetische Untersuchungen zur Rezeption dreier synoptischer Parabeln*. Unpublished thesis, Fribourg, Switzerland.

_____ (1987b), "Gleichnisse—schon in der Grundschule? Ein kognitiv-entwicklungspsychologischer Beitrag zur Frage der altersgerechten Behandlung biblischer Gleichnisse." In *Katechetische Blätter, 112*, 194-203.

Bucher, A./Oser, F. (1988), "Hauptströmungen in der Religionsenpsychologie." In D. Frey et al. (eds.), *Angewandte Psychologie. Ein Lehrbuch*. München: Urban & Schwarzenberg.

Bultmann, R. (1963), *The History of the Synoptic Tradition*. New York: Harper & Row.

Candee, D./Graham, R./Kohlberg, L. (1978), *Moral Development and Life Outcomes*. Harvard: Working paper.

Chisholm, R.M. (1966), *Theory of Knowledge*. Englewood Cliffs: Prentice-Hall.

Colby, A./Kohlberg, L. (1974), "Relations between Cognitive and Moral Stages." In L. Kohlberg, *Moralization, the Cognitive Developmental Approach*. Cambridge, Mass.: Center for Moral Education, Harvard University (photocopy).

Colby, A./Kohlberg, L./et al. (1982), *Standard Form Scoring Manual*. Form A and Form B. Harvard University (photocopy).

Cometa, M./Eason, M. (1978), "Logical Operations and Metaphor Interpretation. A Piagetian Model." In *Child Development, 49*, 649-659.

Damon, W. (1982), "Zur Entwicklung der sozialen Kognition des Kindes. Zwei Zugänge zum Verständnis von sozialer Kognition." In W. Edelstein/M.

Keller (eds.), *Perspektivität und Interpretation. Beiträge zur Entwicklung des sozialen Verstehens*. Frankfurt: Suhrkamp, 110-145.

Dibelius, M. (1971), *From Tradition to Gospel*. Cambridge, Mass.: James Clarke.

Dick, A. (1982), *Drei transkulturelle Erhebungen des religiösen Urteils*. University of Fribourg: Unpublished thesis.

Dietrich, R. (1978), "Erklären und Verstehen als Aufträge der erziehungswissenschaftlichen Forschung." In *Psychologie in Erziehung und Unterricht*, *25*, 357-368.

Döbert, R. (1978), "Sinnstiftung ohne Sinnsysteme?" In W. Fischer/W. Marhold (eds.), *Religionssoziologie als Wissenssoziologie*. Stuttgart: Kohlhammer, 52-73.

Döbert, R./Nunner-Winkler, G. (1975), *Adoleszenzkrise und Identitätsbildung*. Frankfurt: Suhrkamp.

Drehsen, W./Helle, H.J. (1978), "Religiösität und Bewusstsein. Ansätze zu einer wissenschaftlichen Typologie von Sinnsystemen." In W. Fischer/W. Marhold (eds.), *Religionssoziologie als Wissenssoziologie*. Stuttgart: Kohlhammer, 52-73.

Durkheim, E. (1912), *Les formes élémentaires de la vie religieuse*. Paris: Presses Universitaires de France. Engl. (1915), *The Elementary Forms of the Religious Life*. Reprint ed. New York: Macmillan, 1965.

Eckensberger, L.H./Villenave-Cremer, S./Reinshagen, H. (1980), "Kritische Darstellung von Methoden zur Erfassung des Moralischen Urteils." In L.H. Eckensberger/R.K. Silbereisen (eds.), *Entwicklung sozialer Kognition. Modelle, Theorien, Methoden, Anwendung*. Stuttgart: Klett-Cotta, 335-377.

Eicher, P. (1975), *Solidarischer Glaube*. Düsseldorf: Patmos.

_____ (1977), *Offenbarung. Prinzip neuzeitlicher Theologie*. München: Kösel.

Einstein, A. (1981), *Briefe*. Zurich: Diogenes.

Eliade, M. (1955), *Le Sacré et le Profane*. Paris: Gallimard.

Elkind, D. (1961), "The Child's Conception of His Religious Denomination, I. The Jewish Child." In *Journal of Genetic Psychology, 99*, 209-225.

_____ (1962), "The Child's Conception of His Religious Denomination, II. The Catholic Child." In *Journal of Genetic Psychology, 101*, 185-193.

_____ (1963), "The Child's Conception of His Religious Denomination, III. The Protestant Child." In *Journal of Genetic Psychology, 103*, 291-304.

Englert, R. (1986), "Vor einer neuen Phase materialkerygmatischer Erneuerung?" In *Katechetische Blätter. 111 (11)*, 887-888.

Erikson, E.H. (1958), *Young Man Luther*. New York: Norton.

_____ (1963), *Childhood and Society*. New York: Norton.

_____ (1968), *Identity, Youth, and Crisis*. New York: Norton.

_____ (1980), *Identity and Life Cycle*. New York: Norton.

Farley, E. (1983), *Theologia: The Fragmentation and Unity of Theological Education*. Philadelphia: Fortress Press.

Fetz, R.L. (1979), "Die Gegenwart aristotelischen Denkens. Erläutert am Werk Jean Piagets." In *Vierteljahresschrift für Heilpädagogik, 48*, 221-236.

_____ (1979a), "Kreis des Verstehens oder Kreis der Wissenschaften? Anthropologie im Spannungsfeld von Philosophie und Wissenschaft." In *Freiburger Zeitschrift für Philosophie und Theologie, 26*, 163-201.

_____ (1981), "Genetische Semiologie? Symboltheorie im Ausgang von Ernst Cassirer und Jean Piaget." In *Freiburger Zeitschrift für Philosophie und Theologie, 28*, 434-470.

_____ (1982), "Naturdenken beim Kinde und bei Aristoteles. Fragen einer genetischen Ontologie." In *Tijdschrift voor Filosophie, 44*, 473-513.

_____ (1982), "Pour une ontologie génétique. J. Piaget et la philosophie moderne. In *Revue internationale de Philosophie, 142-143*, 409-434.

_____ (1985), "Die Himmelssymbolik in Menschheitsgeschichte und individueller Entwicklung. Ein Beitrag zu einer genetischen Semiologie." In A. Zweig (ed.), *Zur Entstehung von Symbolen. Schriften zur Synmbolforschung, Vol. 2*. Bern: Lang, 111-150.

Fetz, R.L./Bucher, A. (1987), "Stufen religiöser Entwicklung? Eine rekonstruktive Kritik von Fritz Oser und Paul Gmünder: *Der Mensch—Stufen seiner religiösen Entwicklung*. In P. Biehl et al., *Jahrbuch der Religionspädagogik, Vol. 3*. Neukirchen.

Fetz, R.L./Oser, F. (1985), *Weltbildentwicklung und religiöses Urteil*. Fribourg, Switzerland: Berichte zur Erziehungswissenschaft, 47, Pedagogical Institute, University of Fribourg. Abbreviated version in W. Edelstein/G. Nunner-Winkler (eds.), *Zur Bestimmung der Moral*. Frankfurt: Suhrkamp, 1986, 443-469.

Fichte, J.G. (1977), "Instructions for the Blessed Life." In Robinson, D. (ed.), *Characteristics of the Present Age*. Washington, D.C.: University Publications of America.

Filipp, S.H. (ed.) (1981), *Kritische Lebensereignisse*. München: Urban und Schwarzenberg.

Flavell, J.H. (1983, 4th ed.), *Cognitive Development*. New York: Wiley.

Fowler, J.W. (1974), "Stages in Faith—The Structural Developmental Approach." In Th. Hennessy (ed.), *Values and Moral Development*. New York: Paulist Press, 173-211.

_____ (1976), *Mapping Faith's Structure: A Developmental Overview*. Harvard Divinity School, Cambridge, Mass.: Harvard University Press.

_____ (1981), *Stages of Faith—The Psychology of Human Development and the Quest for Meaning*. San Francisco: Harper & Row.

_____ (1986), "Faith and the Structuring of Meaning." In C. Dykstra and S. Parks (eds.), *Faith Development and Fowler*. Birmingham, Ala.: Religious Education Press, 15-42.

_____ (1987), *Faith Development and Pastoral Care*. Philadelphia: Fortress Press.

Fowler, J.W./Lovin, R.W. (1980), *Trajectories in Faith*. Nashville: Abingdon.

Fowler, J.W./Nipkow, K.E./Schweitzer, F. (1991), *Stages of Faith and Religious Development*. New York: Crossroads.

Fraas, H.J. (1973), *Religiöse Erziehung und Sozialisation im Kindesalter*. Göttingen.

_____ (1983), *Glaube und Identität. Grundlegung einer Didaktik religiöser Lernprozesse*. Göttingen.

Fries, H. (1981), "Theologie als Anthropologie." In K. Rahner (ed.), *Theologie in Freiheit und Verantwortung*. Munich: Kösel, 30-70.

Fuchs, G. (1982), "Roter Faden Theologie—eine Skizze zur Orientierung." In *Katechetische Blätter, 107*, 65-180.

Furth, G.H. (1982), "Das Gesellschaftsverständnis des Kindes und der Äquilibrationsprozess." In W. Endelstein/Keller (eds.), *Perspektivität und Interpretation. Beiträge zur Entwicklung des sozialen Verstehens*. Frankfurt: Suhrkamp, 188-218.

Gardner, H. (1981), *The Quest for Mind* (2nd ed.). Chicago: University of Chicago Press.

Gilligan, C. (1977), "In a Different Voice: Women's Conception of Self and Morality." In *Harvard Educational Review, 47*, 481-517.

_____ (1982), "Gibt es eine weibliche Moral?" (Interview). In *Psychologie Heute, 9 (10)*, 21-27, 34.

Ginters, R. (1978), *Relativismus in der Ethik*. Düsseldorf: Patmos.

Gmünder, P. (1979), "Entwicklung als Ziel der religiösen Erziehung." In *Katechetische Blätter, 104*, 629-634.

Goldman, R. (1964), *Religious Thinking from Childhood to Adolescence*. New York: Seabury.

_____ (1971), *Vorfelder des Glaubens*. Neukirchen.

Greive, W. (1975), *Praxis und Theologie*. München.

Grimal, P. (1967), "Der Mensch und der Mythos." In P. Grimal (ed.), *Mythen der Völker*. Frankfurt: Fischer, 12-27.

Grom, B. (1981), *Religionspädagogische Psychologie. Kleinkind, Schüler, Jugendlicher*. Düsseldorf/Göttingen: Patmos/Vandenhoek & Ruprecht.

Gut, U. (1984), "Analyse der Vorraussetzungen der Stufen des moralischen und des religiösen Urteils." In *Der Mensch—Stufen seiner religiösen Entwicklung* (1st ed.). Zurich/Cologne: Benzinger, 230f.

Habermas, J. (1976), *Zur Rekonstruktion des Historischen Materialismus*. Franfurt: Suhrkamp.

_____ (1984), *The Theory of Communicative Action. Volume One: Reason and the Rationalization of Society*. Boston: Beacon Press.

_____ (1988), *The Theory of Communicative Action. Volume Two: Lifeworld and System*. Boston: Beacon Press.

Hager, P. (1987), *Die religiöse Entwicklung von Johann Heinrich Pestalozzi*. Pedagogical Institute, University of Fribourg, Switzerland: Unpublished manuscript.

Halbfas, H. (1968), *Fundamentalkatechetik. Sprache und Erfahrung im Religionsunterricht*. Stuttgart.

_____ (1982), *Das dritte Auge. Religionsdidaktische Anstösse*. Düsseldorf.

_____ (1983), *Religionsunterricht in der Grundschule. Lehrerkommentare, Vol. I*. Zurich, Einsiedeln, Düsseldorf.

_____ (1984), *Religionsunterricht in der Grundschule. Lehrerkommentare, Vol. II*. Zurich, Einsiedeln, Düsseldorf.

_____ (1985), *Religionsunterricht in der Grundschule. Lehrerkommentare, Vol. III*. Zurich, Einsiedeln, Düsseldorf.

Hamann, B. (1982), *Pädagogische Anthropologie*. Bad Heilbrunn: Klinkhardt.

Harnisch, W. (1985), *Die Gleichniserzählungen Jesu. Eine hermeneutische Einführung*. Göttingen.

Hasenhüttl, G. (1979), *Kritische Dogmatik*. Graz: Styria.

Hays, W.L. (1973), *Statistics for Social Sciences*. New York: Rinehart & Winston.

Hoffmann, J. (1979), *Moraltheologische und moralpädaogoische Grundlegung, Vol. I: Moralpädogogik*. Düsseldorf: Patmos.

Holenstein, E. (1980), *Von der Hintergehbarkeit der Sprache. Kognitive Unterlagen der Sprache*. Frankfurt: Suhrkamp.

Holstein, C.B. (1978), "Irreversible Stepwise Sequence in the Development of Moral Judgement—A Longitudinal Study of Males and Females." In *Child Development, 47*, 51-61.

Hoppe-Graf, S./Schell, M. (1987), "The Comprehension of Literary Texts: Developmental Considerations." In D. Meutsch/R. Fiehoff (eds.), *Comprehension of Literary Discourse. Results and Problems of Interdisciplinary Approaches*. Berlin.

Ingarden, R. (1975), "Konkretisation und Rekonstruktion." In R. Warning (ed.), *Rezeptionsästhetik. Theorie und Praxis*. Munich.

Inhelder, B. (1978), "Die Entwicklung von Zufall und Wahrscheinlichkeit bei Kindern." In B. Inhelder/H. Chipman (eds.), *Von der Kinderwelt zur Erkenntnis der Welt*. Wiesbaden: Akademischer Verlag.

_____ (1980), "Language and Learning in a Contextual

Framework." In M. Piatelli-Palermo (ed.), *Language and Learning: The Debate between Jean Piaget and Noam Chomsky*. Cambridge, Mass.: Harvard University Press.

Inhelder, B./Garcia, R./Vonéche, J. (1977), *Epistémologie génétique et èquilibration. Hommage à Jean Piaget*. Neuchàtel: Delachaux et Nestlé.

Iser, W. (1975), "Die Appellstruktur der Texte." In R. Warning (ed.), *Rezeptionsästhetik. Theorie und Praxis*. Munich: Fink.

_____ (1984), *Der Akt des Lesens. Theorie ästhetischer Wirkung* (2nd ed.). Munich: Fink.

Izard, C.E. (1977), *Human Emotions*. New York: Plenum Press.

Jaspers, K. (1967), *Philosophical Faith and Revelation*. New York: Harper & Row.

Jeremias, J. (1966), *Rediscovering the Parables*. New York: Scribner's.

Kasper, W. (ed.), (1985), *Einführung in den Erwachsenenkatechismus*. Düsseldorf: Patmos.

Kaufmann, F.X. (1970), "Zur Rezeption soziologischer Einsichten in die Theologie. Soziologische Anmerkungen." In F. Hausmann et al. (eds.), *Kirchliche Lehre—Skepsis der Gläubigen*. Freiburg i. Br.: Herder, 101-129.

_____ (1979), *Kirche begreifen. Analysen und Thesen zur gesellschaftlichen Verfassung des Christentums*. Freiburg i. Br.: Herder.

Kegan, R. (1982), *The Evolving Self—Problem and Progress in Human Development*. Cambridge, Mass.: Harvard University Press.

Keller, M. (1976), *Kognitive Entwicklung und soziale Kompetenz*. Stuttgart: Klett.

Kesselring, Th. (1981), *Entwicklung und Widerspruch. Ein Vergleich zwischen Piagets genetischer Erkenntnistheorie und Hegels Dialektik*. Frankfurt: Suhrkamp.

Kissinger, W. (1979), *The Parables of Jesus. A History of Interpretation and Bibliography*. New York.

Kitchener, R.F. (1982), "Holism and the Organismic Model in Developmental Psychology." In *Human Development, 25*, 233-249.

Klaghofer, R./Oser, F. (1987), "Dimensionen und Erfassung des religiösen Familienklimas. In *Unterrichtswissenschaft 15*, 190-206.

Kohlberg, L. (1971), "The Ethical Life, the Contemplative Life, and Ultimate Religion—Notes Toward Stage 7." In *Social Sciences, 154*.

_____ (1974), "Education, Moral Development and Faith." In *Journal of Moral Education 4*, 5-16.

_____ (1975), *Towards a Stage 7—Rational Sciences, Rational Ethics and Ultimate Faith*. Cambridge, Mass.: Internal working paper.

_____ (1977), "Eine Neuinterpretation der Zusammenhänge zwischen der Moralentwicklung in der Kindheit und im Erwachsenenalter." In R. Döbert/J. Habermas/G. Nunner-Winkler (eds.), *Die Entwicklung des Ichs*. Cologne: Kiepenheuer & Witsch, 225-252.

_____ (1981a), *The Meaning and Measurement of Moral Development*. Worcester, Mass.: Clark University Press (Heinz Werner Memorial Lecture Series, Vol. 13).

_____ (1981b), *Essays on Moral Development, Vol. I: The Philosophy of Moral Development*. San Francisco: Harper & Row.

_____ (1984), *Essays on Moral Development, Vol. II: The Psychology of Moral Development*. San Francisco: Harper & Row.

Kohlberg, L., et al. (1978), *Assessing Moral Stages. A Manual*. Harvard University (photocopy).

Kohlberg, L./Power, C. (1980), "Religion, Morality, and Ego Development." In C. Brusselmans (ed.), *Toward Moral and Religious Maturity*. Morristown: Silver Burdett, 343-372.

_____ (1981), "Moral Development, Religious Thinking, and the Question of a Seventh Stage." In L. Kohlberg, *Essays on Moral Development, Vol. I*. San Francisco: Harper & Row, 311-372.

Krappmann, L. (1973), *Soziologische Dimensionen der Identität*. Stuttgart: Klett.

Kreft, F. (1982), *Grundprobleme der Literaturdidaktik. Eine Fachdidaktik im Konzept sozialer und individueller Entwicklung und Geschichte*. Heidelberg.

Kreft, J. (1986), "Moralische und ästhetische Entwicklung im didaktischen Aspekt." In F. Oser/W. Althof/D. Garz (eds.), *Moralische Zugänge zum Menschen*. Munich.

Krings, H. (1979), "Der Grundsatz und die Massnahme. Anmerkungen zu einer Logik der Normenbegründung." In W. Oelmüller (ed.), *Materialien zur Normendiskussion, Vol. 3: Normen und Geschichte*. Paderborn: UTB Schöningh, 40-54.

Krings, H./Simons, E. (1973). "Gott." In *Handbuch philosophischer Grundbegriffe*, Vol. III. Munich: Kösel, 614-641.

Kubli, F. (1974), "Einführung." In J. Piaget (ed.), *Abriss der genetischen Epistemologie*. Olten: Walter, 7-22.

Kuhn. D./et al. (1977), "The Development of Formal Operations in Logical and Moral Judgment." In *Genetic Psychology Monographs, 95*, 97-188.

Küppers, W. (1980), *Psychologie des Deutschunterrichts. Spracherwerb, sprachlicher Ausdruck, Verständnis für literarische Texte*. Stuttgart.

Kürthy, T. (1978), *Geschlechtsspezifische Sozialisation*. Paderborn: Schöningh.

Lakeland, P. (1990), *Theology and Critical Theory*. Nashville: Abingdon.

Levine, C.G. (1979), "The Form-Content Distinction in Moral Development Research," In *Human Development, 22*, 225-234.

Lienert, A.G. (1973), *Vorurteilsfreie Methoden der Biostatistik, Vol. I*. Meisenheim: Hein.

Loch, W. (1986), *Die Verleugnung des Kindes in der Evangelischen Pädagogik*. Essen.

Lübbe, H. (1979), "Vollendung der Säkularisierung—Ende der Religion?" In S. Moser/E. Pillik (eds.), *Gottesbilder heute. Zur Gottesproblematik in der säkularisierten Gesellschaft der Gegenwart.* Königstein: Hanstein, 11-21.

_____ (1980), "Religion nach der Aufklärung." In H. Lübbe, *Notwendigkeit pragmatischer Vernunft.* Düsseldorf: Econ, 59-86.

_____ (1986), *Religion nach der Aufklärung.* Graz.

Luhmann, N. (1977), *Funktion der Religion.* Frankfurt: Suhrkamp.

Maier, F. (1978), *Intelligenz als Handlung. Der genetische Ansatz in der Theorie Jean Piagets.* Basel-Stuttgart: Schwab.

Marcia, J.E. (1966), "Development and Validation of Ego-identity Status." In *Journal of Personality and Social Psychology, 5,* 551-558.

Mette, N. (1978), *Theorie der Praxis. Wissenschaftsgeschichtliche und methodologischen Untersuchungen zur Theorie-Praxis-Problematik innerhalb der Praktischen Theologie.* Düsseldorf: Patmos.

_____ (1979), "Religiöse Sozialisation und Entwicklung des Ich." In G. Stachel (ed.), *Sozialisation, Identitätsfindung. Glaubenserfahrung.* Zurich: Benziger, 136-147.

_____ (1982), *Vorraussetzungen der Glaubensvermittlung— Thesen zur religiösen Sozialisation.* Working paper, Münster.

_____ (1983), *Vorraussetzungen christlicher Elementarerziehung.* Düsseldorf: Patmos.

Morgenthaler, C. (1976), *Sozialisation und Religion.* Gütersloh.

Mukarovsky, J. (1974), *Studien zur strukturalistischen Ästhetik und Poetik.* Munich.

Murray, G. (1955), *Five Stages of Greek Religion.* Garden City, NY: Doubleday Anchor Books.

Niggli, A. (1987a), *Familie und religiöse Erziehung in unserer Zeit. Eine empirische Studie über elterliche Erziehungspraktiken und religiöse Merkmale bei Erzogenen.* Bern: Lang.

_____ (1987b), "Untersuchung über Zusammenhänge zwischen religiösem Erziehungsstil der Eltern und religiösen Entwicklungsstufen ihrer Kinder." In *Unterrichtswissenschaft, 15,* 177-189.

Nipkow, K.E. (1987), "Die Gottesfrage bei Jugendlichen—Auswertung einer empirischen Umfrage." In U. Nembach (ed.), *Jugend und Religion in Europa.* Bern.

Nisan, M. (1984), "Content and Structure in Moral Judgement. An Integrative View." In W.M. Kurtines/J.L. Gewirtz (eds.), *Morality, Moral Behavior and Moral Development.* New York: Wiley, 208-224.

Noam, G./Kegan, R. (1982), "Soziale Kognition und Psychodynamik. Auf dem Weg zu einer klinischen Entwicklungspsychologie." In W. Edelstein/M. Keller (eds.), *Perspektivität und Interpretation. Beiträge zur Entwicklung des sozialen Verstehens.* Frankfurt: Suhrkamp.

_____ (1989), "On Boundaries and Externalization: Clinical-

Developmental Perspectives." In *Psychoanalytic Inquiry, Vol. 9(3)*, 397-426.

Oelmüller, W. (ed.) (1984), *Wiederkehr der Religion?* Paderborn.

Oevermann, U./et al. (1979), "Die Methodologie einer objektiven Hermeneutik und ihre allgemeine Forschungslogische Bedeutung in den Sozialwissenschaften." In H.G. Soeffner (ed.), *Interpretative Verfahren in den Sozial - und Textwissenschaften*. Stuttgart: Metzler, 352-433.

Oser, F. (1979), "Zur Entwicklung kognitiver Stufen des religiösen Urteils." In G. Stachel (ed.), *Sozialisation, Identitätsfindung, Glaubenserfahrung*. Zurich: Benziger, 221-249.

_____ (1981), *Moralisches Urteilen in Gruppen. Soziales Handeln, Verteilungsgerechtigkeit. Stufen der interaktiven Entwicklung und ihre erzieherische Stimulation*. Frankfurt: Suhrkamp.

_____ (1987), "Grundformen biblischen Lernens." In A. Stock/E. Paul (eds.), *Glauben ermöglichen. Festschrift für Günter Stachel*. Mainz: Grünewald, 312-246.

_____ (1988), *Wieviel Religion braucht der Mensch? Studien zur Entwicklung und Förderung religiöser Autonomie*. Gütersloh: Mohn.

_____ (1991), "Towards a Logic of Religious Development: A Reply to my Critics." In J.W. Fowler/K.E. Nipow/F. Schweitzer, *Stages of Faith and Religious Development: Implications for Church, Education, and Society*. New York: Crossroads.

Oser, F./Althof, W./Berkowitz, M.W. (1986), "Lo sviluppo della logica argomentativa nei dialoghi fra pari." In *Etá Evolutiva, 24*, 76-85.

Oser, F./Althof, W./Bucher, A. (1986), *Wisdom and Religious Maturity*. Paper presented at the Second European Conference on Developmental Psychology, Rome.

Oser, F./Gmünder, P. (1984), *Der Mensch—Stufen seiner religiösen Entwicklung* (1st ed.). Zurich, Cologne: Benziger.

Oser, F./Patry, J.L. (1985), *Interventionsstudien für sozial-kognitive Kompetenz. Beispiele und Uberlegungen an Treatment-Validität*. Fribourg, Switzerland: Berichte zur Erziehungswissenschaft des Pädagogischen Instituts, 50.

Oser, F./Reich, K.H. (1987), The Challenge of Competing Explanations: The Development of Thinking in Terms of Complementarity. *Human Development 30*, 178-186.

_____ (1990), Moral Judgment, Religious Judgment, World Views and Logical Thought: A Review of their Relationship. *British Journal of Religious Education 12, no. 2*, 94-101 & *no. 3*, 172-181.

Pannenberg, W. (1973), "Anthropology and the Question of God." In W. Pannenberg, *The Idea of God and Human Freedom*. Philadelphia: Westminster Press, 80-99.

_____ (1976) *Theology and the Philosophy of Science*. Philadelphia: Westminster Press.

_____ (1980), "Macht der Mensch die Religion oder macht die Religion den Menschen?" In T. Rendtorff (ed.), *Religion als Problem der Aufklärung. Eine Bilanz aus der religionstheoretischen Forschung.* Göttingen: Vandenhoek & Ruprecht.

_____ (1985) *Anthropology in Theological Perspective.* Philadelphia: Westminster.

Parsons, T. (1977), "Der Stellenwert des Identitätsbegriffes in der allgemeinen Handlungstheorie." In R. Döbert/J. Habermas/G. Nunner-Winkler (eds.), *Entwicklung des Ich.* Cologne: Kiepenheurer & Witsch, 68-89.

Peukert, H. (1981), "Was ist eine praktische Wissenschaft? Handlungstheorie als Basistheorie der Humanwissenschaften. Anfragen an die Praktische Theologie." In Christen für den Sozialismus—Gruppe Münster (eds.), *Zur Rettung des Feuers. Solidaritätsschrift für Kuno Füssel.* Münster, 280-296.

_____ (1982), "Kontingenzerfahrung und Identitätsfindung. Bemerkungen zu einer Theorie der Religion und zur Analytik religiös dimensionierter Lernprozesse." In J. Blank/G. Hasenhüttl (eds.), *Erfahrung, Glaube, Moral.* Düsseldorf: Patmos, 76-103.

_____ (1984), *Science, Action, and Fundamental Theology: Towards a Theology of Communicative Action.* Cambridge, Mass.: MIT Press.

Peukert, U. (1979), *Interaktive Kompetenz und Identität. Zum Vorrang sozialen Lernens im Vorschulalter.* Düsseldorf: Patmos.

Piaget, J. (1930), *The Child's Conception of Physical Causality.* London: K. Paul, Trench, Trubner & Co.

_____ (1947), *The Psychology of Intelligence.* London: Routledge.

_____ (1954), *The Construction of Reality in the Child.* New York: Basic Books.

_____ (1965), *The Moral Judgment of the Child.* New York: The Free Press.

_____ (1967), *The Child's Conception of the World.* London: Routledge & Kegan Paul.

_____ (1968), *Le Structuralisme.* Paris: Presses Universitaires de France.

_____ (1970), *The Child's Conception of Time.* New York: Basic Books.

_____ (1973), *Introduction a l'épistemologie génétique.* Paris: Presses Universitaires de France.

Portele, G. (1977), "Moralisches Urteilen bei Wissenschaftlern verschiedener Disziplinen." In L.H. Eckensberger (ed.), *Entwicklung des Moralischen Urteilens—Theorie, Methode, Praxis.* Bericht über einen Workshop an der Universität des Saarlandes vom 2.-5.10.

Pröpper, Th. (1976), *Der Jesus der Philosophen und der Jesus des Glaubens.* Mainz: Grünewald.

Radding, Ch.M. (1978), "Evolution of Medieval Mentalities: A Cognitive-Structural Approach." In *American Historical Review.*

Rahner, K. (1968), *Spirit in the World.* New York: Herder and Herder.

Raske, M. (1981), "Glaubenserfahrung—Gesellschaftskritik. Schöpferische Aneignung. Drei Fragen zur Didaktik der Korrelation. In *Katechetische Blätter, 106,* 346-350.

Rendtorff, T. (1980), "Religion nach der Aufklärung. Argumentationen für eine Neubestimmung des Religionsbegriffs." In T. Rendtorff, *Religion als Problem der Aufklärung. Eine Bilanz aus der religionstheoretischen Forschung.* Göttingen: Vandenhoek & Ruprecht, 185-202.

Ricoeur, P. (1974), "Stellung und Funktion der Metapher in der biblischen Sprache." In P. Ricoeur/E. Jüngel, *Metapher. Zur Hermeneutik religiöser Sprache.* Munich, 45-70.

_____ (1977), *The Rule of Metaphor.* Toronto: University of Toronto Press.

Ringel, E./Kirchmayer, A. (1985), *Religionsverlust durch religiöse Erziehung. Tiefenpsychologische Ursachen und Folgerungen.* Freiburg i. Br.

Rohrmoser, G. (1980), "Politik und Religion am Ende der Aufklärung." In T. Rendtorff, *Religion als Problem der Aufklärung. Eine Bilanz aus der religionstheoretischen Forschung.* Göttingen: Vandenhoek & Ruprecht, 202-220.

Rosenberg, R. (1977), *Die Entwicklung des Gebetsbegriffs bei jüdischen Kindern in Israel.* (Working Paper), Jerusalem.

_____ (1989), "Die Entwicklung von Gebetskonzepten." In A. Bucher & K.H. Reich (eds.), *Entwicklung von Religiösität.* Fribourg, Switzerland: Universitätsverlag Fribourg.

Rössler, D. (1976), *Die Vernunft der Religion.* Munich: Piper.

Sauter, G. (1980), "Sinn und Wahrheit. Die Sinnfrage in religionstheoretischer und theologischer Sicht." In T. Rendtorff, *Religion als Problem der Aufklärung. Eine Bilanz aus der religionstheoretischen Forschung.* Göttingen: Vandenhoek & Ruprecht, 69-107.

Schaie, K.W. (1979), "Methodische Probleme bei der deskriptiven entwicklungspsychologischen Untersuchung des Erwachsenen und Greisenalters." In P.B. Baltes/L.H. Eckensberger (eds.), *Entwicklungspsychologie der Lebensspanne.* Stuttgart: Klett, 179-208.

Schelling, F.W. (1954), "Philosophie der Offenbarung" In *WW6. Ergänzungsband* (M. Schröter, ed.). Munich.

Schibilsky, M. (1978), "Konstitutionsbedingungen religiöser Kompetenz." In W. Fischer/W. Marhold (eds.), *Religionssoziologie als Wissenssoziologie.* Stuttgart: Kohlhammer, 73-101.

Schildknecht, M. (1984), *Entwicklung von Argumentationsstrategien in moralischen und religiösen Diskussionen.* Fribourg, Switzerland. Unpublished thesis.

Schillebeeckx, E. (1974), *The Understanding of Faith: Interpretation and Criticism.* New York: Seabury.

Schmidt, H. (1986), "Schuld und Vergebung in Religionsuntericht." In *Glaube und Lernen I (2),* 153-166.

Schoonenberg, P. (1977), "Auf Gott hindenken." In *Theologie der Gegenwart, 20,* 193-243.

Schröer, H. (1974), "Forschungsmethoden in der Praktischen Theologie." In F. Klostermann/R. Zerfass (eds.), *Praktische Theologie heute.* Munich/Mainz: Kaiser/Grünewald, 206-224.

Schulz, W. (1974), *Der Gott der Neuzeitlichen Metaphysik.* Pfulingen: Neske.

Schupp, F. (1975), *Vermittlung im Fragment. Überlegungen zur Christologie.* Innsbruck: Fakultätsvertretung der Hochschülerschaft an der Theologischen Fakultät der Universität Innsbruck.

Schütz, A. (1984), *Der sinnhafte Aufbau der sozialen Welt.* Frankfurt: Suhrkamp (1st ed.: 1960).

Seckler, M. (1977), "Theologie, Religionsphilosophie, Religionswissenschaft. Versuch einer Abgrenzung." In *Theologische Quartalsschrift, 157,* 163-176.

Seiler, T.B. (1973), "Die Bereichsspezifizität formaler Denkstrukturen. Konsequenzen für den pädagogischen Prozess." In K. Frey/H. Lang (eds.), *Kognitionspsychologie und naturwissenschaftlicher Unterricht.* Bern: Huber, 249-285.

Selman, R.L. (1973), *A Structural Analysis of the Ability to Take Another's Perspective: Stages in the Development of Role-Taking Ability.* Paper presented to the Society for Research in Child Development, Philadelphia.

_____ (1974), *The Development of Conceptions of Interpersonal Reasoning Based on Levels of Social Perspective Taking.* Cambridge, Mass.: Harvard University (Judge Baker Social Reasoning Project). Unpublished manuscript.

_____ (1975), T*he Relation of Social Perspective-Taking to Moral Development. Analytic and Empirical Approach.* Harvard Graduate School of Education.

_____ (1976), "Toward a Structural Analysis of Developing Interpersonal Relations Concepts: Research with Normal and Disturbed Preadolescent Boys." In A. Pick (ed.), *Minnesota Symposia on Child Psychology, Vol. 10.* Minneapolis: University of Minnesota Press, 156-200.

_____ (1980), *The Growth of Interpersonal Understanding.* New York: Academic Press.

Siegel, S. (1988), *Nonparametric Statistics for the Behavioral Sciences.* New York: McGraw-Hill.

Simons, E. (1974), "Transzendenz." In H. Krings/H.Baumgartner/Chr.

Wild (eds), *Handbuch philosophischer Grundbegriffe, Vol. 6*, Munich: Kösel, 1540-1556.

Singe, G. (1982), *Zur Ontogenese religiösen Bewusstseins. Entwicklung kognitiver Stufen des religiösen Urteils als Element einer religiösen Sozialisationstheorie im Hinblick auf die Praxis der Christen*. Unpublished thesis, Bonn.

Spaemann, R. (1973), "Die Frage nach der Bedeutung des Wortes Gott." In J. Kopperschmidt (ed.), *Der fragliche Gott*. Düsseldorf: Patmos, 45-66.

_____ (1975), "Gesichtspunkte der Philosophie." In H.J. Schultz (ed.), *Wer ist das eigentlich—Gott?* Frankfurt: Suhrkamp, 56-66.

Swanson, G.E. (1960), *The Birth of the God. The Origin of Primitive Beliefs*. Ann Arbor: University of Michigan Press.

Tillich, P. (1958), "The Lost Dimension in Religion." *Saturday Evening Post*, 230, 50 (June 14, 1958); 29, 76, 78-79.

_____ (1964), *The Frage nach dem Unbedingten. Schriften zur Religionsphilosophie*. Stuttgart.

Trautner, H.M. (1978), *Lehrbuch der Entwicklungspsychologie, Vol. I*. Göttingen: Hogrefe.

Turiel, E. (1971), *The Development of Concepts of Social Structure: Social Conventions*. Working paper, Berkeley.

_____ (1978), "Distinct Conceptual and Developmental Domains: Social Convention and Morality," In C.B. Keasey (ed.), *Nebraska Symposium on Motivation 1977*. Lincoln, Nebr.: University of Nebraska Press, 77-116.

Turiel, E./Davidson, P. (1986), "Heterogeneity, Inconsistency, and Asynchrony in the Development of Cognitive Structures." In I. Levin (ed.), *State and Structure. Reopening the Debate*. Norwood, N.J.: Ablex, 106-143.

Van der Ven, J.A. (1984), "Unterwegs zu einer empirischen Theologie." In O. Fuchs (ed.), *Theologie und Handeln. Beiträge zur Fundierung der Praktischen Theologie als Handlungstheorie*. Düsseldorf: Patmos, 102-128.

Vergote, A. (1980), "Neue Perspektiven in den Religionswissenschaften. In T. Rendtorff, *Religion als Problem der Aufklärung. Eine Bilanz aus der religionstheoretischen Forschung*. Göttingen: Vandenhoek & Ruprecht, 36-52.

Vinh-Bang, N. (1978), "Die klinische Methode und die Forschung in der Kinderpsychologie." In B. Inhelder/H. Chipman (eds.), *Von der Kinderwelt zur Erkenntnis der Welt*. Wiesbaden: Akademischer Verlag.

Von Brachel/Oser (1984), "Kritische Lebensereignisse und religiöse Strukturtransformationen." In *Berichte zur Erziehungswissenschaft des Pädagogischen Institute 43*, University of Fribourg, Switzerland.

Waardenburg, D. (1980), "Religion unter dem Gesichtspunkt der religiösen Erscheinungen." In T. Rendtorff, *Religion als Problem der Aufklärung. Eine Bilanz aus der religionstheoretischen Forschung*. Göttingen: Vandenhoek & Ruprecht, 13-36.

Warning, R. (ed.) (1975), *Rezeptionsästhetik. Theorie und Praxis*. Munich.

Wechsler, D. (1972), *Wechsler's Measurement and Appraisal of Adult Intelligence* (5th ed.), Baltimore: Williams & Wilkins.

Weder, H. (1984), *Die Gleichnisse Jesu als Metaphern. Traditions und redaktionsgeschichtliche Analysen und Interpretationen*. Göttingen.

Wegenast, K. (1968), Die empirische Wendung in der Religionspädagogik." In *Der Evangelische Erzieher, 20*, 111-124.

Weiss, K. (1927), *Die Frohbotschaft über Jesu Lohn und Vollkommenheit. Neutestamentliche Abhandlungen XII, 4/5*.

Weitz, S. (1977), *Sex Roles*. New York.

Werbick, J. (1985), "Vom Realismus der Dogmatik. Rückfragen an Walter Kaspers Thesen zum Verhältnis von Religionspadägogik und Dogmatik." In *Katechetishe Blätter, 110*, 459-463.

Ziellessen, D. (1982), *Emanzipation und Religion*. Frankfurt: Diesterweg.

Index of Names

225

Index of Subjects

absurdity, 28f
accommodation, 15, 17, 34, 94, 140, 145
actualization,
   of meaning of texts, 155
adaptive activity,
   and texts, 166
aesthetics,
   and structural developmental theory, 154-156
   literature, 154
     developmental dimension, 155
     and moral development, 155f
   of textual criticism, 154f
affect, see "polarity," "religiosity," and "motivational aspect"
age,
   old age hypothesis, 177
   trend,
     hypothesis, 176
     results, 180-186
animism, 31
   of punishment, 58
anthropology, 150
   and theology, 15
   Christian, 169
anxiety,
   vs. trust, 29f
   vs. fear, 30
applicability, 145
   universal, 16
application(s),
   of deep-structures, 97
   of faith development theory, 44

of theory of religious judgement, 154-169
   semantic, 34
assimilation, 15, 17, 34, 94, 140, 145
atheism,
   research on, 205
autonomy, 38, 149
   ethical, 149
   increased religious, 165
   (stage 4), 12, 68, 76-78
   absolute autonomy orientation (stage 3), 12, 68, 73f

Baal, 156

chance, 10, 32, 36, 87
   –dilemma, 203f
change, see "development," "stage(s)," "transformation," "transition"
climate, religious, study on, 209
clinical,
   method, 98
   interview, semi-, 98-100
closure, lack of and religious development, 143
coding procedures, 109-112, see also "measuring"
cognition, 5, 9
   literary-aesthetical, 158
   religious, 139
cognitive,
   coping with reality, 19
   paradigm, 9
   reconstruction, 32

construal of, 15, 32
coping with, 19, 34
multiple levels of, 148
subjective reconstruction of, 62
ultimate, 50
reasoning, 23, 37f
mathematical, 53
relational, 22, 101
religious vs. other patterns, 58f
reductionism, 4
reequilibration, 146
reflectiveness, 14
Reformation, 152
regression, 74
regularity, 17, 57
regulative system, 20f, 23, 101, 140
relationship,
to an Ultimate, 9, 14f, 18, 20, 23, 53,
62, 85, 140
and polarities, 23-33
relational reasoning, 22, 101
religion, 4, 6, 53
as coping with contingency, 35-38
concept of, 4
critical theory of, 37
history of, 151
irrationality of, 36
nature of, 51
philosophy of, 6, 7, 151
psychological perspective of, 6, 7,
35
psychology of, 151
sociological perspective, 16f, 35, 39
subjective aspect of, 16
religiosity,
affective component, 29, 23-33
and rationality, 14
and the sociology of knowledge, 39
higher form of, 14
temporary vs. permanent, 87
vs. other patterns of world interpretation, 49
religious,
climate, study on, 209
cognition, range of structures of,
139-153
concepts,
development of, 39
consciousness, 9f, 33, 51
content, 139f
deep-structures, 33-34

vs. concept research, 40
as mother-structures, 48-56
development, 10, 44f
and stage chance, 13
constancy, 17
higher vs. lower stages, 14, 23f,
23-33
stimulating, 207
structural view, 14f
universality, 15, 16
vs. faith development
dilemma, 100-102
domain, 3, 5, 49f
dreams, 144
education, 139-142, 154-169
styles of, study on, 209
identity, see "identity"
judgement, 19-23
and coping with contingency, 19,
34-38
and creating security, 20
and deep-structures, 33f
and having-and-being dichotomy,
67-82
and moral judgement, 207f
and objectifying knowing, 19
and plausability, 20
and relationship to the Ultimate,
20
and religious interpretation of
experience, 16f
and motivational aspect, 144
at different ages, 9-12, 13, 23-33
development of, 10, 23-33
and content, 10
and structure, 10, 19
stimulating, study of, 207
as persons' regulative system, 20f
constitutive polar elements, 21,
23f-33
equilibrium/disequilibrium, 23-33,
see also polarity
limits in range of theoretical concept, 144f
measuring, 96-137, 202-205
stages of, 12, 68
stage 0, 69
stage 1, 69f
stage 2, 71
stage 3, 73
stage 4, 76